MW00534653

IMPLEMENTATION FIDELITY IN EDUCATION RESEARCH

Implementation science is an important and underrepresented topic in the literature of educational research, despite the fact that it is inextricably tied to education policy and improvement. Implementation fidelity (the degree to which a program or intervention is delivered as planned) is, in particular, a key issue for every program developer and researcher designing, executing, interpreting, or communicating their work. *Implementation Fidelity in Education Research* provides the first serious developer-evaluator collaborative perspective on the practical considerations of implementation fidelity in program development.

Using case studies from Investing in Innovation (i3) fund grants, this book prepares future researchers for the challenges posed by implementation issues both ideologically and in practice. This book will be an excellent resource for anyone interested in education research and evaluation, and an excellent supplement to research methods courses.

Coby V. Meyers is a Senior Researcher in the Education Program at American Institutes for Research.

W. Christopher Brandt is Executive Director of Assessment and Accountability with the St. Charles School District #303 in St. Charles, Illinois. Previously Dr. Brandt was a Principal Researcher in the Education Program at American Institutes for Research.

IMPLEMENTATION FIDELITY IN EDUCATION RESEARCH

Designer and Evaluator
Considerations

Edited by Coby V. Meyers and
W. Christopher Brandt

Routledge
Taylor & Francis Group

NEW YORK AND LONDON

First published 2015
by Routledge
711 Third Avenue, New York, NY 10017

and by Routledge
2 Park Square, Milton Park, Abingdon, Oxon, OX14 4RN

Routledge is an imprint of the Taylor & Francis Group, an informa business

© 2015 Taylor & Francis

The right of the editors to be identified as the authors of the editorial material, and of the authors for their individual chapters, has been asserted in accordance with sections 77 and 78 of the Copyright, Designs and Patents Act 1988.

All rights reserved. No part of this book may be reprinted or reproduced or utilised in any form or by any electronic, mechanical, or other means, now known or hereafter invented, including photocopying and recording, or in any information storage or retrieval system, without permission in writing from the publishers.

Trademark notice: Product or corporate names may be trademarks or registered trademarks, and are used only for identification and explanation without intent to infringe.

Library of Congress Cataloging in Publication Data
Meyers, Coby V.
Implementation fidelity in education research: designer and evaluator considerations/by Coby V. Meyers and W. Christopher Brandt.
pages cm
Includes bibliographical references and index.
1. Education—Research—Evaluation. I. Brandt, W. Christopher. II. Title.
LB1028.M45 2015
370.72—dc23
2014015463

ISBN: 978-1-138-01380-3 (hbk)
ISBN: 978-1-138-01381-0 (pbk)
ISBN: 978-1-315-79508-9 (ebk)

Typeset in Bembo Std
by Swales & Willis Ltd, Exeter, Devon, UK

Printed and bound in the United States of America by Publishers Graphics, LLC on sustainably sourced paper.

To our wives, Zakia and Katie

CONTENTS

FOREWORD

The editors of and contributors to this volume have provided insights and practical advice on how to conceptualize and measure the extent to which educational interventions are implemented with fidelity. While this topic is interesting from a variety of vantage points (e.g., organizational change, leadership), it is particularly interesting, important, and timely given the current vigorous efforts to identify educational programs, policies and practices (collectively referred to here as interventions) that *work* or *do not work* in live-fire educational settings. Indeed, over the past decade, we have accumulated a great deal of evidence from randomized controlled trials (RCTs) about intervention effects, creating large archives of evidence on interventions that work (or not). This evidence has been largely confined to estimates (like effects sizes, statistical significance tests, confidence intervals) based on the intent-to-treat (ITT) model that, out of technical necessity, overlooks the extent to which the intervention was delivered, received, and enacted (i.e., implemented). Although results from the ITT analyses are correct estimates of the relative effects of the intervention—the extent to which "it works"—augmenting them with evidence about implementation fidelity provides a richer causal understanding of these average relative effects. More specifically, evidence from the assessment of implementation fidelity provides empirical evidence of the putative cause (the "what" of the what works claim) when they are tried in educational settings. Without such assessments, descriptions of the intervention (the cause) are limited to details extracted from treatment manuals or inferred from construct-level labels (e.g., constructivist learning environments, professional development, peer-assisted learning). When we realize that the whole reason for conducting quality tests of interventions is to identify promising educational strategies to replace failing ones, it is imperative that we have detailed evidence on key features of the actual intervention (warts and all) that produced the relative effects. At this point in time the importance of augmenting statistical estimates of effects with descriptive data on the nature of the cause, as implemented, is not controversial. In fact, many funding agencies include implementation fidelity as an element of funding applications, albeit with little guidance on how these might be accomplished. This volume fills a substantial gap in our research skills.

There is a consensus in this volume about the centrality of intervention/program models within implementation fidelity assessment. The intervention model (variously called a logic model, program model, change model) is deliberately constructed to articulate key intervention components, as well as program resources, activities, and processes to be used to operationalize these components. Expected outputs of components and desired short- and long-term outcomes are also included to complete the causal logic of the intervention. Based on these models (especially the logic model) measures and performance benchmarks are developed. These are the explicit basis for assessing the extent to which an intervention is faithfully enacted.

My brief synopsis of these models and the implied measurement of intervention features masks the many and formidable challenges faced by researchers. One of the greatest challenges is to derive an agreed-upon representation of the intervention. This is especially true for complex interventions. As seen in several examples in this book, educational interventions often involve multiple actors (e.g., district personnel, principals, teachers, students), they often involve multiple levels of the educational system (e.g., district, school, classroom), and they may involve multiple links in their causal change model. Although these complexities, per se, are not necessarily troublesome, the presence of multiple actors, levels, and programmatic components affects the magnitude and cost of data collection and analysis. Adding multiple measures of program components (for validation purposes) or variables to explain variation in achieved levels of implementation fidelity across units greatly inflates monetary costs, opportunity costs, and the burden of data collection. Decisions about how much data can be collected need to impose priorities, giving preference to those that involve the essential or unique components of the intervention.

Even if a manageable and cost-efficient set of measures can be specified, a special attribute of implementation fidelity assessment is the need to establish benchmarks of acceptable implementation performance (i.e., a threshold above which a component is said to be implemented with fidelity). Determining how much of the causal component is enough is far from an exact science. Despite the uncertainties in specifying these benchmarks, authors of several chapters illustrate and explain how they arrived at their decisions, thereby providing some much-needed guidance on this important aspect of the implementation fidelity process. Although a number of other important issues are addressed in this volume, the three listed above (model development, specifying measures, and establishing benchmarks), taken together, are what sets implementation fidelity assessment apart from other research endeavors. A further dimension that sets this area apart is that developing models, measures and benchmarks cannot be easily accomplished without collaboration among developers, implementers, internal evaluators, and external/RCT research personnel. In this sense, implementation fidelity assessment is a new kind of endeavor that is nicely illustrated in this volume.

As a final note, in reading these chapters I was struck by the timelines associated with the development of the program and assessments. We can see from these examples that implementation fidelity assessment often unfolds over extended periods of time. Time is needed to develop (and refine) programs, models and measures. As such, having our expectations and funding cycles aligned with these realities is likely to improve the chances that we can learn how to improve the caliber of educational environments.

David S. Cordray
Nashville, TN
June, 2014

ACKNOWLEDGMENTS

A focus on implementation is critical to any evaluation. Implementation measurement sheds light on the black box situated between a program and its outcomes. It helps us understand what actually happened that led to a given set of programs' outcomes. How was the program rolled out, who was involved, and to what extent did those involved do what the program asked of them? On the surface, these questions seem obvious to anyone interested in improving how a program works and scaling it to new locations and groups of learners. Yet for years education research and evaluation treated them as an afterthought. The U.S. Department of Education's Office of Innovation and Improvement deserves credit for requiring that evaluations of innovative programs and practices are "well-designed *and* well-implemented." The proposal language ensures that i3-funded programs provide evidence of implementation essential for practitioners and policymakers to meaningfully interpret results. We are grateful to Beth Boulay and the entire National i3 technical assistance team. They developed a viable method for aggregating and reporting on implementation across well over 100 funded programs, which is not an easy feat. Beth and her team approached us with a genuine sense of partnership to build and implement a high quality research study that met i3 grant requirements. We are especially thankful for Cris Price. Numerous times during the eMINTS evaluation Cris went well beyond expectations to assist with i3 reporting requirements, provide feedback and advise us on all aspects of our evaluation. Cris's expertise in research design is rare, and his humble and thoughtful approach to making other people's work better is refreshing and energizing. We thank Barbara Goodson and Catherine Darrow, whose expert advice influenced the implementation fidelity design and measurement of all three evaluations included in this book. We thank David Cordray, Mark Lipsey, Georgine Pion, Chris Hulleman, Charles Munter, and Michael Nelson, whose research had an enormous influence on our thinking about all aspects of implementation fidelity research. Finally, we are indebted to our colleagues at the American Institutes for Research (AIR)—especially Ayrin Molefe, Dean Gerdeman, Jim Lindsay, Sonica Dhillon, and Pamela Bonsu, who supported our idea to write this book and provided input on chapter drafts. They are regularly generous with their time and inspire us to be our best. It is truly an honor to work with such intelligent and hard-working colleagues who do what they do because they want to improve people's lives.

1

INTRODUCING THIS BOOK ON IMPLEMENTATION FIDELITY IN EDUCATION RESEARCH

Coby V. Meyers and W. Christopher Brandt

Measuring implementation fidelity is an important component of any program evaluation. Although any lasting judgment of a program rests on its impact on participants (e.g., changes in teachers' instructional behavior), the level of fidelity with which a program is implemented is crucial to understanding whether or not the program works as intended, and to what extent. By describing, monitoring, and systematically measuring fidelity, the program developer learns about how to improve application, whether that increased understanding ends with altering training or removing unnecessary or ineffective strategies. Presumably any changes are made with the intention of providing some benefit to the program (e.g., lower cost, higher student achievement).

Fidelity definitions and understandings and the systematic approaches to examining implementation fidelity vary according to the maturity of the program. For instance, developing programs demand formative approaches to evaluation that rely on multiple data sources and prioritize frequent feedback, real-time data, and iterative data analysis to determine what program components to keep, what to refine, and what to discontinue. More mature programs depend on an internally valid set of measures to assess program delivery and participant receptivity, examine relationships between program components and outcomes, and determine the relative influence of dosage levels on outcomes.

Historically, few studies of educational programs have published results of treatment fidelity, especially with the consideration of components and processes necessary to attain high levels of fidelity (Century, Rudnick, & Freeman, 2010; Hulleman & Cordray, 2009; O'Donnell, 2008). Furthermore, few educational programs have traditionally used implementation research to inform the design and refinement of programs and infrastructures, Success for All being an exception (Borman, et al., 2007; Datnow & Castellano, 2000). This has influenced an overall lack of understanding about the implementation process in educational settings (Penuel & Means, 2011; Penuel, Singleton, & Roschelle, 2011) and, more specifically, why and how education policies and programs succeeded or failed to achieve intended outcomes (Munter, Wilhelm, Cobb, & Cordray, 2014).

Investing in Innovation (i3)

Recently, public and private funding agencies have begun to prioritize the role of implementation fidelity in education research (Hulleman & Cordray, 2009). The Investing in Innovation or "i3" Fund was established under section 14007 of the American Recovery and Reinvestment Act of 2009 (ARRA). The purpose of the i3 program is to provide competitive grants to applicants with a record of improving student achievement and attainment in order to expand the implementation of, and investment in, innovative practices that are demonstrated to have an impact on improving student achievement or student growth, closing achievement gaps, decreasing dropout rates, increasing high school graduation rates, or increasing college enrollment and completion rates. The grants allow eligible entities—including local school districts and non-profit entities who partner with local districts—to pursue three main goals:

1. Expand and develop innovative practices that can serve as models of best practice.
2. Allow eligible entities to work in partnership with the private sector and the philanthropic community.
3. Identify and document best practices that can be shared and taken to scale based on demonstrated success.

To be eligible for an award, non-profit applicants such as the eMINTS National Center need to (1) partner with one or more school districts and (2) show that their program or strategy meets minimum evidence standards, which were based on the strength and rigor of research supporting the program's effectiveness on applicable outcomes. Applicants also must identify an external third party to conduct an evaluation of the program's implementation process and impacts on key outcomes.

A unique design feature of the i3 program is how it links funding to a program's quality and extent of existing evidence showing the likelihood that the program can indeed improve student outcomes. The Department awards three types of grants under this program: Development, Validation, and Scale-up. These grants differ in terms of the level of prior evidence of effectiveness required for consideration of funding, the level of scale the funded project should reach, and the amount of funding available to support the project. In terms of evidence requirements, Development grants provide funding to further develop or test programs and practices that are supported by initial "evidence of promise." That is, the program or practice has a strong theory behind it but still needs more systematic study to validate its efficacy. Validation grants provide funding to support expansion of projects supported by "moderate" evidence of effectiveness. Scale-up grants provide funding to support expansion of projects supported by "strong" evidence of effectiveness.[1] The criteria for determining whether a program meets one of these three levels of evidence (initial, moderate, or strong evidence) were established by the What Works Clearinghouse (WWC). The WWC was established in 2002 as an initiative of the Institute of Education Sciences (IES) at the U.S. Department of Education. The goal of the WWC is to be a resource for informed education decision-making. To reach this goal, the WWC identifies studies that provide credible and reliable evidence of the effectiveness of a given practice, program, or policy.

The emphasis on fidelity demonstrated by the i3 Program appears increasingly likely to be a staple of federally funded education research. Annual meetings of the i3 Program have detailed the urgency for effective fidelity measurement at all stages of educational research and evaluation. Moreover, education research increasingly reports on fidelity at conferences such as the Society for Research on Educational Effectiveness and the American Educational Research Association, as well as in peer-reviewed journals. These studies are quickly becoming more sophisticated and nuanced (see Cordray & Pion, 2006; Hulleman & Cordray, 2009; Munter et al., 2014).

The contributors to this book are i3 grantees (program developers and evaluators) and i3 technical assistance providers. Our focus on i3 program grantees is especially relevant because program developers and educational evaluators are working together at various stages of program development. This allows for careful considerations of program fidelity and its measurement at each of three stages—early development, validation, and scale-up. Moreover, differing perspectives, most notably the program developers and the program evaluators, are provided. Notably, in addition to introductory and concluding chapters as well as a chapter reviewing implementation fidelity literature, this book provides three chapter couples that provide program developer and evaluator perspectives for projects at the three different stages. Holistically, this book addresses the following broad questions:

1. What are important implementation fidelity issues and challenges that program developers must consider at various stages, from initial development through scale-up?
2. How can implementation fidelity research be designed and applied to inform program development at three unique stages of the program development process?
3. In what ways can program developers and evaluators work together to improve the fidelity of educational programs?

In the second chapter, Introduction to Implementation Fidelity, Dhillon, Darrow, and Meyers provide a review of health and education implementation fidelity literature, noting specifically that the recent emergence of fidelity in education research imparts some reliance on other fields. The authors provide background on implementation fidelity, including various definitions or conceptualizations as well as its history of use, before engaging in reflection on why it is worth studying. The bulk of the chapter considers how implementation fidelity is assessed as researchers and evaluators begin to grapple with issues of measurement, analysis, and reporting.

In the third chapter, EDUCATION CONNECTION's Center for 21st Century Skills: Development of an Evidence-Based Technology-Enhanced Blended Learning High School, LaBanca, Lorentson, and Oh introduce EDUCATION CONNECTION's STEM21 Digital Academy. STEM21 delivers a standards-based, next-generation 9th–12th grade course sequence in mathematics, science and technology through a "blended learning" environment. In this chapter, program developers explain how the four main elements of coursework—blended learning, experiential learning, a digital portfolio, and proficiency assessments—drive student learning. The authors also consider how the program was systemized before turning their attention to the early stages of grappling with implementation fidelity, including defining it within the framework of a program in its early stages. The authors highlight one nuanced aspect of their work, discussing how having internal and external evaluators interact enable program developers to learn and develop capacity. The authors also expound upon some challenges, including fidelity data collection strategies, making fidelity efforts meaningful to and potentially useful for practitioners, and implementing the program well.

The uniqueness of the overlap in work between internal and external evaluators is also evident in the fourth chapter, STEM21 Digital Academy Fidelity of Implementation: Valuation and Assessment of Program Components and Implementation. Lorentson, Oh, and LaBanca initially provide an overview of their conceptualization of fidelity of implementation in the context of this development evaluation. Then they address related evaluative challenges, including initial ones such as defining roles and developing partnerships, before turning their attention to subsequent programmatic concerns, including shifting EDUCATION CONNECTION's organizational mindset to increase focus on fidelity measurement while simultaneously recognizing that core aspects of the program were not completely finalized (meaning that implementation fidelity measurement was not completely established). Thus, program developers and evaluators, both internal and external, had to determine what to measure, figure out how to measure (and develop instruments to measure), and create fidelity cookbooks to aid developers, evaluators, practitioners, and others in understanding this relatively new world of fidelity of implementation. The authors also discuss how they reported results and how those results informed program development.

In Chapter 5, The eMINTS Professional Development Program and the Journey Toward Greater Program Fidelity, the book shifts to consider fidelity of implementation at the validation stage. Kaplan, Terry, and Beglau detail the eMINTS Comprehensive Program, an intensive professional development model that requires two years and more than 200 hours of professional development for teachers in participating schools. In addition to explaining the eMINTS instructional model, which consists of high-quality lesson design, inquiry-based learning, a community of learners approach to instruction, and classroom technology integration, the authors explicate why program growth drives their need for program fidelity measures. They explain how national policy and program growth necessitated work with an external evaluator to develop and validate instruments to measure aspects of program fidelity. Many of their lessons hinge on the importance of communicating: sharing findings with program participants; involving evaluators in the planning process (and educating them on the details of the program early in the work); working together to find efficiencies; and maintain ongoing communication. They conclude the chapter by considering the future of eMINTS, how they currently think about taking the program to scale, and what that means for measuring implementation fidelity going forward.

Brandt, Meyers and Molefe begin Chapter 6, Placing Evaluation at the Core: How Evaluation Supported Scale Up of the eMINTS Comprehensive Program, by providing an overview of eMINTS's persistent focus on evaluation as part of its growth and highlight some of the research evidence behind the professional development. The authors then provide a high-level explanation of the evaluation design and how it fits the national i3 standards. The chapter goes on to provide a practical demonstration of how implementation fidelity can be determined by detailing the following seven steps taken by the evaluation team: (1) identifying and defining core components of the program; (2) identifying data sources to measure core components; (3) determining the relative importance of each component; (4) developing component indexes; (5) finalizing plans with the program developer; (6) aggregating individual scores to the school level; and (7) determining overall level of implementation fidelity. After walking the reader through the practical example, the authors report on some of the design constraints and limitations, including data constraints and lack of empirical information. They conclude by making some observations regarding next steps.

Slavin and Madden begin the seventh chapter, Success for All Design and Implementation of Whole School Reform at Scale, by detailing the well-known Success for All (SFA) program, including SFA's goals and components. In discussing these components, the authors highlight activities relevant for successful implementation while reporting on potentially successful instructional practices. They detail model program implementation, including discussion of the roles coaches and school leaders have, how data can be used to inform administrative decisions and teacher instructional practices, and how instructional and academic improvements can be attained incrementally. The authors then describe how fidelity measurement in SFA schools has evolved over time. For more than 20 years they have been providing school leaders and teachers feedback to guide continuous school improvement as well as reflect upon results to guide the program's development. They detail one tool that was developed as part of this work, the Success for All snapshot tool, and explain why it remains relevant to continuous improvement in schools and Success for All.

In Chapter 8, Measuring Implementation Fidelity in Success for All, Balu and Quint provide a brief description of the SFA evaluation design followed by a presentation of the Success for All logic model. The authors note that the chapter is one about trade-offs that are most evident when considering the utility of the Success for All snapshot tool for evaluative purposes, which was the decision of MDRC for a number of reasons (for example, financial cost of developing and validating a different-but-similar tool). Still, they explain challenges associated with converting the snapshot from a primarily qualitative instrument designed for school and teacher feedback to a quantitative instrument designed for systematically measuring program fidelity in schools. They also elaborate on the challenges of working with data acquired via developer tools and the related constraints of calculating fidelity. They conclude by weighing the pros and cons of relying on an instrument created by the program developer.

In the final chapter, Measuring Fidelity: The Present and Future, Goodson, Price, and Darrow review what they perceive to be success and challenges in the fidelity work for each evaluation as well as across evaluations. Specifically, they review the articulations of the logic models and identification of key components within them: the identification of data sources and the subsequent development of indexes; revising measures; and more general lessons from the field.

Note

1. Although less clearly defined when the evaluations in this book were funded, current i3 requirements define "moderate" evidence as the program having at least one study that meets What Works Clearinghouse's standards without or with reservations and finds at least one positive, statistically significant outcome while not finding any overriding unfavorable impacts. The current i3 standard for "strong" evidence is the same as "moderate," except two studies meeting standards with reservations are required instead of one.

References

Borman, G. D., Slavin, R. E., Cheung, A. C. K., Chamberlain, A. M., Madden, N. A., & Chambers, B. (2007). Final reading outcomes of the national randomized field trial of Success for All. *American Educational Research Journal, 44*(3), 701–731.
Century, J., Rudnick, M., & Freeman, C. (2010). A framework for measuring fidelity of implementation: A foundation for shared language and accumulation of knowledge. *American Journal of Evaluation, 31*(2), 199–218.
Cordray, D., & Pion, G. (2006). Treatment strength and integrity: Models and methods. In R. Bootzin & P. McKnight (Eds.), *Strengthening research methodology: Psychologica measurement and evaluation* (pp. 103–124). Washington, DC: American Psychological Association.

Datnow, A., & Castellano, M. (2000). *An inside look at Success for All: A qualitative study of implementation and teaching and learning* (Report No. 45). Baltimore: Johns Hopkins University, Center for Research on the Education of Students Placed at Risk. Retrieved May 22, from http://www.csos.jhu.edu/crespar/techReports/Report45.pdf

Hulleman, C., & Cordray, D. (2009). Moving from the lab to the field: The role of fidelity and achieved relative intervention strength. *Journal of Research on Educational Effectiveness, 2*, 88–110.

Munter, C., Wilhelm, A. G., Cobb, P., & Cordray, D. S. (2014). Assessing fidelity of implementation of an unprescribed, diagnostic mathematics intervention. *Journal of Research on Educational Effectiveness, 7*(1), 83–113.

O'Donnell, C. L. (2008). Defining, conceptualizing, and measuring fidelity of implementation and its relationship to outcome in K-12 curriculum intervention research. *Review of Educational Research, 78*(1), 33–84.

Penuel, W. R., & Means, B. (2011). Using large-scale databases in evaluation: Advances, opportunities, and challenges. *American Journal of Evaluation, 32*(1), 118–133.

Penuel, W. R., Singleton, C., & Roschelle, J. (2011). Classroom network technology as a support for systematic mathematics reform: Examining the effects of Texas Instruments' MathForward Program on student achievement in a large, diverse district. *Journal of Computers in Mathematics and Science Teaching, 30*(2), 179–202.

2

INTRODUCTION TO IMPLEMENTATION FIDELITY

Sonica Dhillon, Catherine Darrow, and
Coby V. Meyers

> *The bridge between a promising idea and its impact on students is implementation.*
> *(Berman & McLaughlin, 1976, p.349)*

Over the last 40 years, interest in measuring implementation fidelity has grown substantially. Motivated by challenges to the notion that program implementers are "passive acceptors of an innovation" (Rogers, 2003, p. 180, in O'Donnell, 2008), researchers began to explore how deviations in program delivery influence programmatic outcomes of interest such as adult response to therapeutic interventions in the field of health. The most salient finding of these studies is that increased fidelity of implementation is associated with more positive or anticipated treatment effects (Dane & Schneider, 1998). In addition to providing insight into the extent to which programmatic outcomes met design expectations, studying implementation fidelity can help program developers identify areas of implementation breakdown and support programmatic refinement. Although much progress has been made, the study of implementation fidelity remains a young science. Fidelity definitions and systematic approaches to assessing and reporting implementation fidelity continue to be unstandardized and only a small portion of studies employ measures of fidelity (Dane & Schneider, 1998; Moncher & Prinz, 1991).

The purposes of this chapter are to review the history and current state of implementation fidelity in the fields of health and education and to highlight the importance of continued implementation fidelity studies from the perspective of those that may find this work most useful; program developers, researchers, and evaluators. Given fidelity research is limited in the field of education, this introduction includes evidence from the field of health (O'Donnell, 2008). The knowledge gained from the health sciences has been instrumental in our understanding of the most current and innovative methods of measuring fidelity. We leverage lessons learned in the field of health and translate them to the study of implementation fidelity in the field of education.

Definitions of Implementation Fidelity

Fidelity refers to the degree to which a particular program follows a program model. (Bond, Evans, Salyers, Williams, & Kim, 2000, p. 75)

In 2008, O'Donnell highlighted seven definitions of fidelity in the field of health and six definitions of fidelity in the field of education. O'Donnell noted that although there were variations in the definition of fidelity based on both the field and type of study being conducted, most definitions were synonymous and focused on adherence to a program model. For example, Bond et al. (2000) defined fidelity as the "degree to which a particular program follows a program model" (p. 75). Dusenbury, Brannigan, Falco and Hansen (2003) described fidelity as "the degree to which … program providers implement programs as intended by the program developers" (p. 240), and Moncher and Prinz (1991) described fidelity as the "confirmation that the manipulation of the independent variable occurred as planned" (p. 247).

Although there is general agreement on implementation fidelity being defined as the degree to which a program model is instituted as intended, interpreting the extent or quality of implementation is far more complex. How implementation fidelity is conceptualized and measured varies greatly. This is exemplified in the variation of terminology used to describe implementation fidelity itself (e.g., program integrity, compliance, dose, adherence, and clinical effectiveness) and its associated dimensions and measures (Dane & Schneider, 1998; Dusenbury et al., 2003; Eccles et al., 2009; Mowbray, Holter, Teague, & Bybee, 2003; O'Donnell, 2008). For instance, Dane and Schneider (1998) presented fidelity in terms of five constructs: adherence, exposure, quality of delivery, participant responsiveness, and program differentiation.[1] Conversely, Yeaton and Sechrest (1981) discuss fidelity in terms of three components: strength, integrity, and effectiveness of treatment. Yeaton and Sechrest (1981) prioritized elements of fidelity related to the treatment. Participant responsiveness has the potential to influence the degree of fidelity, but was not included in their discussion and is absent from more recent definitions of fidelity (Darrow, 2013). Moreover, confirming program differentiation is a desirable outcome of any fidelity analysis. As Darrow notes, "The concept of program differentiation is a byproduct of a well-implemented intervention and is made evident through data collected via fidelity measures, yet is no longer included in the definition of fidelity" (p. 1140).

The focus of measurement and the terms associated with it also varies among researchers. For example, Nelson et al. (2012) make a distinction between "intervention fidelity," which is implementation of the core components of a program model, and what Fixsen, Naoom, Blase, Friedman, and Wallace (2005) describe as "organizational fidelity," which is the implementation of program supports such as training, coaching, and staff selection. More so, Century, Cassata, Freeman, and Rudnick (2012) present and discuss the organization of a program model in terms of "structural" and "interactional" components. These variations in how fidelity is described and conceptualized make alignment of implementation constructs across program evaluations difficult. It impedes the field's common interpretation of what it means to be faithful to a program, as well as the ability to report implementation findings in a consistent and interpretable manner. Despite these challenges, the integration of implementation fidelity measurement into project proposals has become more prominent in recent years (Hulleman & Cordray, 2009). Greater attention and funding for implementation fidelity affords research and evaluators alike more opportunities to address implementation fidelity measurement issues as well as build an evidence base upon which best practices for implementation fidelity measurement can be determined. In the next section, the history of implementation fidelity is discussed in an effort to better understand the progress of this field of study.

History of Implementation Fidelity

> *Increasingly, measures of program model fidelity have become standard requirements in mental health services research (Heflinger, 1996; Henggeler, Pickrel, & Brondino, 1999) and in other applied fields, such as criminal justice, education, and medicine (Leithwood & Montgomery, 1980; Rezmovic, 1984; Schreier & Rezmovic, 1983). Despite this attention, no systematic body of theory and research on fidelity has yet appeared. (Bond et al., 2000, p. 75)*

Although implementation fidelity remains a young science, the field of education has benefited from the efforts of early implementation fidelity researchers. According to Bond et al. (2000), the history of implementation fidelity is rooted in psychiatric research from the 1960s, growing out of an interest in "sorting out methodological and interpretative problems in the early outcome studies" (p. 76). Early psychotherapy research included little to no documentation of how therapeutic models were expected to be implemented. This made replication studies difficult. Critics, including Eysenck (1952, in Bond et al., 2000) challenged the notion that adoption of a psychotherapeutic model guaranteed accurate model implementation. In time, research revealed program implementers, in fact, did not implement programs as intended and modified components to fit their own needs (Berman & McLaughlin, 1976; Rogers, Eveland, & Klepper, 1977). According to Bond et al. (2000), the introduction of fidelity measurement "accelerated the maturation of psychotherapy research by making standardized treatment possible and by providing methods to document differences between different forms of treatment" (p. 76). Research focus shifted towards studying issues related to adherence to program models such as treat-ment integrity[2] and treatment differentiation,[3] eventually yielding a surge of research on which programmatic elements had the most influence on therapeu-tic outcomes (Bond et al., 2000).

The field of psychotherapy has demonstrated the necessity for understanding program measurement irrespective of an individual's domain of research. Specifi-cally, challenging the assumption that program implementers were "passive accep-tors of an innovation, rather than active modifiers of a new idea," encouraged further examination of how modifications to intended program models influence desired outcomes (Rogers, 2003, p. 180, in O'Donnell, 2008). Berman and McLaughlin's (1976) report, which examined how federally supported educa-tional programs were implemented, demonstrated that the field of education suffered from similar implementation issues encountered in the health field. The study found that no educational program in their study was immune to modifica-tion and noted that overall fidelity of program implementation was deficient (Berman & McLaughlin, 1976, in Dusenbury et al., 2003). The field of education leveraged lessons learned in the health field and supported the advancement of implementation fidelity through subsequent research. Hall and Loucks (1977) helped further the study of implementation fidelity by challenging the assump-tion that the use of educational innovations occurred in isolation in the treatment condition and not the non-treatment condition. They demonstrated that there can be varied "levels of use" or quality of implementation, and through their exploratory analysis cautiously suggested that a relation may exist between vari-ation in level of use and anticipated outcomes.

Despite growing interest in developing measures to examine fidelity of imple-mentation between the 1960s and 1980s, research suggests that the study of implementation had not yet been fully adopted and perhaps valued. Moncher and Prinz (1991) reported that between 1980 and 1988, 55 percent of psychotherapy studies did not employ any measures of fidelity. Additionally, Dane and Schnei-der's (1998) seminal work suggested that only 39 of 162 of the behavioral, social, and/or academic prevention programs published between 1980 and 1994 pro-vided information on fidelity.

Although the study of implementation fidelity has not been systematically adopted in the field of health or education, interest in implementation fidelity continues to grow. This is best demonstrated by public and private funding agen-cies' increased focus on examining implementation fidelity in education research (Hulleman & Cordray, 2009), as well as the strides being made towards develop-ing implementation fidelity models or best practices (e.g., Century et al., 2012; Gearing et al., 2011; Koop et al., 2004; Nelson et al., 2012; Teaue, Bond, & Drake, 1998). Moreover, researchers continue to refine fidelity measurement. For instance, Mowbray et al. (2003) offer examples on how to construct valid fidelity indices, and Hulleman and Cordray (2009) explore different methods of calculat-ing fidelity and examine how these methods influenced the Achieved Relative

Strength (ARS) of a program—the actual strength of the intervention accounting for differences in levels of program implementation in both treatment and control conditions.

Why Study Implementation Fidelity?

It is difficult to determine whether nonsignificant results are due to a poorly conceptualized program or to an inadequate or incomplete delivery of prescribed services. (Dane & Schneider, 1998, p. 23)

Fidelity is necessary for the accurate interpretation of treatment effects. (Perepletchikova & Kazdin, 2005, in Gearing et al., 2011, p. 79)

We know that outcomes cannot be changed unless programs are adopted into practice (Bergman & McLaughlin, 1976, in Dusenbury et al., 2003; Eccles et al., 2009). Developing a program from concept to real-world implementation is often a complex, iterative process that requires an extensive amount of time (Fixsen et al., 2005). In this section, we explore the value of studying implementation fidelity from the perspective of intervention developers as well as researchers and evaluators. The study of implementation fidelity has shown promise in helping developers, researchers, and evaluators alike better understand the factors that hinder program adherence as well as understand how the quality of implementation impacts outcomes of interest in real-world settings.

Several studies have shown that outcomes suffer when there are changes to implementation. Hulleman and Cordray (2009) note reductions in treatment effectiveness when moving from the lab or controlled setting to the field, and Dobson and Cook (1980) show outcomes vary based on the amount of services received. One of the most compelling and salient arguments for the study of fidelity is "without documentation and/or measurement of a program's adherence to an intended model, there is no way to determine whether unsuccessful outcomes reflect a failure of the model or failure to implement the model as intended" (Chen, 1990, in Mowbray et al., 2003, p. 317). In this respect, program evaluations that do not include measures of implementation fidelity may be considered "high stakes" for program developers as evaluations "may underrepresent the potential value of a prevention program, putting effective interventions at risk of discontinuation" (Felner et al., 1994, in Dane & Schneider, 1998, p. 24–25).

In program evaluation settings, the study of implementation fidelity can inform more accurate interpretation on treatment effects (Mowbray et al., 2003; Perepletchikova & Kazdin, 2005). At a minimum, measuring fidelity can be used as a "manipulation check" to ensure the absence of treatment in the control condition (Bond et al., 2000, p. 78; Mills & Ragan, 2000, in Mowbray et al., 2003, p. 317) and in more refined studies can be used to examine threats to internal validity by providing additional evidence disproving alternative explanations of effects (Moncher & Prinz, 1991). As succinctly articulated in Nelson et al. (2012), the strongest statistical test of cause and effect is the Randomized Control Trial (RCT) in which individuals are randomly assigned to treatment or control conditions. By randomizing assignment, a study can assume that external factors outside of what is being studied will vary randomly across groups as well, and as a result will not bias one group's results more than the other. However, given that treatment occurs after assignment, it is possible that non-random factors influence the extent to which treatment is implemented as expected (e.g., number of PD hours, attitudes, access to materials, or administrative supports) (Dusenbury et al., 2003). Without the study of implementation fidelity it is possible to interpret negative research results as "indications of inadequacies or incompleteness in the conceptualization of the program model, rather than in its delivery" (Dane & Schneider, 1998, p. 36). In essence, in cases where programs are not implemented properly, the study of implementation fidelity can help researchers avoid erroneously attributing research findings to a program model (Dobson & Cook, 1980, in Dusenbury et al., 2003). It may also help researchers understand the impact of these non-random factors on both mediating and distal outcomes (Dusenbury et al., 2003), opening the figurative "black box" between assignment to condition and outcomes.

Moreover, Bond et al. (2000) indicated that the study of measures of implementation fidelity is

> Equally valuable when program evaluations do yield significant treatment outcomes. In addition to increased confidence in the study's internal validity, the fidelity measures provide a roadmap for replication. With significant findings, the research question shifts to asking what the critical ingredients of program success are. Fidelity measures provide the basis for more fine-grained inquiry into such questions. (p. 79)

In addition, "fidelity assessment in both the treatment and counterfactual conditions allows the researcher to capture intervention strength as implemented (i.e., Achieved Relative Strength)" (Nelson et al., 2012, p. 377). By developing and answering more refined questions, depth can be added to the evidence base for a given program (Mowbray et al., 2003) and further the field's understanding of "what works in education, for whom, and under what circumstances" (IES, 2007, in Nelson et al., 2012, p. 377).

Beyond program evaluation, the study of implementation offers insight into the factors that influence programmatic uptake as well as enacting an intervention in practice (Dusenbury et al., 2003). A key aspect of studying fidelity is documentation of differences in ideal and actual implementation of core program components; programmatic elements needed to bring about short-term outcomes of interest and required for future replications of the program. Breakdowns in implementation can be caused by a number of factors, including but not limited to complexity of the intervention, teacher attitude, and organizational readiness to adopt new programs (Dusenbury et al., 2003; Fixen et al., 2005). Beyond circumventing the misattribution of negative or null findings, assessing differences between ideal and actual implementation can highlight where deviations from the intended model exist (Bond et al., 1997; Mowbray et al., 2003) and, once identified, can guide developers to augment the types of supports and the areas that are needed to ensure better implementation. Furthermore, implementation fidelity can be used for program monitoring (Bond et al., 2000). Perepletchikova and Kazdin (2005, in Gearing et al., 2011) showed that over time participants deviate from the program model. By assessing fidelity over time, developers are better able to see changes in implementation and, if they deem necessary, development of additional intervention supports or programmatic refinements (e.g., refresher courses, re-certification tests, etc.) (Bond et al., 1997; Dane & Schneider, 1998; Koop et al., 2004; Mowbray et al., 2003).

How Is Implementation Fidelity Assessed?

As demand increases for broader penetration of evidence-based treatments in the services marketplace, so does the expectation that service providers and organizations be held accountable for their outcomes. Whether implementing a particular treatment model or treatment elements common across a class of empirically tested treatments (e.g., cognitive-behavioral treatments, interpersonal treatments; see, e.g., Chorpita and Daleiden, 2009; Garland et al., 2008a; McHugh et al., 2009), indices of implementation fidelity are needed to determine whether client improvement or lack thereof is a function of the failure of the treatment (or treatment element) or of its application. (Schoenwald et al., 2011, p. 33)

How implementation fidelity is conceptualized and measured continues to vary, making interpretation of what it means to be faithful to an intervention nebulous (Dane & Schneider, 1998; Dusenbury et al., 2003; Mowbray et al., 2003; O'Donnell, 2008). In the education domain, several researchers have worked to address this issue by developing frameworks to assess fidelity (e.g., Century et al., 2012; Gearing et al., 2011; Koop et al., 2004; Nelson et al., 2012). In the remainder of this chapter, we synthesize four emergent themes found in implementation fidelity literature: articulation of the change and logic model; identification of critical components; selection of appropriate indices and benchmarks of fidelity; and computation and application of fidelity score.

Articulate the Change and Logic Model

According to Gearing et al. (2011), "design is the first core component of fidelity" and should include "elements essential to the design of the trial as well as elements needed to evaluate or replicate the study" (p. 80). In well-developed programs, program models are often outlined in treatment manuals (Bond et al., 2000). These manuals can provide guidance on minimal acceptable standards of implementation and offer guidance on acceptable amounts of model variation (Santacroce, Maccarelli, & Grey, 2004, in Gearing et al., 2011). Understanding how a program is designed provides a framework upon which one can start to understand how program developers believe their interventions impact change and provides a baseline upon which deviations from anticipated implementation can be assessed.

To study implementation fidelity, developers and researchers alike must understand the change model[4]—"constructs that intervention designer believed will be involved in the causal process" (Nelson et al., 2012, p. 379). Or, in other words, developers must be able to articulate and understand how, theoretically, their program will bring about change or desired outcomes. According to the authors, "specifying this model is crucial in identifying the core intervention components which are theorized to drive the effect of the intervention" (p. 380).

Once a change model has been established, a logic model[5] can be overlaid. A program logic model "links outcomes (both short- and long-term) with program activities/processes and the theoretical assumptions/principles of the program" (W. K. Kellogg Foundation, 1998, p. 35). It "serves as a roadmap for implementing the intervention" and "consists of the resources and activities (both of implementers and of participants) necessary to operationalize the change model components for the treatment condition of the experiment" (Nelson et al., 2012, p. 382–383). Using a logic model "presents a plausible and sensible model of how the program will work under certain conditions to solve identified problems" and is seen as a "useful strategy for identifying program components and outcomes, as well as important conceptual factors affecting program operations and outcomes" (McLaughlin & Jordan, 1999, p. 66). In essence, for both program developers and evaluators, it "helps create shared understanding of and focus on program goals and methodology; relating activities to projected outcomes" (W. K. Kellogg Foundation, 1998, p. 5).

Identify Critical Components

Most programs contain both essential and non-essential components. However, practical limitations such as funding, capacity, and time may hinder developers' and researchers' abilities to review all components of a program. Identification of critical components of a program is a practical next step in assessing fidelity of implementation. Taking the time to isolate critical components allows researchers and developers to "ensure that each core component of the intervention is fully assessed, and that any extraneous activities are excluded from fidelity assessment" (Nelson et al., 2012, p. 385). More so, this approach allows researchers and developers to establish an a priori framework to assess whether key implementation components were present at all, the extent to which they were present, and whether they are related to final outcomes (Century et al., 2012). Identification of critical elements is prevalent in the implementation fidelity models and is extensively supported throughout the literature (Century et al., 2012; Fullan & Pomfret, 1997; Gottfredson, 1984, in Dusenbury et al., 2003; Koop et al., 2004; Mowbray et al., 2003; Nelson et al., 2012; Saunders et al., 2013).

In recent years, there has been a shift to further categorizing critical elements as components that address two measures of fidelity—commonly referred to in i3 evaluation work as measures of "fidelity of intervention" and "fidelity of implementation." Fidelity of intervention has been defined as assessing the variation between the planned and delivered program mediators (i.e., the heart of the intervention itself), whereas fidelity of implementation is seen as assessing the variation between the planned and delivered program inputs and activities (Boulay, Goodson, & Darrow, 2012). Although there is variation in terminology, this distinction in components is pronounced. Mowbray et al. (2003) argued that evaluation include both "structure" and "process." Moreover, what is referred to as "implementation fidelity" in i3 is described by Fixsen et al. (2005) and Nelson et al. (2012) as "organizational fidelity." Similarly, what is described by i3 evaluators as "fidelity of intervention" is described as "personnel fidelity" or "intervention fidelity" by these two researchers respectively.

Selection of appropriate indices and benchmarks of fidelity, setting their thresholds, and creating the fidelity measure are contingent on the development of a strong change and logic model and identification of critical components. Moreover, the creation of a strong implementation fidelity evaluation plan relies on clear communication and collaboration between developers and evaluators. These communications help to ensure that to the extent possible, program designs as seen by evaluators conform to both the expectations of key stakeholders and the reality of program operations. Clear communication and collaboration also "help shape stakeholders' expectations by informing key policy makers and managers of the expectations and priorities of others, by confronting them with the reality of the program as it is currently operating and in some cases by helping them to explore the implications of possible changes in program activities and goals" (Wholey, ch. 2, in Newcomer, Hatry, & Wholey, 2004, p. 37). Without clear articulation of a logic model and its critical components, establishing measures of fidelity is difficult and may result in ambiguous findings (Bond et al., 2000; Eccles et al., 2009).

Select Appropriate Indices and Benchmarks of Fidelity

Once critical components have been identified, the next step is to select appropriate measures for each. For each critical component, one or more aspects of fidelity may be measured. However, selection of what aspect of fidelity to measure for each component will, again, be contingent on what developers and researchers are interested in examining and, potentially, how developed a program is. As articulated by Mowbray et al. (2003),

When programs are initially being evaluated and fidelity criteria are first developed, an emphasis on structure over process items may be appropriate. Then if evaluations do show positive outcomes, measures of structure may permit more rapid initial replication of the program model, assuring fidelity at least to some significant component. However, for enduring programs and to facilitate movement toward more valid, mature replication, time should be invested in the careful development and testing of reliable and valid measures of process criteria associated with critical components and based on program theory at a deeper level. (p. 333)

Once developers and researchers have established what aspects of fidelity are important to study, two additional steps need to be taken: (1) appropriate indices of fidelity should be selected or developed, and (2) appropriate weights and measurement thresholds should be set.

Select or Develop Indices

Using indices is viewed as a method of quantifying fidelity (Drake et al., 2001, in Mowbray et al., 2003). Indices are used to examine whether components of the logic model were implemented as expected (Nelson et al., 2012). Common indices include teacher self-report, observations, logs, checklists, attendance, participant surveys, and interviews (Dusenbury et al., 2003; Nelson et al., 2012). Identification of indices for both treatment and counterfactual is encouraged as a means to produce findings associating fidelity of implementation with program impacts (Cordray & Pion, 2006; Hulleman & Cordray, 2009). Selection of appropriate indices can be a complicated and difficult process. Unrau (2001) "advises that measurement of fidelity should not use client data alone, but rather, that client data should complement other evaluations approached" (Mowbray et al., 2003, p. 329). Researchers encourage the use of multiple measures, maintaining that "if indices of intervention components involve … a binary scale or with a single item, then there is a risk that the index cannot detect sufficient variance in implementation to link it to outcomes" (Nelson et al., 2012, p. 392). In addition to supporting analysis, using multiple indices offers other benefits. Some indices run the risk of being biased. For example, social desirability bias, or the tendency to respond in a manner that will be viewed favorably by others, has been associated with self-report (Arnold & Feldman, 1981). Using a single measure may skew findings. Multiple indices allow researchers and developers to triangulate information from an assortment of sources and allow for more accurate interpretation of results. In the same vein, if indices have not been deemed a valid or reliable measure of the construct of interest, it will be difficult to "ensure that valid conclusions are drawn from an experiment about the intended intervention" (Nelson et al., 2012, p. 387).

Set Appropriate Weights and Measurement Thresholds

Following the selection of appropriate fidelity indices, thresholds for each metric must be set. These thresholds are the benchmarks against which fidelity is measured. Darrow and Goodson (under review) keenly point out that depending on a program/intervention's stage of development, creating these thresholds can be challenging. If an intervention has been tested in the past, thresholds can be set empirically (e.g., based on post-hoc analysis of effectiveness and implementation studies). However, interventions early in development that lack data require thresholds to be created theoretically. In cases where benchmarks cannot be set empirically, researchers can make informed threshold decisions through other means, such as consultation with experts, review of literature, or through polling key program developers or constituents (Mowbray et al., 2003). This is another area in which communication between researcher and developers may be vital. In addition, weights can be included in cases where there are several core components which developers believe differentially influence outcomes. Weights allow researchers and developers to give more analytic value to certain components over others.

Compute and Apply Fidelity Scores

Once fidelity data has been collected and appropriate thresholds have been set, fidelity can be established. Fidelity data can be used descriptively and/or can be linked to outcome measures to help explain both intermediate and distal outcomes (Nelson et al., 2012; Saunders et al., 2012). As mentioned earlier, employing multiple indices for each critical component is encouraged. By combining indices for the critical components being studied, researchers can "evaluate the implementation and effectiveness of each core component individually," and minimize "bias due to type of measure" (Nelson et al., 2012, p. 389). For example, if there is a risk of social desirability bias in self-report, independent researcher observations could be added to increase objective interpretation of results. Adopting this method has been shown to account for more variation when predicting outcomes (Abry, Rimm-Kaufmann, & Hulleman 2012, in Nelson et al., 2012).

Although no consensus exists around best practices when computing implementation fidelity scores, Cordray and Hulleman (2009) offer three methods for calculating fidelity, each of which is constrained by its own limitations. In order to calculate an absolute fidelity we must know the maximum value that can be achieved on an index. Once this is known, absolute fidelity is calculated as a percentage by dividing the overall mean of conditional group (treatment or control) by the maximum value and then multiplied by 100. Calculating an average fidelity index does not require knowledge of the maximum value that can be achieved. It is simply calculated by taking the mean of the conditional group (sum of indices values over the number of group members). The binary compiler index requires that a cut point be established, theoretically or empirically, differentiating sufficient and insufficient completion of the component of interest. The binary compiler index is calculated by assigning a 1 to all individuals that meet or exceed the cut point and a 0 to those that fall short. Participant scores are then summed and divided by the number of participants in the condition.

Researchers have proposed several methods of connecting fidelity data to observed outcomes. These methodologies include but are not limited to analysis of variance (ANOVA), hierarchical linear modeling (HLM), and correlations trend analysis (Nelson et al., 2012). Methods used to examine the relationship between outcomes and implementation may vary based on a number of factors such as complexity of intervention, quality of instructional training materials, participant attitudes, organizations' willingness to adopt intervention, etc. (Dusenbury et al., 2003, p. 249–251). Currently, limited research exists linking fidelity to outcomes (Nelson et al., 2012). Although this may be the state of this field of study, researchers continue to encourage the study of implementation fidelity as variations in fidelity may explain variations in outcomes. Nelson and colleagues (2012) identify three reasons for why there is value in linking fidelity to outcomes. In cases where outcomes do not reach significance, assessing fidelity may explain or account for the lack of differences between treatment and control. Alternatively, in cases where outcomes are significant despite breakdowns in implementation, this may indicate that there is room for growth for outcomes if a program is implemented as expected and/or components assumed to be critical to the program may, in fact, not be crucial at all. The third benefit to connecting fidelity measures to outcomes is the "ability to determine empirically a cutoff point for sufficient fidelity: that level of fidelity above which variation in implementation has little impact on outcomes" (p. 391).

Summary

Implementation fidelity has gained traction over the last year, in part, due to the strides made in the health and education fields. Research has shown that deviations in program delivery can influence programmatic outcomes of interest (Dane & Schneider, 1998). The study of implementation fidelity offers a mechanism by which program developer, researcher, and evaluators can better understand the factors that may dampen or drive these programmatic outcomes. However, despite the advances made in the study of implementation fidelity thus far, more is needed. Integration of the study of implementation fidelity measurement in evaluation designs as well as identification of systematic definitions and approaches to measure implementation fidelity are areas where more attention is needed.

Notes

1. See Dane and Schneider (1998) for definitions of the five aspects of program integrity: adherence, exposure, quality of delivery, participant responsiveness and program differentiation.

2. Treatment integrity is defined as the "degree to which a treatment condition is implemented as intended" (Moncher & Prinz, 1991, in Bond et al., 2000, p. 76).
3. Treatment differentiation is defined as "whether treatment conditions differ from one another in the intended manner such that the manipulation of the independent variable offered as planned" (Moncher & Prinz, 1991, p. 247, in Bond et al., 2000).
4. As noted by Nelson et al. (2012) change model is also referred to as "theory of change," "conceptual logic model," or "conceptual model."
5. As noted by McLaughlin & Jordan (1999) logic models have been described as "chains of reasoning," "theory of action," "performance frameworks" and "logical frameworks."

References

Abry, T., Rimm-Kaufman, S. E., & Hulleman, C. S. (2012). Using intervention core components to identify the active ingredients of the Responsive Classroom approach. Unpublished report.

Arnold, H. J., & Feldman, D. C. (1981) Social desirability response bias in self-report choice situations. *The Academy of Management Journal, 24*(2), 377–385.

Berman, P., & McLaughlin, M. W. (1976). Implementation of educational innovation. *The Educational Forum, 40*(3), 345–370.

Bond, G. R., Evans, L., Salyers, M. P., Williams, J., & Kim, H. W. (2000). Measurement of fidelity in psychiatric rehabilitation. *Mental Health Services Research, 2*(2), 75–87.

Boulay, B., Goodson, B., & Darrow, C. (2012). NEi3 standards for high-quality implementation studies. Technical assistance training provided by National Evaluation of i3, Cambridge, MA.

Century, J., Cassata, A., Freeman, C., & Rudnick, M. (2012). *Measuring implementation, spread and sustainability of educational innovations: Innovating for coordinated collaborative research*. Chicago: Center for Elementary Mathematics and Science Education (CEMSE), University of Chicago. Paper presented at the annual meeting of the American Educational Research Assocation, Vancouver. Retrieved from http://www. academia.edu/2242502/Measuring_Implementation_Spread_and_Sustainabilityof_ Educational_Innovations_Innovating_for_Coordinated_Collaborative_Research

Chen, H. (1990). Theory-driven evaluations. Thousand Oaks, CA: Sage.

Chorpita, B. F., & Daleiden, E. L. (2009). Mapping evidence-based treatments for children and adolescents: Application of the distillation and matching model to 615 treatments from 322 randomized trials. *Journal of consulting and clinical psychology, 77*(3), 566.

Cordray, D. S., & Pion, G. M. (2006). Treatment strength and integrity: Models and methods. In R. R. Bootzin & P. E. McKnight (Eds.), *Strengthening research methodology: Psychological measurement and evaluation* (pp. 103–124). Washington, DC: American Psychological Association.

Dane, A. V., & Schneider, B. H. (1998). Program integrity in primary and early secondary prevention: Are implementation effects out of control? *Clinical Psychology Review, 18*(1), 23–45.

Darrow, C. L. (2013). The effectiveness and precision of intervention fidelity measures in preschool intervention research. *Early Education & Development, 24*(8), 1137–1160.

Darrow, C. L., & Goodson, B. (under review). Methods in developing systematic measures of implementation fidelity in evaluation research.

Dobson, L. D., & Cook, T. J. (1980). Avoiding Type III error in program evaluation: Results from a field experiment. *Evaluation and Program Planning, 3*, 269–276.

Drake, R. E., Goldman, H. H., Leff, H. S., Lehman, A. F., Dixon, L., Mueser, K. T., & Torrey, W. C. (2001). Implementing evidence-based practices in routine mental health service settings. *Psychiatric Services, 52*(2), 179–182.

Dusenbury, L., Brannigan, R., Falco, M., & Hansen, W. B. (2003). A review of research on fidelity of implementation: Implications for drug abuse prevention in school settings. *Health Education Research, 18*(2), 237–256.

Eccles, M. P., Armstrong, D., Baker, R., Cleary, K., Davies, H., Davies, S., et al. (2009). An implementation research agenda. *Implementation Science, 4*(1), 18.

Eysenck, H. (1952). The effects of psychotherapy, an evaluation. *Journal of Consulting Psychology, 16,* 319–324.

Felner, R. D., Brand, S., Mulhall, K. E., Counter, B., Millman, J. B., & Fried, J. (1994). The parenting partnership: The evaluation of a human service/corporate workplace collaboration for the prevention of substance abuse and mental health problems and the promotion of family and work adjustment. *Journal of Primary Prevention, 15,* 123–146.

Fixsen, D. L., Naoom, S. F., Blase, K. A., Friedman, R. M., & Wallace, F. (2005). Implementation research: A synthesis of the literature. Tampa, FL: University of South Florida, Louis de la Parte Florida Mental Health Institute, The National Implementation Research Network (FMHI Publication #231). Retrieved from http://ctndisseminationlibrary.org/PDF/nirnmonograph.pdf

Fullan, M., & Pomfret, A. (1997). Research on curriculum and instruction implementation. *Review of Educational Research, 47*(1), 335–397.

Garland, A. F., Hawley, K. M., Brookman-Frazee, L., & Hurlburt, M. S. (2008). Identifying common elements of evidence-based psychosocial treatments for children's disruptive behavior problems. *Journal of the American Academy of Child & Adolescent Psychiatry, 47*(5), 505–514.

Gearing, R. E., El Bassel, N., Ghesquiere, A., Baldwin, S., Gillies, J., & Ngeow, E. (2011). Major ingredients of fidelity: A review and scientific guide to improving quality of intervention research implementation. *Clinical Psychological Review, 31,* 79–88.

Gottfredson, G. D. (1984) A theory-ridden approach to program evaluation: A method for stimulating researcher–implementer collaboration. *American Psychologist, 39,* 1101–1112.

Hall, G. E., & Loucks, S. F. (1977). A developmental model for determining whether the treatment is actually implemented. *American Educational Research Journal, 14*(3), 263–276.

Heflinger, C. A. (1996). Implementing a system of care: Finding from the Fort Bragg Evaluation Project. *Journal of Mental Health Administration, 23,* 16–29.

Henggeler, S. W., Pickrel, S. G., & Brondino, M. J. (1999). Multisystemic treatment of substance-abusing and -dependent delinquents: Outcomes, treatment fidelity, and transportability. *Mental Health Services Research, 1,* 171–184.

Hulleman, C. S., & Cordray, D. S. (2009). Moving from the lab to the field: The role of fidelity and achieved relative intervention strength. *Journal of Research on Educational Effectiveness, 2*(1), 88–110.

Institute of Education Sciences (IES). (2007). Education Research Training Grants. RFA No. IES-NCER-2008–02. Washington, D.C.: U.S. Department of Education.

Koop, J. I., Rollins, A. L., Bond, G. R., Salyers, M. P., Dincin, J., Kinley, T., Shimon, S. M., & Marcelle, K. (2004). Development of the DPA fidelity scale: Using fidelity to define an existing vocational model. *Psychiatric Rehabilitation Journal, 28*(1), 16.

Leithwood, K. A., & Montgomery, D. J. (1980). Evaluating program implementation. *Evaluation Review, 4*(2), 193–214.

McHugh, R. K., Murray, H. W., & Barlow, D. H. (2009). Balancing fidelity and adaptation in the dissemination of empirically-supported treatments: The promise of transdiagnostic interventions. *Behaviour Research and Therapy, 47*(11), 946–953.

McLaughlin, J. A., & Jordan, G. B. (1999). Logic models: A tool for telling your programs performance story. *Evaluation and Program Planning, 22*(1), 65–72.

Mills, S. C., & Ragan, T. J. (2000). A tool for analyzing implementation fidelity of an integrated learning system (ILS). *Educational Technology Research and Development, 48,* 21–41.

Moncher, F. J., & Prinz, R. J. (1991). Treatment fidelity in outcome studies. *Clinical Psychology Review, 11*(3), 247–266.

Mowbray, C. T., Holter, M. C., Teague, G. B., & Bybee, D. (2003). Fidelity criteria: Development, measurement, and validation. *American Journal of Evaluation, 24*(3), 315–340.

Nelson, M. C., Cordray, D. S., Hulleman, C. S., Darrow, C. L., & Sommer, E. C. (2012). A procedure for assessing intervention fidelity in experiments testing educational and behavioral interventions. *The Journal of Behavioral Health Services & Research, 39*(4), 374–396.

Newcomer, K. E., Hatry, H. P., & Wholey, J. S. (2004). Meeting the need for practical evaluation approaches: An introduction. In J. S. Wholey, H. P. Hatry, and K. E. Newcomer (Eds.), *Handbook of practical program evaluation* (p. xxxiii–xliv). San Francisco, CA: Jossey-Bass.

O'Donnell, C. L. (2008). Defining, conceptualizing, and measuring fidelity of implementation and its relationship to outcomes in K–12 curriculum intervention research. *Review of Educational Research, 78*(1), 33–84.

Perepletchikova, F., & Kazdin, A. E. (2005). Treatment integrity and therapeutic change: Issues and research recommendations. *Clinical Psychology: Science and Practice, 12*(4), 365–383.

Rezmovic, E. L. (1984). Assessing treatment implementation amid the slings and arrows of reality. *Evaluation Review, 8*, 187–204.

Rogers, E. (2003). *Diffusion of innovations.* New York: Free Press.

Rogers, E. M., Eveland, J. D., & Klepper, C. (1977) *The Innovation Process in Organizations.* Department of Journalism, University of Michigan, Ann Arbor, MI.

Santacroce, S. J., Maccarelli, L., & Grey, M. (2004). Intervention fidelity. *Nursing Research, 53*(1), 63–66.

Saunders, R. P., Evans, A. E., Kenison, K., Workman, L., Dowda, M., & Chu, Y. H. (2013). Conceptualizing, implementing, and monitoring a structural health promotion intervention in an organizational setting. *Health Promotion Practice, 14*(3), 343–353.

Schoenwald, S. K., Garland, A. F., Chapman, J. E., Frazier, S. L., Sheidow, A. J., & Southam-Gerow, M. A. (2011). Toward the effective and efficient measurement of implementation fidelity. *Administration and Policy in Mental Health, 38*(1), 32–43. doi:10.1007/s10488-010-0321-0

Schreier, M. A., & Rezmovic, E. L. (1983). Measuring the degree of program implementation: A methodological review. *Evaluation Review, 7*, 599–633.

Teague, G. B., Bond, G. R., & Drake, R. E. (1998). Program fidelity in assertive community treatment: Development and use of a measure. *American Journal of Orthopsychiatry, 68*, 216–232.

Unrau, Y. A. (2001). Using client exit interviews to illuminate outcomes in program logic models: A case example. *Evaluation and Program Planning, 24*(4), 353–361.

W. K. Kellogg Foundation. (1998). *W. K. Kellogg Foundation evaluation handbook.* Battle Creek, MI: Author. Retrieved from http://www.wkkf.org/resource-directory/resource/2010/w-k-kellogg-foundation-evaluation-handbook

Yeaton, W. H., & Sechrest, L. (1981). Critical dimensions in the choice and maintenance of successful treatments: Strength, integrity, and effectiveness. *Journal of Consulting and Cinical Psychology, 49*(2), 156–167.

3

EDUCATION CONNECTION'S CENTER FOR 21ST CENTURY SKILLS

Development of an Evidence-Based Technology-Enhanced Blended Learning High School Program

Frank LaBanca, Mhora Lorentson, and Youn Joo Oh

Program Launch

Humble Beginnings

In 1989, eighteen Hartford children led by lead plaintiff 4th-grade student Milo Sheff began a civil action suit against the State of Connecticut, including then Governor William A. O'Neill (Eaton, 2006; Dougherty, et al., 2006). The suit argued that the State of Connecticut violated students' fundamental rights to education and equal protection through the use of an educational system based on the provision of separate city and suburban school districts, which was described as leading to racially segregated schools (Sheff Movement, 2013). The Connecticut State Supreme Court, in this landmark legal case *Sheff vs. O'Neill*, determined that the state had an obligation to provide Hartford's schoolchildren with equal educational opportunities that were not substantially and materially impaired by racial and ethnic isolation (Delaney, 2000).

In 2003, a settlement was reached between the plantiffs and the state primarily focused on voluntary desegregation. As a result, a number of educational programs were established to facilitate desegregation, including interdistrict magnet schools, open choice programs, and interdistrict cooperative grants. The interdistrict cooperative grant program was established as a competitive grant program with the goals of providing funding for programs to increase student achievement and reduce racial, ethnic, and economic isolation (Connecticut State Department of Education (CSDE), 2013a). The Connecticut Department of Education, Office of Choice Programs, recognized that socioeconomic and racial isolation was not limited to Hartford and expanded the availability of interdistrict cooperative funds to other urban centers statewide that included low-performing schools (CSDE, 2013b).

Much of the work associated with interdistrict cooperative grants occurred through Connecticut's six regional education service centers (RESCs). RESCs are public non-profit education agencies created under state statute for the main purpose of cooperative action to furnish programs and services to public school districts (Sec. 10-66a, 1965). Each RESC, including EDUCATION CONNECTION, is locally governed and designed to provide multi-district program support to Connecticut's 169 school districts.

In 1998, EDUCATION CONNECTION received interdistrict cooperative grant funding to develop a co-curricular high school leadership academy that emphasized the use of technology to create and showcase innovative student-created products and businesses. Several years later, in response to a need for increased student workforce preparedness in K-12 education in Connecticut's emerging STEM (Science, Technology, Engineering and Mathematics) workplaces, Connecticut's Office of Workforce Competitiveness (OWC) established the Connecticut Career Choices (CCC) program to address Connecticut's pressing STEM workforce needs. In 2002, EDUCATION CONNECTION led this initiative and advocated for scalable program delivery through the use of a technology-enhanced blended learning model. As an emerging teaching and learning strategy, the blended learning model used a learning management system (LMS) to deliver content in collaboration with a face-to-face teacher environment. The model coordinated digitally mediated learning and a variety of experiential learning activities, bringing together urban, suburban, and rural students for career mentoring, company tours, guest speakers, student internships, and teacher externships essentially connecting the classroom to the work world. To more formally codify this work, in 2005, EDUCATION CONNECTION established the Center for 21st Century Skills (the Center). Operating as one of EDUCATION CONNECTION's programs, the Center began to achieve state-wide recognition for the development, implementation, and scaling of innovative high school programs (e.g., Broderick, 2008; Leonard, 2003; O'Neill, 2003; Simkewicz & Mino, 2009). These programs assumed various forms: after-school technology-based clubs, enhanced curriculum modules for pre-existing courses, and full-year, stand-alone courses.

The key innovative curricular design for the Center's programs and courses was an extended challenge project (Apple, 2009). These research and development projects incorporated real-world experiences into education to allow students to develop skills in technical writing, research, computer-assisted design, computer animation, design work, field experiments, and web presence. They were designed to immerse students in an experience that replicates a professional environment, in which students take on roles and responsibilities, departmentalize, and make choices based on expertise and interest. Challenge projects are most successful when they are designed with no predetermined outcomes but, instead, when students clarify an ill-defined problem (Jonassen, 1997) and create diverse solutions. A sample challenge project used by Center students is provided in Figure 3.1.

Create and implement a new product or service that addresses the theme ***Adaptability***. Teams will:

- define adaptability that is meaningful to your team
- identify an issue or topic that will be addressed by the project
- investigate the topic via research, experimentation, and data analysis
- develop an innovative solution (product or service) that addresses the issue
- demonstrate application of the product or service
- document and communicate the project using digital media.

FIGURE 3.1 Challenge project scope

The system of students from multiple districts working on similar work created a need to better define expectations. In 2004, the Center created the Student Innovation Exposition, a day-long program designed to bring participating students together to showcase their work. The Student Innovation Exposition took the form of a trade show: each student group was provided with an 8 x 10 foot exhibition space so the public, other students, and judges from industry and academia could view and evaluate it. Students were also required to make a 3-minute elevator pitch oral presentation in a more formal theater-style format. These projects took on a variety of designs: students created or developed mobile apps, public health campaigns, e-businesses, digital media, environmental remediation tools, and sustainable energy products, to name a few.

Projects were evaluated using standardized rubrics that elucidated the intended learning outcomes without defining the specifics of the student-derived products. As many students from multiple school districts were participating, the Student Innovation Exposition became the means for consistent program implementation by the nature of students being evaluated on projects by judges that were external to the schools and the Center. Teachers were provided with a system that focused solely on student project results and there were diverse, unmonitored instructional methods to get to this "end product." Best teaching and learning practices that promoted achievement and engagement and also resulted in successful student projects were not well understood. However, this informal learning system created a feedback loop that provided a method to revise and improve Student Innovation Exposition challenge projects. One of the early lessons learned is that problem ideation and definition (problem finding) by students, an often overlooked and under-taught creativity skill process (Torrance, 1987; Turner, 2013), was critical to project success. Over the years, the rigor and quality of these projects rose quickly, and ultimately we realized that the development of a meaningful idea is the most important factor in group success (LaBanca & Ritchie, 2011).

National Recognition

The synergistic work between EDUCATION CONNECTION, the Connecticut State Department of Education Interdistrict Grants Program, and the Office of Workforce Competitiveness CCC program elicited formative evaluation feedback that suggested students were highly motivated and engaged by the work they were completing. In the mid-2000s, EDUCATION CONNECTION formed a key partnership with the Connecticut Community Colleges' College of Technology (CoT). The CoT is a statewide initiative providing career pathways for students to earn certificates and degrees in engineering and technology disciplines and acting as an umbrella for Connecticut's twelve community colleges and six public and private partner universities (Connecticut Board of Regents for Higher Education (BoR), 2013).

The CoT operationalizes much of its work through the National Science Foundation-funded Regional Center for Next Generation Manufacturing (RCNGM). The RCNGM develops skilled workers in the manufacturing workplace by constructing programs that provide resources to educators and students interested in learning new technologies in manufacturing. The CoT-RCNGM also provided seamless pathways with full credit articulation for community college students who earned STEM technologist associates degrees who wanted to pursue 4-year technology and engineering degrees at all state universities and a number of private Connecticut universities. As the Center and the CoT established its partnership, a model was developed in 2006 to articulate the relation and pathways for student trajectories to STEM workforce to include high school students (see Figure 3.2).

As the partnership blossomed, the Center applied for and received its first federal grant in 2008 in the National Science Foundation Advanced Technological Education program. The CoT, also participated in this funding stream and was a partner on the application. This funding supported the complete development, pilot testing, and validation of the initial three courses in the Center's portfolio: Information Technology Leadership Academy, Biology21 (Biology in the context of Biotechnology) and E-Commerce Entrepreneurship. Previously program modules were designed only around the challenge, with supporting resources. The evolution to a standards-aligned program that scaffolded essential content in conjunction with project-based challenges provided courses that had broader impact and use.

In addition, the curriculum development process was systematized and formalized. In 2009, the Center was awarded a second Advanced Technological Education grant as well as an Innovative Technology Experiences for Students and Teachers grant, both from the National Science Foundation. This funding enabled further program development and implementation in technology, science, and mathematics. As course development and implementation throughout Connecticut occurred, the need was recognized to capitalize on this success, strengthen the role of these programs, and increase the impact of course participation on the knowledge, skills, and abilities of students.

In 2010, with the support of the US Department of Education's Investing in Innovation (i3) program, the model was expanded into a 4-year high school

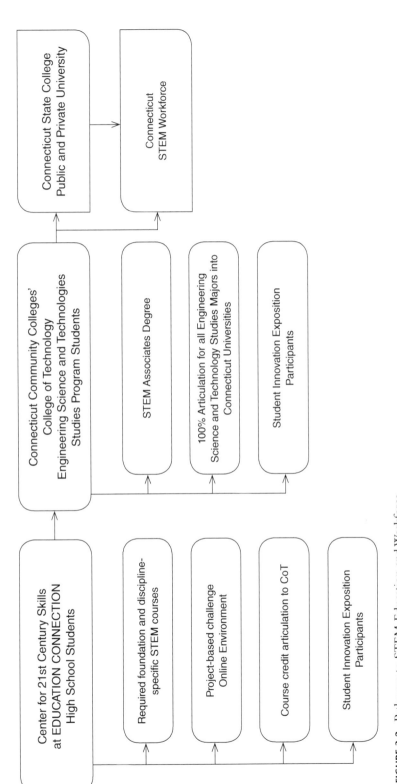

FIGURE 3.2 Pathways to STEM Education and Workforce

career-themed Academy of Digital Arts and Sciences (STEM21). The STEM21 colloquialism was used to reference the Center for 21st Century Skills but also to indicate a program taught in a forward-thinking 21st-century context. All courses were purposefully aligned to meet all state standards and frameworks. However, STEM21 courses were designed to be contextual with specific focus on relevance and authentic learning. In addition, participation in STEM21 would result in students exceeding all district graduation requirements for science and technology and the potential to earn college credits through articulation agreements with the CoT. To generate an articulation agreement, the CoT assigned a group of professors to review the course curriculum and evaluate its rigor and relationship to CoT level courses. If appropriate alignment was determined, the course was articulated.

STEM21 was operationalized as the participation of students in a specific sequence of STEM courses in a high school. The required sequence includes a minimum of one technology and one science-related class during each of grades 9–12 (see Figure 3.3). However, through the process of rapid growth and expansion (the portfolio of full-year courses went from one technology program (e.g., the program took place as an after-school activity, a co-curricular program during the school day, or a formal course in the school) to 15 formal school-day courses, including the 13 in STEM21), the Center recognized that, while the scope and sequence was defined, the instructional model was not well articulated or described.

In addition to i3 funding, the Nellie Mae Education Foundation Research and Evaluation program provided funding in 2011 to better define the instructional model. The refinement process and definition have successfully resulted in a model termed *blended instruction*, with four key components: blended learning, experiential learning, digital portfolio, and proficiency assessments (LaBanca, Worwood, Schauss, LaSala, & Donn, 2013). Prior to this time, the model was not described in detail. From a programmatic standpoint, the Center "knew the things it did" but could not articulate these things or provide a conceptual definition that could be used to complete research on the program. Therefore, the influence of external funders and partners provided the impetus to more formally commit to a description of intervention that was based on learning theory and, ultimately, a fidelity framework to measure implementation.

Theoretical Framework

Design Guided by Learning Theory

The underlying learning theory operationalized in STEM21 is inquiry. Simply and elegantly defined as learning by questioning and subsequent investigation (Shore et al., 2009), inquiry is based on constructivism, where students learn through authentic experience to construct and conditionalize knowledge. It

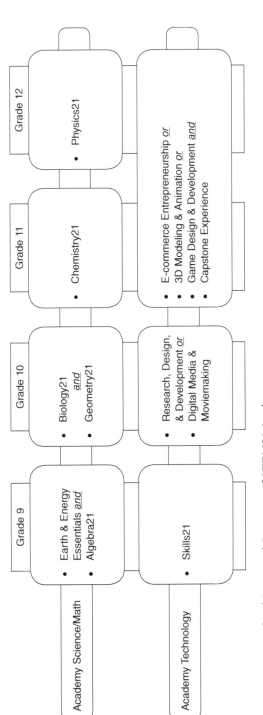

FIGURE 3.3 Articulated Scope and Sequence of STEM21 Academy

manifests as problem-based adaptive learning that challenges faulty schema, integrates new and existing knowledge, and allows for creation of original work (Driscoll, 2004). Students are challenged to engage in both problem-finding and problem-solving processes.

Inquiry

Beginning with Dewey (1938) and Bruner (1961), inquiry strategies have been described as foundational to the promotion of high-quality teaching and learning. Inquiry, as defined by the National Research Council (NRC) (1996), encompasses "diverse ways in which scientists study the natural world and propose explanations based on the evidence derived from their work" (p. 23). Inquiry also refers to activities of students in which they acquire knowledge and understanding of concepts, as well as problem-solving skills. High-quality inquiry requires learning *to do* and learning *about* at the same time (Shore et al., 2009): knowledge, skills, and process are inseparably linked.

Inquiry learning has the goals of teaching the knowledge and processes of research while nurturing a commitment to inquiry and promoting open-mindedness and a cooperative spirit and skill (Joyce, Weil, & Calhoun, 2008). Educational benefits of the use of inquiry learning include the development of imaginative, evidence-based explanations, improved higher-order thinking skills (Mao & Chang, 1998; Smith, 1996), gains in student learning (Jackson & Ash, 2012; Kanter & Konstantopoulos, 2010; Shore, Aulls, & Delcourt, 2007; Shymansky, Hedges, & Woodworth, 1990), and improved engagement via increased use of sophisticated resources for research and improved performance (Spronken-Smith, Walker, Batchelor, O'Steen, & Angelo, 2012; Summerlee & Murray, 2010).

Instructionally, levels of inquiry can take many forms and span a continuum of learning activities. Martin-Hansen (2002) described a continuum including three major levels of inquiry: structured, guided, and open. Structured inquiry is the most teacher-centered and least student autonomous. This is typically exemplified by a hands-on learning experience where students follow the step-by-step directions provided by the teacher. Students are provided with a problem and a procedural and analytic strategy, but they are not informed of the predetermined results. Student behavior is focused on following teacher-derived instructions. Structured inquiry activities are predictable: students are studying a well-known question with a well-known outcome using a reliable and reproducible method.

Guided inquiry provides more independence and problem-solving responsibilities for students and offers more higher-order thinking and cognitive development strategies than a structured inquiry approach (Lynch et al., 2007; Smith & Wittman, 2007). When students participate in a guided inquiry learning activity, however, more of the responsibility for learning is transferred to them (Nwagbo, 2006). The students become responsible for many of the cognitive structures and learning associated with the inquiry activity. They also become responsible for constructing their knowledge. A teacher poses a question, often curricular in nature, and students work to develop a solution by designing their own methods and strategies. In guided inquiry, more problem-solving responsibilities are given to students.

At the far end of the inquiry spectrum is highly student-centered open inquiry. In open inquiry, students are responsible for asking their own questions, designing and conducting investigations, and analyzing and reporting results. In essence, an additional creative element is added because students must problem-find before they can problem-solve (LaBanca & Ritchie, 2011). Students observe raw phenomena, identify a problem, and determine a solution. Students conducting an open-inquiry project are often given the opportunity to showcase their work; challenged to do more; given autonomy; and engage in more higher-order thinking as compared to a structured or guided approach (Buldyrev, 1994; Shepardon, 1997; Shore et al., 2007; Tytler, 1992).

Constructivism

Underlying an effective inquiry program are philosophies associated with problem solving, reasoning, critical thinking, oral and written communication and the active and reflective use of knowledge. These philosophical goals are commensurate with a constructivist instructional strategy. Kauchak and Eggen (1998) define constructivism as a "view of learning in which learners use their own experiences to construct understandings that make sense to them, rather than having understanding delivered to them in already organized form" (p. 184). Therefore, learning activities based on constructivism put learners in the context of antecedent knowledge to apply their understanding to authentic situations.

Driscoll (2004) outlines conditions for constructivist learning which dovetail philosophy of inquiry instruction. First, learning is embedded in complex, realistic, and relevant environments. Authentic learning tasks and assessment are critical to creating an environment that promotes critical thinking. As such, learning tasks must be complex in nature because simplistic tasks will not allow for the long-term development of mature problem-solving skills (Cognition and Technology Group at Vanderbilt, 1991). When diverse, irregular, and complex ill-defined problems are provided, students have the opportunity to develop unique solutions that are not predetermined (Jonassen, 1997; Spiro, Feltovich, Jacobson, & Coulson, 1995).

Integral to these learning experiences are social interactions between students and between students and teachers. "Learning becomes . . . a communal activity, a sharing of culture" (Bruner, 1986, p. 127). Effective collaborative skill development and content acquisition are joint learning goals. Students are encouraged to own their learning in a positive, self-effective way (Bandura, 1986). In a constructivist setting, students cannot be passive learners of instruction but must actively determine their own learning needs and develop strategies to address them (Honebein, 1996; Perkins, 1991). Finally, students must be self-aware of their learning processes. In essence, there must have a reflective mind and epistemic flexibility to learning (Cunningham, 1992).

Model Description

Blended instruction, as defined by the Center, is an innovative, transformative teaching and learning model that embodies the following student-centered approaches: (a) specific intentional approaches to meet the needs of students, particularly those starting at the lowest levels; (b) transparent systems for formative and summative assessment; (c) curriculum, instruction and assessment embrace skills and knowledge needed for college and career success; (d) community assets provide support and deepen learning experiences; (e) time is flexible and includes learning opportunities outside of the traditional school day and year; and (f) mastery-based strategies provide pacing based on skills and knowledge gains. All curriculum is aligned to state and national standards, including the International Society for Technology in Education National Educational Technology Standards (International Society for Technology in Education (ISTE), 2007), National Science Education Standards (NRC, 1996), Connecticut Science Frameworks (Connecticut State Department of Education (CSDE), 2004), Common Core State Standards in English for language arts and literacy in history, social studies, science, and technical subjects (Common Core State Standards Initiative (CCSSI), 2010a), and Common Core Standards in Mathematics (CCSSI, 2010b). The model features four key pedagogies: blended learning, experiential learning, digital portfolios, and proficiency assessments (see Figure 3.4).

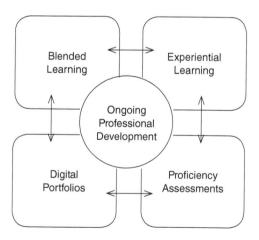

FIGURE 3.4 Blended Instruction Model

Blended Learning

Blended learning uses a highly engaging student-centered environment, integrating teacher-facilitated online coursework rich in experiential components to deepen content knowledge, self-directed learning competencies, and the acquisition of 21st century skills. In parallel with in-classroom activities, online components provide flexibility and support differentiated instruction. Coursework is delivered using an open-source, web-based learning management system (LMS). Embedded assessments allow teachers to monitor student progress and provide instant feedback and customized support based on individual learning progressions. The LMS provides varied options for learning and opportunities for online collaboration. Students interact asynchronously, via forums, blogs, and wikis; and synchronously via chats, videoconferencing, and virtual worlds.

Experiential Learning

Experiential learning is incorporated into coursework and transports students and teachers beyond the classroom to apply learning in authentic, real-world environments. The proficiency-based challenge project develops standards-based competencies and 21st century skills. As a culminating experience, student teams present their "challenge" solution at the Student Innovation Exposition. Projects are evaluated by college faculty and STEM professionals in multiple venues in a trade show-style exhibition, and as an oral presentation.

Digital Portfolios

Students and teachers collaborate to submit work via a digital portfolio, reflecting knowledge and skill mastery over time. Digital portfolios are an organized collection of artifacts and reflections that have the added benefit of being housed online with easy access for a wide audience that can provide feedback and comments in an organized, structured format. Portfolios enable students to demonstrate and recognize growth in knowledge and skills, identify interests, and communicate thinking and personal values.

Proficiency Assessments

Formative and summative assessments inform the pace of learning and differentiate content and instructional approaches to individual learning styles and trajectories. The model capitalizes on the anywhere/anytime paradigm, where access to learning tools is not restricted to classroom time, but rather available from any Internet-enabled device 24 hours a day. Students complete learning and assessments individually and in teams and receive individualized teacher feedback. Each curriculum provides an outcome-focused, standards-aligned learning unit that scaffolds student development. Essential learning is measured through authentic, open-ended, inquiry-based "unit performance assessments" (UPAs). In addition, a long-term challenge project that requires extensive collaboration, research, design, and testing is integrated into each course. This definition of proficiency assessments was challenging and required a review and discussion of a wide variety of descriptors and content.

Ongoing Professional Development

The role of the teacher in program implementation is key to the successful design and facilitation of cognitive and social learning necessary to validate educationally worthwhile learning outcomes (Allen, Witt, & Wheeless, 2006; Hughes, 2005). Students share their responsibilities with the instructor. Face-to-face learning has advantages in the development of group processes and complementary relationships for students, and therefore requires a compassionate, caring adult to facilitate the process. Updated knowledge and skills are critical and require ongoing development. The Center provides intensive professional development through a summer learning conference; site visits for team teaching, coaching, and mentoring; virtual support via WebNR, chats, and other online-delivered learning activities.

Systemizing Program Development

After some minor fidelity of implementation strategies (i.e., developing and implementing program-wide rubrics for challenge projects common to all schools), the Center's more significant foray to fidelity was at the program level. Much of the Center's initial work was developed based on a just-in-time philosophy where products and services were created and delivered as they were needed (Hutchkins, 1998). While this innovation was producing novel programs and services, formative program evaluation demonstrated that this success hindered the development of a coordinated, systems-based strategy.

Program and Course Development

We started program systemization by developing a procedure for course development. Using the Understanding by Design[1] model (Wiggins & McTighe, 1998), each course or program was created following guidelines of essential questions and linked directly to standards. Essential questions are "questions that are not answerable with finality in a brief sentence ... Their aim is to stimulate thought, to provoke inquiry, and to spark more questions—including thoughtful student questions—not just pat answers" (Wiggins & McTighe, 1998, p. 106). Essential questions identify "big ideas" or concepts of learning.

In the early days of the Center, the nationally recognized International Society for Technology in Education's National Educational Technology Standards (ISTE/NETS) guided the development of learning activities, performance assessments, and the course challenge project. The development process was designed in order to develop a cohesive, standards-based curriculum that could be implemented in a comprehensive manner. As diversity of programs grew (e.g., advent of the science program: Biology21, Chemistry21, Physics21), other relevant state and national standards were incorporated. Programs and courses were designed by processes that include development teams, orientation to standards, pilot testing, review and examination of pilot student work, design revisions, and ultimately scaled implementation.

Considering True Fidelity of Implementation: Beginning Stages

Most of the initial work of the Center was student-centric. Programs were designed for students as the primary customer, not teachers. Our view at the time was that student outcomes (e.g., Expo challenge projects) were the measure of fidelity. At the time, our oversimplification led us to, in essence, ignore the process and the teaching and learning mechanisms that could produce a positive engagement or achievement outcome. The essence of our learning was based on the question: *What did students produce that was showcased at the end-of-year Student Innovation Exposition?* What happened during the initial presentation of the challenge to the students and the final results were somewhat nebulous.

In essence, an educational "black box" was created where we could view the system in terms of our input (presenting a challenge) and output (student presentations at the Student Innovation Exposition), but we had very little knowledge of the internal workings and processes occurring in the classrooms at partner school sites. Occasionally we were able to observe some inner workings by bringing students together for experiential education events at colleges and universities. Site visits were sporadic and more observational in nature than collaborative and developmental.

It became obvious that in order to unpack the black box to more properly allow our program to be implemented in similar ways across different schools and districts, a centralized management system was necessary. In 2005, the Center determined that the open-source LMS Moodle (Modular Object-Oriented Dynamic Learning Environment) should be used based on its large user community (Moodle currently represents 19 percent of all LMS usage [Green, 2011]), and robust features (Dougiamas & Taylor, 2003).

Moodle provided options for resources, including the administration, documentation, tracking, reporting, and delivery of the Center's blended instruction courses (Ellis, 2009). As a method to deploy a student-centered learning environment, the LMS was configured to provide assessments, opportunities for student authoring, collaboration tools, content management, and teacher resources—all with back-end analytics to examine usage. We commissioned a registration system integration to systemically collect data on student demographics. This was our critical step to create a systematized method for program curriculum delivery that had anytime-anywhere, just-in-time access.

In conjunction, the Center had developed a summer teacher professional development program that was more technology skill-driven than learning-centered. For example, teachers would learn the mechanical aspects of using the open-source online LMS, Moodle (i.e., how to navigate the website, how to register students, and how to upload PDFs). Little time was spent engaging in discussions of how to use an LMS to promote student-student and teacher-student interaction or how to create learning experiences that empowered students to gain knowledge of content while developing 21st century skills.

The Original "Definition" of Fidelity

From 2005 to 2010, the Center's original fidelity definition was "Doing 80 percent of the activities in the LMS." This was an attempt to codify teacher use of the LMS with students in conjunction with conducting a challenge project. However, it was extremely problematic. The LMS was robustly populated with content, resources, and activities that were designed to be "pick-and-choose." The Center's guiding philosophy was based on relationships that students build with their teachers: Teachers should have the autonomy to determine the best, differentiated choices to engage their students in meaningful learning.

There was no effective way to measure the 80 percent threshold. No structures existed, and what did 80 percent mean anyway? If a teacher chose content that was more consumption-based (i.e., students were completing tasks designed to gain knowledge from external sources) rather than production-based (i.e., students creating products such as digital media, digital posters, wikis, and blogs), was that representative of creating a student-centered environment? In addition, each unit had essential questions and outcomes, but it would be feasible that, based on teacher selection of learning activities, the student would have never demonstrated proficiency to them.

Program Feedback via Internal Evaluation

Since 2000, EDUCATION CONNECTION has had an evaluation arm to the agency. Initially, evaluation services were provided to internal and external clients by one qualified evaluator on staff. In 2008, EDUCATION CONNECTION's Center for Collaborative Evaluation and Strategic Change (CCESC) was formally established to provide external evaluation services to schools, districts, stage agencies, and non-profit organizations (Lorentson, 2012). From CCESC's inception, the Center and CCESC worked in close partnership to provide feedback—primarily formative in nature—to address program quality and implementation. Although CCESC was internal to the agency, it was external to the Center and the Center's projects and was able to provide a satisfactory level of feedback objectivity.

Beginning in 2000, EDUCATION CONNECTION's CCESC staff collected data on Center programs primarily through focus groups and attitudinal surveys. Focus groups with teachers and students were conducted annually to obtain qualitative formative information. Data was used to inform understanding of fidelity of program improvement. In addition, teacher and student satisfaction surveys were conducted to examine perceptions of achievement of desired goals and outcomes. Non-validated self-perception content knowledge pre/post tests were also collected. These surveys were descriptive in nature and developed by CCESC in partnership with program staff. In essence, course objectives were developed based on state standards, reworded as questions, and administered pre/post. Data was descriptive in nature: Inferential analysis was not conducted. However, detailed commentary with rich and thick description provided keen insight as to what was occurring: student preferences, teacher implementation, and barriers to implementation. Because multiple focus groups were conducted, data could be triangulated, providing a high level of credibility, dependability, and confirmability to the results (Krefting, 1991). The Center consistently incorporated the results of the implementation evaluation and program impact feedback to make design changes for program improvement.

CCESC conducted a small, non-rigorous, and exploratory quasi-experimental study in 2009 to examine differences in outcome achievement between students taking part in Center courses and those who did not. Prior to this study, any differences were examined using pre-post methods without inferential comparison. Although there was extensive data examining teacher and student dispositions and satisfaction, this was EDUCATION CONNECTION's first attempt to mitigate external threats to validity. The quasi-experimental pilot study utilized univariate analysis. Significant gains in student achievement based on perceptions when compared with a group of students who were not in the program were identified (Lorentson, 2009).

Honest Discussions

In 2010, having received a U.S. Department of Education Investing in Innovation Development Grant, the Center was positioned to grow, implement, and evaluate its programs in a significantly meaningful way. The Investing in Innovation Fund, established under section 14007 of the American Recovery and Reinvestment Act of 2009 (ARRA), provided funding to support organizations and school districts by providing competitive grants to applicants with a record of improving student achievement and attainment in order to expand the implementation of innovative practices with demonstrated impacts on student achievement (US Department of Education (USDoE), 2013). Development grants were designed to support the enhancement and evaluation of innovative models that have already demonstrated effectiveness in improving students' academic performance.

Our innovation and "development" was to take the instructional model that had demonstrated success—currently being implemented as individual courses—and expand it into a 4-year articulated STEM Academy. Local teachers in the STEM fields would teach the program with support from the Center utilizing the blended instruction model. We identified 12 public comprehensive and magnet high schools, almost all of whom were participating in individual programs, for participation. The student population in these schools were comprised of 72 percent underserved in STEM as measured by ethnicity, socioeconomic status (free/reduced lunch status), and gender (female).

The i3 development grant included a significant research component to assess impact. We partnered with the Education Development Center (EDC) to conduct and manage the research and serve in the role of external evaluator. In addition, the i3 evaluation criteria required the Center to consider fidelity of implementation in a meaningful way for the first time. The Center charged CCESC with this task in consultation with EDC, and technical assistance and quality assurance for the i3 program was managed nationally by Abt Associates. EDC was instrumental in providing an objective feedback loop to both CCESC and the Center.

Program fidelity had to be more concretely articulated because we had no way to clearly describe what we expected teachers and students to do while participating in the program. Up to this point, program implementation was akin to a black box. The Center decided that we could not be satisfied with impact but needed to know if schools, teachers, and students were implementing our program in the intended way. When we initially started the conversation in collaboration with CCESC, a laundry list of tasks and outcomes were generated. What we quickly realized is that we had to discuss our values. *What was important to us? What were our program "non-negotiables"?* We eventually settled on the following overarching question: *What are the technology-enhanced and student-centered practices that our instructional model mandates?* Our challenge was to determine how we could fairly and succinctly identify the key and necessary program activities and behaviors as subcomponents of the instructional model and collect data crucial to intended outcomes. Figure 3.5 depicts this transition.

As we considered "what students did" in our programs, our discussion evolved into "why we wanted them to do it" (see Figure 3.6). Take blended learning, for example. Computer-assisted instruction is often designed to "deliver" content. And although our curricular resources are housed in an LMS, we knew there was more to using an LMS than just delivery. First and foremost, we knew that technology should enhance interaction rather than isolate students (Jonassen & Kwon, 2001; Offir, Lev, & Bezalel, 2008; Vonderwell, Liang, & Alderman, 2007). To operationalize increased interaction, we decided that forums, one of our underutilized interactive but perhaps most powerful platforms that allow students to asynchronously discuss and collaborate on curricular topics, would be the best venue. After some debate, we decided that the fidelity measure would be to

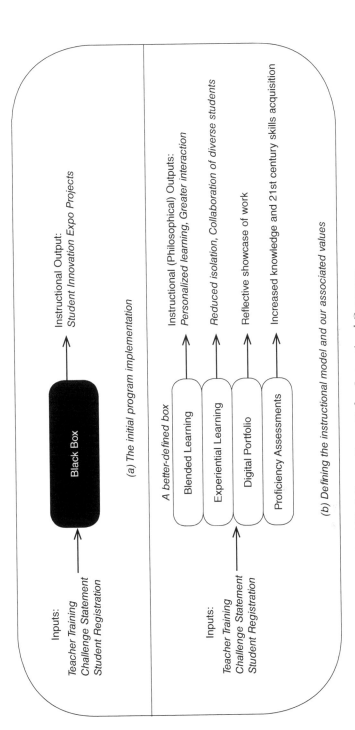

Inputs:
Teacher Training
Challenge Statement
Student Registration

Black Box

Instructional Output:
Student Innovation Expo Projects

(a) The initial program implementation

Inputs:
Teacher Training
Challenge Statement
Student Registration

A better-defined box

Blended Learning

Experiential Learning

Digital Portfolio

Proficiency Assessments

Instructional (Philosophical) Outputs:
Personalized learning, Greater interaction

Reduced isolation, Collaboration of diverse students

Reflective showcase of work

Increased knowledge and 21st century skills acquisition

(b) Defining the instructional model and our associated values

FIGURE 3.5 Unpacking the Instructional Black Box to Better Define Instructional Outcomes

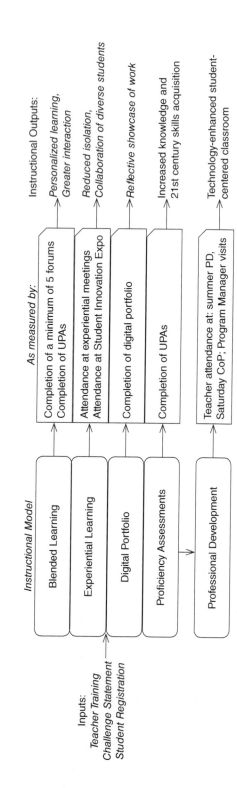

FIGURE 3.6 Operationalization of Fidelity Measures to Align With Value Output

require each student to complete a minimum of five forum posts. Most courses have 2–3 forums per unit with a range of 7–10 units per course. As a postscript, we have found that teachers have really come to value the forums, and we often see many more forum posts per student than the required five.

The Center also came to the realization that the main reason to use an LMS was not to use technology but rather to promote project-based authentic performance learning. We consider technology simply as a tool—one of many tools a teacher might use to facilitate instruction. So therefore, we did not want technology to be used for the sake of technology, but rather to promote 21st century skill acquisition in conjunction with conceptual understanding of content.

To formalize the importance of the performance assessment, we decided that each learning unit would require a Unit Performance Assessment (UPA) as a final project. The UPAs were designed to align with the unit's essential questions and learning outcomes. In essence, if a student completed a UPA, he or she should have been able to demonstrate proficiency of *all* of the unit's essential questions. All of our science courses were using this convention, and some units in our technology and mathematics courses were as well. We decided to systematize our unit module design, use common vocabulary, and carefully evaluate the content and purpose of our UPAs. The opportunity for students to complete the UPA became the measure of fidelity. With a strong emphasis on UPAs, the Center began to receive more concrete and specific feedback on the quality of UPAs, which became a feedback loop for continuous improvement.

Experiential learning was measured in a much simpler way – attendance. The Center decided to record attendance at each event, including the end-of-year Student Innovation Exposition. At that point, digital portfolios were a very underutilized feature of the program even though we knew the importance of showcasing and reflecting on work (Abrami & Barrett, 2005). The Center determined that portfolios should be measured for completion as a measure of fidelity. Portfolios suffered from personal value to the students. When students are asked why they use an academic portfolio, their responses often amount to "because my teacher made me do it." Students often do not recognize the value of it because there is no authentic audience to view it and provide feedback. Although we would be hard-pressed to say that our work has totally mitigated this problem, the Center has designed strategies to help.

The Center designed an end-of-year digital portfolio rubric to provide teachers and students with a scaffold to assist in the process. The rubric provided indicators with links to the six skills, as well as indicators for organization, aesthetics, and enhancements. We asked teachers to score the portfolios and provide us with a score. Although the score was not used in the fidelity calculation (rather portfolios were fidelity-scored by criterion—complete/not complete), the rubric was a structure that assisted teachers with imparting value.

Issues and Challenges of Fidelity of Implementation

Collecting Fidelity Data

Since fidelity of implementation was a new concept to the Center and unfamiliar to our program teachers and schools, we knew we had to be very careful to properly disseminate the process to all of our stakeholders: teachers primarily, but students, administrators, and even our own staff. We started by creating a Fidelity of Implementation Guidebook (LaBanca & Lorentson, 2013). We took extra care to give it a professional look: stock covers, spiral-bound, and careful attention to detail on formatting and layout. The Center brought CCESC and our external evaluators from EDC to attend the intensive summer professional development institute to discuss the fidelity process. The guidebook, affectionately referred to as the fidelity cookbook by the evaluation team, included a checklist of tasks as well as the impact measures. We did not want to convolute the process for the teachers, so we put the data requirements in one location. We included a description of the model, templates for data collection, rubrics for analyzing student work, student templates and guides for portfolio guidelines, and UPA checklists. We also made a digital version of the Fidelity of Implementation Guidebook available for teachers electronically in the LMS.

At the end of the first year of program implementation, CCESC, through the Center, requested teachers to submit fidelity of implementation data. Data was to be submitted electronically to CCESC. While we received the majority of the data, what we received was nothing short of a logistical nightmare. There was relatively no consistency in the data presentation: some data came on handwritten sheets; some in Excel spreadsheets; some in Excel spreadsheets with multiple tabs; some data was alphabetized by student last name and some was not; and some data lacked the teacher or school name. Frequently, components of fidelity measurements were missing. In most instances, it was not because of non-compliance to the instructional intervention, it was just missing. CCESC worked diligently to collect missing pieces and identify mis- or non-coded data.

The Center, too, was guilty of inconsistent data collection. Center program managers were responsible for collecting attendance data at experiential learning events and the Student Innovation Exposition. Similar problems occurred: data was not properly labeled; teacher names were disassociated from student names; signatures were illegible; and event dates were sometimes missing. Program managers created their own version of an attendance sheet for experiential learning, lacking organization.

The Center and CCESC had an earnest conversation to discuss the problematic nature of a lack of systemization to the data collection process of fidelity. We determined that we needed a technology-based platform to collect data and elected to use SurveyMonkey. On the back end, CCESC created a customized data collection instrument in the survey format for each individual. Each fidelity document included the required course activities and, when necessary, the student names to create matrices. Each teacher received his or her fidelity template, filled it out, and submitted it online. Data, although still cumbersome, became much more manageable since it was all now in a consistent form. It was much easier to identify missing data and contact teachers.

Navigating the Research-Practitioner Nexus

EDUCATION CONNECTION is primarily a practitioner organization. As a regional educational service center, the agency promotes the success of school districts and their communities by providing educational and related services. Although the process of data is not new in the educational milieu, experience and expertise with the rigorous nature of actual valid and reliable research processes was limited to two people at the agency—the Director of CCESC and the Director of the Center. We became responsible for disseminating and building capacity for the value of the research process to our Center staff and subsequently to our stakeholders. Many originally viewed the research activities as "extras," not necessarily related to a practitioner's work. It became incumbent upon us to articulate the necessary integration and interplay of research and practice. They could not, from a philosophical standpoint, operate independently from one another.

As an example, consider the following illustrative partial email exchange where a program manager was writing to STEM21 teachers:

> Unfortunately, at the [experiential learning] meeting on Tuesday we must hold a teacher focus group. Due to the challenges of space it is likely this will take place at 9:30AM. Sadly you will miss the opening of the event. I want to apologize in advance. Further instructions will be provided on your arrival.

The Center Director needed to respond to ensure that there was a positive interplay fostered between program and research:

> While I totally appreciate your frustration with having students/teachers having to miss parts of program, I think we need to be very careful in phrasing this to teachers. Data collection is an absolutely critical, valuable, and necessary part of our grants and it very much informs the way we program. I don't want research components to have the perception of being "extra," "add-ons," or "inconvenient." Rather, we want teachers and students to feel that they are very valuable and important and that their voice is critical to the improvement and measurement of program success.

Center staff responsibility and accountability to fidelity is critical. As we observed, challenges in program implementation in schools, we felt compelled to use this data to provide targeted feedback and assistance to teachers. During onsite visits to schools, program managers needed to make an effort to assist with both the implementation of program components and management of the program component fidelity data collection. Although Center and CCESC leadership spent time working with Center program managers both in the development of fidelity standards and the rollout of the fidelity data collection process, knowledge gaps persisted. For example, reference to the 80 percent rule came up again (i.e., "You have to do 80 percent of the UPAs"—an incorrect statement). In addition, questions to the number of required forums to complete were repeated, although we had identified five as a group. Questions were even asked about whether digital portfolios were required. Consistent messaging and training for the Center staff became important as they were not reading the fidelity document with discipline.

Program Implementation

One of the Center's greatest struggles was implementing the course sequence as prescribed. We had initially articulated clearly the scope and sequence (Figure 3.3) but soon realized that this might not be ideal for schools in different districts. Our minimum requirement was to implement a cohort that participated in a science and technology course together. Some schools also chose to implement the mathematics component, but some did not. For example, more often than not, local school districts have students taking a wide variety of math courses in a specific grade (i.e., some 9th-grade students may take Algebra, while others take Geometry or Algebra II). To entice a diverse group of students to participate in STEM21, some schools could not successfully schedule a complementary mathematics course. Others thought the math component was critical. We came to realize that implementing STEM21 as exactly prescribed might not be as critical as revising the model to enable broader use.

Because we were working in 12 different schools in eight different school districts, scope and sequence often differed. For example, some of our schools offer Biology as a freshman course and some offer Earth and Energy Essentials. In order to meet the needs of having a program that had the potential for scalability, we quickly recognized that we had to be flexible with the courses that schools could offer during specific years. The Center had to design challenge projects that were malleable to different course matchups. Our evaluation of implementation fidelity was going to need to somehow reflect these necessary changes.

Some schools have 45-minute traditional period schedules, some use the A–B alternating day block format, some use other formats such as the semester block format. The ability to be flexible was critical to maintaining our relationships with school partners and ensuring that our program could do what we wanted it to do— improve student learning. This flexibility would also be critical to allow us to scale up the program in diverse environments. We found that 45-minute periods and A–B block format tended to work well, as students had the chance to meet with all of their STEM21 teachers on a regular basis throughout the school year.

The semester block schedule was much more problematic. The curriculum was designed to be delivered over the course of a full year: time for research, development, and problem finding is necessary to conduct a high-quality challenge project (LaBanca & Ritchie, 2011). In addition, on a semester block schedule, schools would need to schedule, for example, a science course in the fall and a technology course in the spring. The teachers would generally lack the ability to collaborate with the students, leading to less diverse expertise for students as they worked through their challenge project.

Individual program elements also had challenges for implementation. Most experiential learning events took place at college campuses and business and industry sites. Even though Connecticut is not a large state, it is notorious for heavy highway traffic, especially along the southern coast. If we had an event on one side of the state, it could produce potentially long (>2 hours each way) bus rides for some students. Within the confines of a 6.5 hour school day, students could theoretically be travelling for four of those hours, making attendance impractical in some instances. Schools would weigh the potential benefits of the experiences against the disadvantages of travel and would sometimes conclude that the travel would not be viable. This of course would have an impact on grade-level fidelity scoring. Also, as our program began to scale to include more schools, we had an unintended consequence: Most experiential sites are not physically big enough to handle the size of the program. This led to the development of a sophisticated mapping and planning of individual school programs and different types of external experiences, based on geographic location and restrictions of the hosting organization. From a programmatic level, we needed to ensure that there was equity of experiences available for participating schools.

While the full-year, large-scale, challenge project was conducted with high levels of fidelity, we had more variation with completion of individual unit (module) performance assessments. Indeed, our qualitative evaluation research has indicated that both students and teachers are less satisfied and compliant with the unit performance assessments and highly satisfied with the challenge project (Oh, Lorentsen, et al., 2014). We have come to understand that unit performance assessments hold less value to teachers and students even though they were carefully designed to provide an assessment for all of an individual unit's objectives. Unlike the extended challenge projects, unit performance assessments are not evaluated by panels of judges outside of the classroom. Therefore, we find there is more variation to their implementation. Considering that the purpose of unit performance assessments is to create a project-based learning environment, we are currently evaluating how we can promote this broader goal. We recognize that we may need to re-engineer and/or provide more choice for performance assessments as well as provide more professional development for teachers to build capacity for our broader goal.

As STEM21 was in the early stages of development, we recognized that there was a need to constantly review and revaluate our approach to measuring fidelity.

The key was collaboration between the Center's program staff, CCESC evaluation staff, and the external evaluation team from EDC. We were obligated to frequently review data and regularly engage in collaborative discussion.

Experiences with Fidelity as a New Aspect of Program Implementation

Operationalizing Fidelity Compared to Our Abstraction of Fidelity

The Center crafted our fidelity model to represent our core values. We want to promote a technology-enhanced, student-centered, inquiry-based learning environment that increases student engagement and achievement. By using our instructional model as the foundation, we identified ways that we could approach these indicators (blended learning, experiential learning, digital portfolio, proficiency assessments) by delineating specific student practices. However, our indicators are binary in nature: task completed/task not completed. We do not measure quality as an indicator of fidelity of implementation.

As an example, consider the forum. The forum, a fidelity indicator in blended learning, is designed to use technology to promote student interaction asynchronously. A teacher should use forums throughout the year to promote discourse and sense-making through a social process where students utilize each other to construct their knowledge. Key to the process is students reacting to each other, challenging each other's conceptions, and building upon each other's understandings. We do not measure that. We just measure that a post happened. Feasibly, a student could make a post, not read any of his or her classmates' ideas, and remain isolated. Other students could then make the same comments, not adding to the conversation. This would still meet the requirements of the fidelity indicator. A teacher could operably not conduct any forums with students the entire year, assign five the last week of school, have the students complete them in isolation, and still receive full credit for the fidelity indicator. While this meets the requirements of fidelity of implementation, it certainly does not meet the spirit of it.

Next Steps

The process of defining and examining fidelity of implementation has provided an excellent feedback loop for the Center's learning to improve program design and implementation. We have learned that maximizing fidelity of implementation leads to program improvement and achievement of intended outcomes. However, we have also learned that fidelity measurements need to evolve over time to better indicate what is happening in the proverbial black box. Currently our implementation fidelity measures are like a light switch. We have "on" and "off" positions. The indicator is happening or it is not happening.

Our categorical measurement scheme can be better tailored to use impact data as a fidelity measurement. Take, for example, digital portfolios. We ask teachers to score them based on a rubric, but that quality factor is not used in the calculation of fidelity, making it harder to link fidelity of implementation to student impact. This is not a requirement in the i3 program for development grants, but it is the natural next step in the progression to overall quality improvement. For us, fidelity takes on a checklist perspective. *Did I, as a teacher, do the task or not?* Rather, we would like to see if there is a link allowing quality of the digital portfolio leading to potential increased achievement.

Fidelity has also helped us examine our own practices. For example, the Center provides in-class support in the form of demonstration teaching, co-teaching, mentoring, and coaching. However, we now recognize that these processes are not formalized. Just as we have evolved into an instructional model, we need to further develop our instructional support model. What happens when we coach, what are the outcomes, and how do we know it happened? Fidelity of implementation applies here too and this is our identified next great endeavor for program improvement. We have begun the process in our professional development institute. We have a quality rubric that we use to evaluate ourselves during the institute and we use that feedback to provide insight to improve our own practices. CCESC has helped us define and refine this measure.

Working with Evaluators

The Center has been extremely fortunate to have both our CCESC internal evaluator and our EDC external evaluator to support us and facilitate our ability to gain powerful insight about our work with schools. Having expertise in measurement and evaluation on the programmatic side makes it much easier to understand the needs and challenges of evaluators. Center leadership consistently promotes the work of evaluation to make the integration of program and evaluation more seamless.

Consistent and frequent interaction is critical. The Center has regular face-to-face meetings with our internal CCESC team and we collaborate on research options, choices, and decisions. We try not to make decisions in isolation from one another. Our external partners from EDC, although a 3-hour drive away, regularly communicate by email and by phone conversation. We did realize early on that face-to-face meetings were important, too, and established a face-to-face quarterly meeting alternating locations. We find that these collaborative meetings help build capacity and trust. It supports program development and facilitates close interaction.

When we began our work, we realized that our evaluators may have had a conceptual understanding of the work, but may not understand the mechanics, day-to-day challenges, and idiosyncrasies of our partner schools. This is important to us and our evaluators as well. Both our internal and external teams have taken the time to engage in the process. This project is being implemented in 12 schools in eight different school districts, each with its own unique parameters, values, and priorities. Recognizing the programmatic challenges associated with building capacity, not only with teachers, but with principals, district leadership, parents, and students creates practical implementation difficulties that are often hard for evaluators to understand. Our collaboration between programmers and evaluators has helped to mitigate those challenges.

Our evaluators have attended our professional development institutes not only to observe but to present to the teachers. This is not only valuable to the evaluators to understand what we are doing, but it gives them a face with the teachers. Instead of being this type of conceptual individual operating in an ivory tower, they become authentic and they can build relationships with the teachers not only though presentation, but by sharing a meal during lunch. In addition, this interaction allows evaluators to really gain meaningful understanding of the challenges associated with being a teacher. Having expectations that data collection occurs without challenge because it needs to is not a reality in a school setting. Even the best-laid intentions are interrupted by school assemblies, fire drills, and changes in the daily schedule. Having evaluators that understand the dynamics of running a school often deprioritizes the agreed-upon research obligations. Having evaluators that recognize the need for this type of flexibility and have the ability to adapt quickly is a necessity.

Each year, our external evaluator attended our Student Innovation Exposition. In 2013, we engaged her as a judge, so she could go beyond just observing the experience but actually delve into the process of student work evaluation and meet our students. She gets to experience, first hand, student challenges, student successes, teacher roles, and how students use their knowledge and skills to form high-quality products. From the opposite perspective, as academic publications have been produced, the research team has engaged the program team to participate in the process (e.g., LaBanca, Oh, Lorentson, Jia, & Sibuma, 2014; Lorentson, Oh, & LaBanca, 2014; Oh, Jia, Lorentson, & LaBanca, 2013; Oh, Jia, Sibuma, LaBanca, & Lorentson, 2014; Oh, Jia, Sibuma, Lorentson, & LaBanca, 2013).

As programmatic and research teams, we make a concerted effort to collaborate in meaningful ways where both programmatic and research work products are produced. This synergistic relationship allows us to understand each other better. As a program implementation team we can better understand our evaluation feedback and simultaneously provide critical feedback to improve research. As a Center, we also want to make sure the work we do is appropriately represented to an academic audience.

We appreciate that our evaluators take a positivist, rather than critical, stance in their work. They are committed to honoring, dignifying, and appreciating the challenging work of educational reformers. They continue with a commitment to helping the Center, as innovators, learn to do our work better, by opening it to thoughtful and critical examination and by bringing to bear multiple perspectives.

Note

1. Understanding by Design (Wiggins & McTighe, 1998) is a curricular model utilized for educational planning focused on the practice of examining student outcomes in order to design curriculum units, performance assessments, and classroom instruction. The model stresses "backward design" whereby outcomes for units of learning become foundation to plan the curriculum followed by the selection of activities and materials that are designed to scaffold learning in order to allow students to reach proficiency. The backward design approach begins with educators identifying the desired learning outcomes for students by establishing the overall goal linked to content standards. The goals are described as essential questions, conceptual "big idea" questions that create clarity and precision and for communicating pivotal parts of ideas of the learning unit (Jacobs, 1997). As students problem-solve, create, communicate, collaborate, and inquire, essential questions become outcome-based end points. The focus of essential questions identifies what students will know and will be able to do. After the design of essential questions, assessment is designed that allows students to demonstrate evidence of understanding. Generally assessment takes the form of culminating performance tasks that allow students to demonstrate understanding of concepts. Well-designed performance tasks measure all essential questions of the unit. Finally, in the design process, learning activities that scaffold learning that will build the requisite knowledge and skills are developed and organized so students have a progression to be able to complete the performance task and demonstrate competency to the essential questions and unit standards.

References

Abrami, P., & Barrett, H. (2005). Directions for research and development on electronic portfolios. *Canadian Journal of Learning and Technology, 31*(3). Retrieved from http://cjlt. csj.ualberta.ca/index.php/cjlt/article/viewArticle/92

Allen, M., Witt, P. L., & Wheeless, L. R. (2006). The role of teacher immediacy as a motivational factor in student learning: Using meta-analysis to test a causal model. *Communication Education, 55*(1), 21–31.

Apple, Inc. (2009). Challenge based learning: Taking action and make a difference. Cupertino, CA: Apple, Inc.

Bandura, A. (1986). *Social foundations of thought and action: A social cognitive theory.* Englewood Cliffs, NJ: Prentice-Hall.

Broderick, M. (2008). Local schools show that science is no game. *Republican-American*, p. 2B.

Bruner, J. S. (1961). The act of discovery. *Harvard Educational Review, 31*, 21–32.

Bruner, J. S. (1986). *Actual minds, possible worlds.* Cambridge, MA: Harvard University Press.

Buldyrev, D. V. (1994). Science research in the classroom. *The Physics Teacher, 32*, 411–415.

Cognition and Technology Group at Vanderbilt. (1991). Technology and the design of generative learning environments. *Educational Technology, 31*, 34–40.

Common Core State Standards Initiative (CCSSI). (2010a). Common core state standards for English language arts & literacy in history, social studies, science, and technical subjects. Washington, DC: Council of Chief State School Officers and the National Governors Association.

Common Core State Standards Initiative (CCSSI). (2010b). Common core state standards for mathematics. Washington, DC: Council of Chief State School Officers and the National Governors Association.

Connecticut Board of Regents for Higher Education (BoR). (2013). Connecticut Community Colleges College of Technology. Retrieved from http://www.ct.edu/academics/cot

Connecticut State Department of Education (CSDE). (2004). Core science curriculum framework: An invitation for students and teachers to explore science and its role in society. Retrieved from http://www.sde.ct.gov/sde/cwp/view.asp?a=2618&q=320890

Connecticut State Department of Education (CSDE). (2013a). Interdistrict Cooperative Grants. Retrieved from http://www.sde.ct.gov/sde/cwp/view.asp?a=2681&q=320446

Connecticut State Department of Education (CSDE). (2013b). Priority School Program. Retrieved from http://www.sde.ct.gov/sde/cwp/view.asp?a=2618&Q=321612

Cunningham, D. J. (1992). Beyond educational psychology: Steps towards and educational semiotic. *Educational Psychology Review, 4*(2), 165–194.

Delaney, S. B. (2000). Sheff vs. O'Neill, Connecticut's landmark desegregation case. Unpublished doctoral dissertation. Amherst, MA: University of Massachusetts.

Dewey, J. (1938). *Logic: The theory of inquiry.* New York: Holt, Rinehart and Winston.

Dougherty, J., Estevez, N., Wanzer, J, Tatem, D., Bell, C., Cobb, C., & Esposito, C. (2006). A visual guide to Sheff vs. O'Neill school desegregation. Hartford, CT: Trinity College.

Dougiamas, M., & Taylor, P. (2003). Moodle: Using learning communities to create an open source course management system. In World conference on educational multimedia, hypermedia and telecommunications (Vol. 2003, No. 1, pp. 171–178).

Driscoll, M. P. (2004). Psychology of learning for instruction. Boston: Pearson/Allyn & Bacon.

Eaton, S. (2006). The children in room E4: American education on trial. Chapel Hill, NC: Algonquin Books of Chapel Hill.

Ellis, R. K. (2009). *Field guide to learning management systems.* Alexandria, VA: ASTD Learning Circuits.

Green, K. C. (2011). The Campus Computing Project. Paper presented at the 2011 EDUCAUSE Conference, Philadelphia, PA.

Honebein, P. C. (1996). Seven goals for the design of constructivist learning environments. In B. G. Wilson (Ed.), *Constructivist learning environments: Case studies in instructional design.* Englewood Cliffs, NJ: Educational Technology Publications.

Hughes, J. (2005). The role of teacher knowledge and learning experiences in forming technology-integrated pedagogy. *Journal of Technology and Teacher Education, 13,* 277–302.

Hutchins, D. (1998). *Just in time.* Surrey, UK: Gower Publishing, Ltd.

International Society for Technology in Education (ISTE). (2007). The National Educational Technology Standards and Performance Indicators for Students. Eugene, OR: International Society for Technology in Education.

Jackson, J. K., & Ash, G. (2012). Science achievement for all: Improving science performance and closing achievement gaps. *Journal of Science Teacher Education, 23*(7), 723–744.

Jacobs, H. H. (1997). *Mapping the big picture: Integrating curriculum and assessment K–12.* Alexandria, VA: Association for Supervision and Curriculum Development.

Jonassen, D. H. (1997). Instructional design models for well-structured and ill-structured problem-solving learning outcomes. *Educational Technology Research and Development, 45,* 65–94.

Jonassen, D. H., & Kwon, H. I. (2001). Communication patterns in computer mediated versus face-to-face group problem solving. *Educational Technology Research & Development, 49*(1), 35–51.

Joyce, B., Weil, M., & Calhoun, E. (2008). *Models of teaching.* Boston: Pearson/Allyn & Bacon.

Kanter, D. E., & Konstantopoulos, S. (2010). The impact of a project-based science curriculum on minority student achievement, attitudes, and careers: The effects of teacher content and pedagogical content knowledge and inquiry-based practices. *Science Education, 94*(5), 855–887.

Kauchak, D. P., & Eggen, P. D. (1993). *Learning and teaching.* Boston: Pearson/Allyn & Bacon.

Kauchak, D. P., & Eggen, P. D. (1998). *Learning and teaching: Research-based methods* (3rd ed.). Boston: Allyn & Bacon.

Krefting, L. (1991). Rigor in qualitative research: The assessment of trustworthiness. *The American Journal of Occupational Therapy, 45*, 214–222.

LaBanca, F., & Lorentson, M. (2013). *Fidelity of implementation guidebook v. 3.0*. Litchfield, CT: EDUCATION CONNECTION.

LaBanca, F., & Ritchie, K. C. (2011). The art of scientific ideas: Teaching and learning strategies that promote effective problem finding. *The Science Teacher, 78*(8), 48–51.

LaBanca, F., Oh, Y. J., Lorentson, M., Jia, Y., & Sibuma, B. (2014). Development of a 21st century and inquiry skill assessment in science, technology, engineering and mathematics for high school students. Paper presented at the American Educational Research Association Annual Meeting, Philadelphia.

LaBanca, F., Worwood, M., Schauss, S., LaSala, J., & Donn, J. (2013). *Blended instruction: Exploring student centered pedagogical strategies to promote a technology-enhanced learning environment*. Litchfield, CT: EDUCATION CONNECTION.

Leonard, Q. (2003, April 27). Technical wonderkids on display. *Republican-American*, pp. 1B–2B.

Lorentson, M. (2012). The Center for Collaborative Evaluation and Strategic Change: Using data to make change work [Brochure]. Litchfield, CT: EDUCATION CONNECTION.

Lorentson, M., Oh, Y. J., & LaBanca, F. (2014). Assessment of fidelity of implementation: The experience of the STEM21 Digital Academy High School program development. Paper presented at the American Educational Research Association Annual Meeting, Philadelphia.

Lynch, S., Taymans, J., Watson, W. A., Ochsendorf, R. J., Pyke, C., & Szesze, M. J. (2007). Effectiveness of a highly rated science curriculum unit for students with disabilities in general education classrooms. *Exceptional Children, 73*(2), 202–223.

Mao, S., & Chang, C. (1998). Impacts of an inquiry teaching method on Earth science students' learning outcomes and attitudes at the secondary level. *Proceedings of the National Science Council ROC (D), 8*, 93–101.

Martin-Hansen, L. (2002). Defining inquiry. *The Science Teacher, 69*, 34–37.

National Research Council (NRC). (1996). *National science education standards*. Washington, DC: National Academy Press.

Nwagbo, G. (2006). Effects of two teaching methods on the achievement in and attitude to biology of students of different levels of scientific literacy. *International Journal of Educational Research, 45*(3), 216–229.

O'Neill, P. (2003). Student brainpower: Students drawn to career choices pilot programs testing strategies for IT industry. *Connecticut's Journal of Business and Economic Development, March/April*, 52–54.

Offir, B., Lev, Y. & Bezalel, R. (2008). Surface and deep learning processes in distance education: Synchronous versus asynchronous systems. *Computers & Education, 51*(3), 1172–1183.

Oh, Y. J., Jia, Y., Lorentson, M., & LaBanca, F. (2013). Development of the Educational and Career Interest Scale in science, technology, and mathematics for high school students. *Journal of Science Education and Technology, 22*(5), 780–790.

Oh, Y. J., Jia, Y., Sibuma, B., LaBanca, F., & Lorentson, M. (2014). Examining the relationship between educational goals, self-efficacy and science academic achievement in high school students: A latent moderated structural model. Paper presented at the American Educational Research Association Annual Meeting, Philadelphia.

Oh, Y. J., Jia, Y., Sibuma, B., Lorentson, M, & LaBanca, F. (2013). Development of the STEM College-Going Expectancy Scale for high school students. *International Journal of Higher Education, 2*(2), 93–105.

Oh, Y. J., Lorentson, M., Jia, Y., Sibuma, B., Snellback, M., & LaBanca, F. (2014). *BLENDED INSTRUCTION: Measuring the impact of a technology-enhanced student-centered learning environment on underserved student engagement, 21st century inquiry skill acquisition, and science achievement.* Quincy, MA: Nellie Mae Education Foundation.

Perkins, D. N. (1991). What constructivism demands of the learner. *Educational Technology, 31*, 19–21.

Sec. 10–66a. (1965). Establishment of Regional Educational Service Centers. Hartford, CT: State of Connecticut.

Sheff Movement. (2013). About Sheff vs. O'Neill. Retrieved from http://www.sheffmovement.org/aboutsheffvoneill.shtml

Shepardon, D. P. (1997). The nature of student thinking in life science laboratories. *School Science and Mathematics, 97*, 37–44.

Shore, B. M., Aulls, M. W., & Delcourt, M. A. B. (2007). *Inquiry in education volume II: Overcoming barriers to successful implementation.* Mahwah, NJ: Erlbaum.

Shore, B. M., Birlean, C., Walker, C. L., Ritchie, K. C., LaBanca, F., & Aulls, M. W. (2009). Inquiry literacy: A proposal for a neologism. *LEARNing Landscapes, 3*, 139–156.

Shymansky, J. A., Hedges, L. V., & Woodworth, G. (1990). A reassessment of effects of inquiry-based science curriculum of the '60s on student performance. *Journal of Research in Science Teaching, 27*, 127–144.

Simkewicz, M., & Mino, M. (2009). Governor Rell proclaims May 9 CT Student Innovators' Day: Connecticut students to exhibit, present sustainable energy/environmental projects at Expo [Press Release]. Retrieved from http://www.skills21.org/press/

Smith, D. (1996). *A meta-analysis of student outcomes attributable to teaching science as inquiry as compared to traditional methodology.* Unpublished doctoral dissertation, Temple University, Philadelphia.

Smith, T. I., & Wittman, M. C. (2007). Comparing three methods for teaching Newton's third law. *Physics Education Research, 3*(2), 1–8.

Spiro, R. J., Feltovich, P. J., Jacobson, M. I., & Coulson, R. L. (1995). Cognitive flexibility, constructivism, and hypertext: Random access instruction for advanced knowledge acquisition in ill-structured domains. In L. P. Steffe & J. E. Gale (Eds.), *Constructivism in Education* (pp. 85–107). Mahwah, NJ: Lawrence Erlbaum Associates.

Spronken-Smith, R., Walker, R. Batchelor, J., O'Steen, B., & Angelo, T. (2012). Evaluating student perceptions of learning processes and intended learning outcomes under inquiry approaches. *Assessment & Evaluation in Higher Education, 37*(1), 57–72.

Summerlee, A., & Murray, J. (2010). The impact of enquiry-based learning on academic performance and student engagement. *Canadian Journal of Higher Education, 40*(2), 78–94.

Torrance, E. P. (1987). Teaching for creativity. In S. G. Isaksen (Ed.), *Frontiers of creativity research: Beyond the basics* (pp. 189–215). Buffalo, NY: Bearly Limited.

Turner, S. (2013). Teachers' and pupils' perceptions of creativity across different key stages. *Research in Education, 89*, 23–40.

Tytler, R. (1992). Independent research projects in school science: Case studies of autonomous behavior. *International Journal of Science Education, 14*, 393–411.

U.S. Department of Education (USDoE). (2013). Investing in Innovation Fund (i3). Retrieved from http://www2.ed.gov/programs/innovation/index.html

Vonderwell, S., Liang, X., & Alderman, K. (2007). Asynchronous discussions and assessment in online learning. *Journal of Research on Technology in Education, 39*(3), 309–328.

Wiggins, G., & McTighe, J. (1998). *Understanding by Design.* Alexandria, VA: Association for Supervision and Curriculum Development.

4

STEM21 DIGITAL ACADEMY FIDELITY OF IMPLEMENTATION

Valuation and Assessment of Program Components and Implementation

Mhora Lorentson, Youn Joo Oh, and Frank LaBanca

The STEM21 Digital Academy

EDUCATION CONNECTION was established as a Regional Education Service Center in Connecticut in 1966, under Connecticut Statutes. As a 501(c) 3 non-profit organization, the agency is funded primarily through grant awards and contracts and fee-for-service activities. Our Center for 21st Century Skills (the Center) has, through the STEM21 Digital Academy program, provided student-centered, blended learning instruction integrating innovative, real-world, performance-based learning experiences across STEM content areas, for 14 years. The program began in 2000 as a single course in one high school and, in 2012–2013, has grown to involve 1889 students from 34 Connecticut high schools in 15 blended learning classes.

In 2010, we expanded the model into a 4-year career-themed Academy of Digital Arts and Sciences. We defined the Academy as student participation in a specific sequence of rigorous STEM21 courses, taught using blended instruction pedagogy (LaBanca, Worwood, Schauss, LaSalsa, & Donn, 2013), aligned with state and national standards, and providing graduation credit. The pedagogical model incorporates four key components: blended instruction, experiential education, performance-based proficiency assessments, and a digital portfolio. The model has been shown to increase student engagement, science academic achievement, and 21st century inquiry and learning skills and to have the potential to decrease the achievement gap (Oh, et al., 2014).

A high school can choose to participate in the Academy sequence or to offer only a select number of courses. During 2012–2013, twelve schools and 500 9th- and 10th-grade students participated in the Academy sequence and an additional 14 schools and 1,740 students participated in at least one STEM21 course. During 2013–2014, our first cohort of Academy students entered 11th grade. The STEM21 Academy course scope and sequence is in Table 4.1.

Table 4.1 STEM21 Academy Scope and Sequence

Subject/Grade	9th Grade	10th Grade	11th Grade	12th Grade
STEM Course Sequence	Earth & Energy Essentials (E3) Algebra21 Skills21	Biology21 Geometry21 Digital Media Movie Making Research Design & Development	Chemistry21 Video Game Design & Development E-Commerce Entrepreneurship	Physics21 Research Capstone

Developing an Understanding of Implementation Fidelity

To sustain the rapid growth of the STEM21 program and support its evolution into the Digital Academy, we needed to clearly define the program model. Additionally, we needed to develop a deeper understanding of the degree and impact of implementation, the effect of each model component on students and teachers, and the degree to which program implementation was meeting stakeholder needs. As a result, evaluation and research activities focused on the STEM21 Digital Academy have increased over time in parallel to the expansion of implementation.

In 2005, EDUCATION CONNECTION created the Center for Collaborative Evaluation and Strategic Change (CCESC). CCESC's mission was to provide research and evaluation services to EDUCATION CONNECTION programs and to education, health, and human service organizations in Connecticut and surrounding states.

From inception, a major responsibility of CCESC was to conduct annual data collection to support improvement of the Center's STEM21 program (Blase & Fixsen, 2013; Century, Cassata, Rudnick, & Freeman, 2012; Cresswell, 2009; Rossi, Lipsen, & Freeman, 2004). During the early years of program development, evaluation questions related to implementation fidelity included the following:

- How are courses actually being implemented within the classroom setting?
- How are the program components and the implementation of the program model meeting the needs of teachers and students?
- How can the program model and implementation process be improved?
- What challenges and opportunities are faced by schools while implementing these courses?

CCESC collected qualitative and quantitative data annually to obtain information regarding implementation processes and outcomes. Methods included document and student and teacher attendance reviews, qualitative interviews, and focus groups with teachers and students, classroom observations, and satisfaction surveys. Results were analyzed, shared with program staff at quarterly meetings, and used to refine program implementation and evaluation activities.

Findings supported the improvement and refinement of the program model and implementation processes. Results indicated a high degree of enthusiasm and support by teachers and students for the STEM21 program. Model components, including the blended approach to instruction, experiential learning opportunities, digital portfolio, and proficiency assessments received enthusiastic support from teachers and students. Feedback was used continuously to refine the program model and improve the program. Local and national recognition was received.

As the program's popularity grew and demand increased, program planners, educators and funders increasingly requested information on the STEM21 model's implementation process and corresponding impacts on classroom instruction and student performance. We knew that the design and implementation of research and evaluation studies necessary to address these questions were beyond the capacity of CCESC. In 2009, CCESC and the Center for 21st Century Skills identified several research questions to address stakeholders' questions:

- What does ideal implementation of the Academy of Digital Arts and Sciences look like?
- To what degree is the Academy of Digital Arts and Sciences being implemented with fidelity?
- How does implementation fidelity vary by school, grade, and district?
- What is the relationship between implementation fidelity and desired program outcomes?

To address these questions and ensure that results were generalizable to broader populations, CCESC and the Center began to establish partnerships with external research and evaluation organizations, including the Education Development Center (EDC). These partnerships proved to be invaluable to program success and allowed EDUCATION CONNECTION to focus research activities, design and implement research and evaluation processes, and collect data necessary to document success while simultaneously implementing a rapidly expanding and highly successful project. In 2010, funding from the United States Department of Education Investing in Innovation (i3) program was received and facilitated the initiation of rigorous evaluation of implementation fidelity.

Initial Evaluation Challenges

EDUCATION CONNECTION's i3 program award was our first large influx of funding specifically designated for research and evaluation. The U.S. Department of Education was also our first funder to require, and provide intensive technical assistance for, rigorous research and evaluation design and implementation related to outcome and implementation fidelity.

Prior evaluations of the STEM21 model were on a much smaller scale than the i3 grant required. Although CCESC had developed several useful instruments to gather data on implementation and key outcomes, we did not have the capacity to conduct an evaluation that met i3 program evaluation criteria. Our evaluation team was keenly aware of the need to balance research and programming activities to allow the program to support, and benefit from, data collection efforts. We knew that we needed to build evaluation capacity in a way that enhanced learning, performance, and change at program and organizational levels, and develop an evaluation structure that was appropriate for use in a small program within a small non-profit educational organization (Morariu, Athanasiades, & Emery, 2012).

The first challenge we faced was to clearly define the roles and expectations of CCESC staff and research partners. In addition to CCESC, the implementation of research activities supported through i3 funding involved the Education Development Center (EDC), and the i3 national evaluation contractor, Abt Associates (Abt).

Our experience had identified the critical importance of a strong partnership between program staff and evaluation experts. We knew that the ability of these individuals to work together to develop a shared understanding of the program, the impact of data collection on program implementation, and the impact of necessary program changes on research design and implementation would be crucial to success. We needed to define the roles and responsibilities of each of the internal and external evaluators clearly and in a way that maximized the skills and experience of each.

Additionally, in a growing program, assessment of implementation fidelity can be expected to impact and be impacted by programmatic changes (Fixsen, Naoom, Blase, Friedman & Wallace, 2005; Joyce & Showers, 2002; Kitsen, Havey, & McCormack, 1998). This relationship between research activities and programmatic changes strengthened our conviction that we needed a strong partnership between program and evaluation staff and external evaluation partners. The role of project staff therefore, also needed to be clearly delineated. Through a collaborative process incorporating input from CCESC, Abt, EDC, and the project director, we defined the roles of these entities as follows.

Center for Collaborative Evaluation and Strategic Change

The long-term partnership between CCESC and the Center for 21st Century Skills, CCESC's knowledge of Center needs and experiences, and CCESC's close proximity to Center staff, pointed to a role for CCESC as an internal evaluator. The understanding CCESC had of the STEM21 program and its early stage of development implied that CCESC would be most appropriately involved in research design and data collection related to assessment of implementation fidelity. CCESC's role was defined as that of an internal evaluator with primary responsibility for directing the implementation fidelity study. Specifically, CCESC developed the implementation fidelity research design, developed data collection measures, conducted implementation data collection activities, and designed the analysis plan.

Education Development Center, Inc.

The Center had previously worked with EDC through activities funded by the National Science Foundation's Advanced Technological Education and Innovative Technology Experiences for Students and Teachers programs. This experience provided EDC with a working knowledge of Center programs and an established relationship with CCESC and program staff as an external evaluator. EDC's primary responsibilities included research design, measurement development and validation, data collection and analysis of program outcomes. As external evaluator, EDC provided insight and feedback to CCESC on the assessment of implementation fidelity, implementation measurement development and analysis techniques, and research and evaluation design and activities.

Abt Associates

As the prime contractor for the national i3 program evaluation, Abt Associates had developed standards for high-quality implementation studies for i3 program grantees. These standards included the use of a program-specific logic model for the intervention and the development of a related system for measuring fidelity of implementation of intervention at classroom, school, and program levels over time. Abt provided support to evaluation teams to ensure that the evaluations were high quality and met i3 standards.

Center for 21st Century Skills

EDUCATION CONNECTION's Center for 21st Century Skills was most closely acquainted with program goals and processes. The Center was responsible for supporting data collection activities with EDC and ensuring that data collection and design activities were in line with national i3 evaluation standards.

Subsequent Challenges: Paradigm Shifts and Lessons Learned

Our evaluation team faced a number of additional challenges, the resolution of which required paradigm shifts and key learnings for the partnership as a whole, and for each individual member. The initial challenge was the need to identify exactly what was meant by rigorous and valid quantitative evaluation of implementation fidelity within the Digital Academy program.

As described in Chapters 1 and 2, little research exists on fidelity measurement in education. As a result, when i3 funding was received, Abt was in the initial stages of identifying the desired nature of data collection and research expectations related to implementation fidelity for i3 funded programs. Clear guidelines for the collection of implementation fidelity data had not yet been articulated.

The quantitative evaluation of implementation fidelity was a relatively new concept for CCESC, EDC, and the program director. Our evaluation team needed to develop a shared understanding of quality evaluation of implementation fidelity; appropriate levels of implementation fidelity expectations for the Academy; and the importance and value of the collection of implementation fidelity data.

EDUCATION CONNECTION and EDC staff also experienced their own separate challenges. Initially, for EDUCATION CONNECTION leadership, program, and evaluation staff, the high degree of rigor and expectations associated with the successful collection of data for the i3 program increased accountability and visibility and resulted in anxiety, uncertainty of expectations, and occasional resistance on all sides. We needed to put structures and processes in place to support successful research and evaluation activities.

Both the EDUCATION CONNECTION program director and CCESC staff had the majority of their experience with, and commitment to, qualitative data collection. This commitment resulted in a struggle to understand and support the value of using numbers to understand implementation fidelity in STEM21 program schools. Initially, collection of quantitative fidelity data seemed to assign numerical values to qualitative information. We note that this initial opinion changed drastically over the 2 years of implementation as it became clear that the collection of quantitative implementation fidelity supported rather than replaced our qualitative data collection efforts.

The early stage of the Academy's development meant, for practical purposes, that the Academy was in the beginning stages of learning about and revising its program model (Blase & Fixen, 2013; Fixsen, et al., 2005; Macallair & Males, 2004). Our team knew that program model components needed to be more clearly defined to accommodate the collection of rigorous implementation fidelity data.

The evaluation team also realized that the collection of quality implementation fidelity data would require a change in mindset for Center staff. We knew that Center staff would need to support research and data collection activities in an ongoing and consistent fashion. A shift in thinking would be required to change from a culture in which evaluation responsibilities were seen as an occasional, additional, and unwanted chore to a view in which these responsibilities were considered to be an integral component of the ongoing work.

The resolution of these challenges required intensive interactions and frequent meetings between CCESC and the program director and between CCESC and

EDC. We needed to address these challenges while developing and implementing an evaluation plan that met national i3 standards and the needs of our growing program.

As a result of each discussion, we adapted either the evaluation plan or the program implementation process as needed. Challenges faced during the initial program year included the identification of appropriate survey administration procedures (online versus hard copy administration), the development of strategies to support teachers, students and staff with the additional workload related to data collection (combine impact and fidelity data collection tools or keep them separate when collecting data from students and teachers? Require completion of templates for data collection or allow flexibility?), and the development of strategies to develop a positive culture related to data collection within the program.

Developing a positive culture related to data collection was perhaps the biggest challenge. The evaluation team knew that program personnel were dedicated, talented, committed to program development, and constrained by time and fiscal limitations. The majority did not have a background in research design or implementation and were unfamiliar with the relationship between research and program change and growth. Evaluation activities added to an already full workload and occasionally resulted in the need to pull students or school staff from valuable program activities. As a result, there was a tendency for program staff to perceive evaluation as a limitation to program implementation and, therefore, to resist evaluation requirements and data collection activities.

The collection of quality data required that the program director and evaluation team develop a shared understanding of the importance of evaluation activities at the program and school levels to ensure that data collection proceeded smoothly. The evaluation team supported these efforts through attendance at Center meetings or experiential education activities, formal and informal discussions with program staff, revision of data collection procedures as needed to minimize burden on program and school staff, and presentations and discussion of research findings with an emphasis on the implications of findings on program development and growth.

EDC external evaluators also experienced their own challenges. In addition to learning about the requirements of data collection for implementation fidelity evaluation, EDC needed to design the outcome evaluation and determine the most appropriate strategies to collect data from 12 Connecticut school districts. The external evaluator, although highly experienced and familiar with the implementation of rigorous research activities, required time to learn about the Academy program, the challenges faced by this program within a school setting, and to develop appropriate data collection techniques for both fidelity and outcome assessment. She needed time to develop strategies for data sharing and communication with school-level site coordinators necessary to monitor data collection and collect data in a timely and efficient manner.

The resolution of the majority of these challenges occurred over a 6-month period and required consistent and collaborative interactions. Monthly, and sometimes more frequent, conference calls with Abt provided an opportunity for interaction between

Abt and the evaluation team, a collaboration that supported the development of the fidelity implementation evaluation plan, data collection process, and analysis of the results. These conversations enhanced the ability of evaluation partners to understand and clarify the research design and data collection methodology required for high-quality and rigorous implementation research and evaluation. Additionally, EDC external evaluators, the program director, and the internal evaluator met in person on a quarterly basis to identify concerns, review progress, and develop or identify appropriate and useable data collection tools and structures to meet the needs of the research and evaluation, program development, and participating schools.

Measuring Program Fidelity

Determining What to Measure

The first task for our evaluation team was to clearly define the program inputs/activities, key components, and related mediators necessary to achieve program outcomes. Intervention inputs/activities are defined by Goodson and Darrow (2013) as the resources, activities, or structural changes necessary to accomplish the desired changes or, similarly, as program components, activities, and processes for which the developer is responsible. Program mediators are considered to be short-term outcomes through which inputs/activities as implemented are expected to lead to intended short-term outcomes. Finally, outcomes are defined as the change objectives that the intervention is designed to achieve (Goodson & Darrow, 2013; W. K. Kellogg Foundation, 2004). Our first task was to incorporate these components into a visual depiction of the program using a logic model.

CCESC and the program director initiated conversations to develop the STEM21 logic model. The visual depiction of the relationship between program inputs, mediators, and short- and long-term outcomes provided by a logic model made it easy to identify areas in which the relationships between the four levels were unclear or inconsistent on either the program or the evaluation side. EDC, in consultation with Abt, reviewed the logic model in relation to the impact study and provided feedback to CCESC. This process was ongoing and iterative as the program developed. As the impact and implementation studies and the program implementation model were refined, the evaluation team revised the logic model and shared, as needed, with the program director.

As an example of these interactions, during the first program year the external evaluator reviewed the logic model, elaborated upon the mediators at the student and teacher levels, and refined the short-term outcomes. Specifically, improved student interest/self-efficacy was removed from the short-term outcome level and incorporated into the long-term outcomes as achievement of these outcomes could be expected to require more long-term exposure to the program. CCESC worked with the project director to obtain consensus and to incorporate changes into program implementation as needed. The final program logic model is depicted in Figure 4.1.

FIGURE 4.1 STEM21 Digital Academy Logic Model

INPUTS	MEDIATORS:INSTRUCTIONAL PRACTICES	SHORT TERM OUTCOMES	LONG TERM OUTCOMES
Yearly Professional Development	**Teachers**	**Teachers**	**Teachers**
Summer Institute: Face to face intensive 28 hour group training covering inquiry-based education, 21st century skills, use of on-line curricula and lesson delivery. **Coaching**: 2 in person coaching activities **Reflection Session**: End of year reflection session	Teachers use at least 65% of on-line curricula	Increased teacher efficacy with use of intervention materials and activities Increased teacher ability to teach inquiry-based learning and 21st century skills in CT schools	Teachers implement activities with high fidelity Teachers improve use of appropriate instructional practices Teachers improve use of digital environment
Grade-level Implementation	**Students**	**Students**	**Students**
Digital Portfolio: Digital portfolio used to record student progress **LMS Forums**: Used by students to communicate with peers and teacher in one science and one technology class per grade **Experiential Education**: Students participate in three regional meetings and an annual Innovation Expo **Curricula Completion**: Teachers implement online curricula in one science and one technology class per grade measured by completion of proficiency assessments	Students use online curricula, digital portfolios and LMS forums Students participate in experiential education activities Students apply content knowledge, inquiry and 21st century skills to completion of proficiency assessments	Students increase use of digital environment and 21st Century and inquiry-skills	Increased student interest/self-efficacy in STEM Increased student enrollment in STEM college and careers Increased student achievement in STEM Increased student learning and application of 21st century and inquiry skills to STEM
Course Implementation and Development: Courses implemented with fidelity in 12 sites **Course Articulation**: 6 courses articulated with the Connecticut Community College System **Expected Student and Teacher Participation**: 960 students and 80 teachers participate **Underrepresented Student Participation**: 51-100% of students are under-represented. **Annual Quality Professional Development Provided to Teachers**: Including summer professional development, two hour coaching sessions and one end-of-year reflection session	**Program** Courses implemented in 12 sites Teachers and students participate Data collection for outcome and fidelity of implementation assessment		**Program** Comprehensive understanding of success of Academy in 12 CT sites Increased understanding of success of assessments in improvement of teaching practice in 12 CT sites Quality assessment of fidelity of implementation, student achievement and growth Impact on STEM interest/self-efficacy, content knowledge and college readiness/ entry identified

STEM21 Digital Academy logic Model

The logic model depicts linkages between program components (teacher professional development, grade-level implementation, and program implementation), mediators or short-term outcomes, and expected long-term outcomes. Expected short-term teacher outcomes include implementation of activities with fidelity, improved use of instructional practices, and improved use of the digital environment. Short-term student outcomes include increased use of a digital environment and increased 21st century and inquiry skills. Long-term teacher outcomes are increased teacher efficacy with the use of intervention materials and activities and increased ability to teach inquiry learning and 21st century skills. Long-term student outcomes include increased interest/self-efficacy in STEM; increased enrollment in STEM-related college programs and careers; increased achievement in STEM; and increased application of 21st century and inquiry skills to STEM. Long-term program outcomes include development of a comprehensive understanding of Academy success; increased understanding of the success of assessments; assessment of fidelity of implementation and student achievement on growth; and an understanding of the impact of program participation on STEM interest/self-efficacy, content knowledge, and college readiness.

The assessment of implementation fidelity informs program improvement and examines the degree to which the program is implemented as intended, both across sites and at different levels of implementation. Three levels of implementation identified within the logic model include teacher, student, and program levels of implementation. After these levels were identified, our evaluation team needed to select indicators that could be used to measure implementation at each level. The development of indicators was facilitated by discussions revolving around the following questions:

- What do teachers have to do if they are participating in the program with fidelity?
- What has to happen at the grade or classroom level if the program is implemented with fidelity?
- What does the program itself have to do if the program is implemented with fidelity?

Specific indicators identified within each component are described in Table 4.2.

Instrument Development and Data Collection

CCESC collected qualitative implementation fidelity data annually using teacher and student focus groups and interviews and administration of perception surveys linked to the program goals. Results were used to adjust the program in Years 1 and 2. Summative data collection was initiated in 2011 in line with the expectations of

Table 4.2 STEM21 Digital Academy Implementation Fidelity: Final Selected Indicators

Teacher Professional Development Indicators	Grade-level Implementation Indicators	Program Implementation Indicators
Participation in Summer Academy (Year 1: all teachers, Years 2–4: first-year teachers only)	Percent of students completing the digital portfolio	Summer Institute: 28 hours of quality professional development including inquiry and 21st century skills
		-or-
		Make-up Session: 6 hour session for individuals unable to attend the Summer Institute
Participation in two coaching sessions annually (Years 2–4)	Percentage of curriculum units completed by teacher	Participation of each teacher in two coaching sessions (Years 2–4)
Participation in one end-of-year reflection session (Years 2–4)	Percentage of students attending three experiential meetings and an Innovation Expo	Participation of teachers in one reflection session (Years 2–4)
	Percentage of students completing five on-line forums in one science and one technology class	At least 51% of students in study from underrepresented groups as defined by gender, minority status and SES
		Expected number of students participating in high school program (Calculated at 20 students/grade/school/year)
		Eight courses in 12 schools implemented as planned (Year 4)
		Six courses articulated with College of Technology (Year 4)

Note: Changes in specific indicators over time are identified.

the i3 program and previously identified program needs. This data provided more comprehensive and detailed information linked to expected program outcomes.

CCESC and EDC identified summative data sources for implementation fidelity assessment for each model component. Data sources for teacher professional development fidelity included attendance records at the Summer Institute, the make-up session, coaching sessions, and the end-of-year reflection session. Attendance was collected by Center staff and provided to CCESC for analysis. Grade-level fidelity consisted of two primary subcomponents—student participation in classroom activities and teacher completion of the curricula. Required student data was identified as attendance records at regional student meetings and the Innovation Expo, portfolio grades, and records of online forum use. Attendance information was collected by Academy staff at regional meetings. Student portfolio grades and forum completion records were collected by the classroom teacher and provided to the internal evaluator for analysis. Completion of the curricula by the teacher in each class was assessed through examination of the number of unit performance assessments (UPAs) within the curricula that had been completed. Finally, program fidelity data was collected including professional development agendas and observation data collected on each professional development session, coaching schedules, and reflection session agendas. Additional data required for program fidelity included course schedules and student registration.

CCESC developed qualitative and summative instruments prior to initial data collection. These instruments included an interview protocol to conduct teacher and student focus groups and a perceptual survey instrument to assess student and teacher program perceptions. EDC reviewed and commented on these instruments in relation to program activities and goals and student learning. In addition, qualitative data collection instruments were reviewed by program staff to ensure linkages and connections with program needs and expectations of funding agencies.

Instruments used to collect summative data can best be described as tools to ensure that necessary high-quality data was obtained in a form that was consistent and easy to use. As with other key activities and instruments, we changed the strategies and tools for summative data collection over time as we learned what worked and what did not. During the evaluation's first year, we asked teachers to provide existing data to evaluators, such as portfolio grades or forum participation results. We gave teachers limited guidance as to how the data should be provided—that is, in what format and using what structure. As a result, data was provided to CCESC in a wide variety of confusing formats that were difficult-to-understand or manage. Although data collection during this first year resulted in the attainment of all necessary data, the mechanism used was highly inefficient and time-intensive for program staff, site coordinators, teachers, and CCESC staff.

As a result of the difficulties experienced during the first year of data collection, we incorporated a number of substantive changes into data collection for subsequent years including the development of specific instruments for implementation fidelity data collection. These changes have been very successful and have expedited the data collection process for all stakeholders. Each change is described in detail below.

Development of Templates to Collect Data from Teachers

CCESC developed a template to guide the collection of fidelity data from teachers. The template was provided to each teacher to collect information specific to that teacher's students and subject area. The template prompted the teacher to provide portfolio grades for each student, the number of unit performance assessments completed (differing by subject area), and the number of online forums completed by each student. We used Survey Monkey—an online survey development tool—to administer the template and support data collection among teachers (Survey Monkey, Inc., 2014). The names of students in a teacher's classroom were obtained from the registration database and incorporated into the survey. The survey, with class-specific attendance, was shared with each individual teacher and used to provide required information for students in the class. This strategy was highly successful and provided quality data, suitable for rapid and efficient data analysis. Additionally, the collection of teacher-specific data in this fashion facilitated the ability of the evaluator to map results back to a specific teacher and examine relationships between the data and outcomes for students in the class.

Development of Templates to Track Student Attendance

Similarly, we developed a template to collect student attendance at experiential education events. Prior to each event, the registration database was used to develop an attendance form for students in each class who were expected to attend the meeting. The form included the teacher's name and school district, the name of the event, the class taught, and the names of students in the class. The form was provided to the teacher upon arrival at each meeting. The teacher checked the names of students present, marked an "A" if the student was absent, and crossed off the names of students who had dropped the course. This template also allowed the revision of the student registration database as needed.

Use of Online Portal for Data Collection

In addition to the collection of data for implementation fidelity analysis, the evaluation team used a variety of tools to collect outcome and satisfaction data related to program expectations. Requirements for data collection were dependent on grade or classroom. To ease complexity and minimize confusion, we incorporated all necessary instruments into an online portal. Each teacher could access the portal and identify which survey or data collection forms were required for their particular class and grade level. This portal was extremely useful to minimize confusion and complexity of the data collection process.

Fidelity Cookbook

A critical tool used to support data collection was the development of a "fidelity cookbook" for teachers and administrators (see Appendix A). We provided this cookbook in hard copy form to school staff and incorporated the use of the cookbook into professional development for teachers during the Summer Institute. The cookbook included a description of the need for and purpose of data collection for implementation fidelity, the types of data to be collected, the time frame required for data collection, and the role of teachers in the data collection process. Additionally, the cookbook outlined program incentives to support data collection. Incentives included the development of memorandums of agreement with participating teachers that outlined the data collection expectations and authorized the withholding of payment until all data was received, and the development of a lottery system in which teachers who had completed all data requirements were eligible to participate in a lottery to win an iPad.

We implemented data collection primarily through four staff roles: the project director, the internal evaluator, site coordinators, and teachers. We put procedures in place to reduce participant burden and strengthen the response rates and overall quality of data collected to ensure reliable and rigorous results. We scheduled school visits by coordinators well in advance and made efforts to provide schools and teachers with all information they needed well in advance.

Development of Approach to Implementation Fidelity Measurement

Research questions for the evaluation of implementation fidelity were developed and included:

1. What was the overall level of fidelity of implementation and how much variation in implementation fidelity was there across sites (schools, classrooms)?
2. How did the model as implemented differ from the model as planned?

These research questions guided the development of a measurement plan for implementation fidelity assessment. However, we faced a number of issues during the development process that challenged both the evaluators and program staff. Accurate measurement of implementation fidelity was initially extremely challenging. The concept of and strategies used to measure fidelity were new ways of thinking to program staff, and internal and external evaluation staff. We had very little understanding of or experience in the use of scorings of key components to determine implementation fidelity of a program at the teacher, grade, and program levels.

Our evaluation team experienced a variety of questions related to the development of appropriate scoring levels for each level of fidelity. Examples include the following:

- How much of a 28-hour Summer Institute does a teacher need to attend to have a high fidelity score for professional development?
- What percentage of students in a grade need to complete a portfolio for the grade to have a high fidelity score for portfolio use?
- How should scores for different components be weighted to reflect the relative importance of that component in the program outcome?

This last question became the most challenging to address. We had initially set scores for each indicator using 0 = low fidelity, 1 = moderate fidelity, and 2 = high fidelity. However, we realized that the relative importance of indicators in the determination of the final student outcome might not be identical, and, therefore, potentially each indicator should not be weighted equally. For instance, we decided that the number of curriculum components (and therefore unit performance assessments) completed by a teacher might be expected to have a greater impact on student outcome than the percentage of students who participated in a specific event (attended a single experiential meeting, for instance). Therefore, we developed scores for completion of unit performance assessments based on a range of 0 = low fidelity and 4 = high fidelity.

It should be noted that decisions related to the weighting of scores for various components were required frequently. Getting through the learning curve related to measurement of implementation fidelity was difficult and required time, practice, and discussion on the part of all key stakeholders.

Additionally, educational programs like the Digital Academy experience a number of challenges resulting from their early stage on the organizational development continuum (Blase & Fixsen, 2013; Darrow, Goodson, & Caven, 2013; Fixsen, et al., 2005; James Bell Associates, 2009). Developing programs face more stringent budget, time, and resource limitations than their larger and more developed peers. As data is collected, it is used to revise the program as needed. These changes, although necessary and appropriate, pose challenges to the evaluation of implementation fidelity.

As each change is incorporated into the program, the evaluator must decide whether to adapt the implementation fidelity evaluation plan to address these changes and potentially decrease the ability to compare results from one year to another, or to replicate the same data collection each year regardless of programmatic changes. Our evaluation team found that the key to good decision-making is to focus on the determination of which changes are essential to the program model, and therefore must be reflected in the data collection process, and which components can or should be modified, added, or eliminated.

The Academy implementation data collection experienced this challenge when, after the first data collection year and based on feedback from participating teachers, the program director identified the need to change the professional development structure significantly. During the first program year, all teachers attended the Summer Institute regardless of previous experience with the program model. Subsequent to the first year, only teachers new to the program were expected to attend the Summer Institute. Additionally, during the second year coaching sessions and an end-of-year reflection session were added to the professional development model and were required of all teachers. CCESC, in partnership with the program director and the external evaluator, determined that these changes were substantial and, if not incorporated into the data collection for assessment of implementation fidelity, would result in data which did not represent well the implementation of the Academy model. As a result, professional development indicators and measures were changed for the second program year.

Last, the Academy evaluation team, after the first year of data collection, realized that assessment of completion of professional development activities, as initially incorporated into the model, did not adequately assess the implementation of quality in the professional development activities. The evaluation team was interested in measuring the implementation of quality professional development activities, not simply the implementation of professional development. As a result, during the second program year, the quality of the Summer Institute sessions was assessed through the use of rubric-based observations of each Summer Institute Session. Each observation was graded using a five-point, standardized rubric. This measurement of quality was incorporated into the measurement plan for implementation fidelity.

Reporting Fidelity Results

Given that the goal of an implementation analysis is to describe the intervention, reporting efforts involve the development of quantitative measures of implementation that accurately describe the intervention and treatment conditions (Century, Freeman, & Rudnick, 2008; Century, et al., 2012; Goodson & Darrow, 2013). Key data must be tabulated in a way that accurately describes the type and amount of services delivered in treatment conditions using data from attendance records, registration databases, grades, and other data sources.

Participation in the Digital Academy is defined as completion of one science and one technology class at each grade level. We developed quantitative indices based on this definition to establish implementation benchmarks regarding the extent to which the program is implemented with fidelity in each treatment classroom and in all Academy schools and grades.

In the development of the scoring calculations, we needed to identify a construct-level score and to define a threshold at the construct level. For instance, the construct of classroom-level fidelity consists of four separate indicators. The score for these four indicators needs to be calculated at the construct level and a level of acceptability, or "threshold," defined a priori. Based on the logic model, the key constructs were: teacher professional development fidelity, grade-level fidelity, and program-level fidelity. The first step, therefore, in the development of appropriate calculations for each key construct was to assign weights to each indicator appropriate to the relevance and importance in program implementation and to develop calculations to measure indicators in each construct using different metrics. Subsequent to the calculation of construct-level scores, each score needed to be categorized into levels of implementation fidelity and a threshold for "adequate implementation" needed to be defined.

Additionally, as the Academy program implementation process changed after the initial data collection year, we needed to develop calculations for each year and to develop a structure to incorporate these changes into the construct level score. As with each step in the completion of the Academy implementation fidelity assessment process, consistent interaction between the evaluation team and the project director was required to accomplish these goals in a manner that met the research needs and fairly and adequately represented the program implementation process. Through multiple revisions and iterations, the evaluation team, the project director, and Abt refined the three constructs (e.g., component 1 = teacher PD level, component 2 = grade level, and component 3 = program level), specific implementation indicators for each construct, scorings of the activities and key components (low = 0, moderate = 1 and high = 2, or 0 = incomplete and 1 = complete for binary items), data sources and scheduled data collection plans, and yearly calculation and an a priori threshold for each construct set at 65 percent. Ranges in total score may vary by year, dependent on the indicators measured that year. The final scoring calculations were developed and are provided for each construct separately in Tables 4.3–4.5.

Using these calculations, implementation fidelity scores were successfully calculated by school and overall during the first and second years of implementation. Results are provided in Table 4.6.

Challenges of Measuring Implementation

The Center for 21st Century Skills and its evaluation partners have experienced a number of challenges related to the introduction of fidelity implementation research and evaluation in a small and growing program. These challenges are summarized below.

Balancing Research and Practice

Balancing research and programming needs is particularly challenging in a developing program (Blase & Fixsen, 2013; Darrow, et al., 2013; Shapley, Sheehan, Maloney, & Caranikas-Walker, 2010). We found that the need to balance research and practice in this setting, particularly in implementation fidelity research, required the development of fidelity measures that meet the needs of and accurately reflect a growing and changing program.

Our experience has identified the critical importance of a strong partnership between the program staff and the internal and external evaluation experts. Each

Table 4.3 Digital Academy Implementation Fidelity Scoring and Calculations: Teacher PD Implementation Fidelity

Component 1 = Teacher PD	Source of Data	Schedule	Scoring of Level of Implementation at Teacher Level
Year 1			
Participation in Summer Institute: All teachers	Attendance records	July, 28 hours Summer Institute	0 = 0–9 hours of participation in training (Low) 1 = 10–19 hours of participation in training (Moderate) 2 = 20–28 hours of participation in training (High) -Or- 2 = Completion of make up if summer session is missed
Calculations			
Teacher-level teacher participation score			0 = Low participation 1 = Moderate participation 2 =High participation
Grade-level teacher participation score			0 = Low Grade-level Participation Score: <34% of teachers in grade have high participation (score = 2) 1 = Moderate Grade-level Participation Score: 34–59% of teachers in grade have high participation (score = 2) 2 = High Grade implementation = 60–100% of teachers in grade have high participation (score = 2)
School-level teacher participation score			0 = Low School-level Participation Score: <0% of teachers in school have high participation (score = 2) 1 = Moderate School-level Participation Score: 34–59% of teachers in school have high participation (score = 2) 2 = High School implementation = 60–100% of classes in school have high participation (score = 2)

Sample-level Thresholds

Sample-level fidelity threshold			Implemented "with fidelity" = 65% of schools with high implementation of teacher PD (score = 2)

Years 2–4

Participation in Summer Institute: **first-year teachers only**	Attendance records	July, 28 hours Summer Institute	0 = 0–9 hrs of participation in training (Low) 1 = 10–19 hrs of participation in training (Moderate) 2 = 20–28 hrs of participation in training (High Adequacy) Or 2 = Completion of make up if summer session missed is missed
Participation in 2 (45) minute coaching	Coaching schedules	Twice per year	0 = No participation (low) 1 = One coaching session completed (moderate) 2 = Two coaching sessions completed (high)
Participation at Reflective Session	Attendance	June, 6 hours.	0 = No participation (low), 1= Participation (high)

Calculations

Teacher-level Teacher Participation Score			**First-year teachers (0–5)** 0 = Low participation = score of 0–1 1 = Moderate participation = score of 2–3 2 = High participation = score of 4–5 **Returning teachers (0–3)** 0 = Low participation = score of 0–1 1 = Moderate participation = score of 2 2 = High participation = score of 3

(Continued)

Table 4.3 (Continued)

Component 1 = Teacher PD	Source of Data	Schedule	Scoring of Level of Implementation at Teacher Level
Grade-level teacher PD score			0 = Low Grade-level Participation Score: <34% of teachers in grade have high participation (score = 3) 1 = Moderate Grade-level Participation Score: 34–59% of teachers in grade have high participation (score = 3) 2 = High Grade implementation = 60–100% of teachers in grade have high participation (score = 3)
School-level implementation score for teacher PD			0 = Low School-level Participation Score: <0% of grades in school have high participation (score = 2) 1 = Moderate School-level Participation Score: 34–59% of grades in school have high participation (score = 2) 2 = High School implementation = 60–100% of grades in school have high participation (score = 2)
Thresholds **Sample-level teacher PD fidelity threshold**			**Implemented "with fidelity" = 65% of schools with high teacher participation in professional development (score = 2)**

Table 4.4 Digital Academy Implementation Fidelity Scoring and Calculations: Classroom and Grade-Level Implementation Fidelity

Component 2 = Classroom/Grade Implementation Fidelity	Source	Schedule	Score	Grade-level Score (Same students in 2 classes per grade)
Student Participation in Digital Portfolio	Rubric Grade for Portfolio	June, annually	0 = No portfolio grade 2 = Portfolio grade	0 = Low = <50% of students with portfolio grade 1 = Moderate = 50–74% of students with portfolio grade 2 = High = 75% of students or more with portfolio grade
Student Participation in Regional Meetings and Innovation Expo	Attendance Records	Regional Meetings: 1. Oct/Nov 2. Jan/Feb 3. March 4. Expo: May June	0–4 Each student is scored in terms of the # of events attended (one point per event)	0 = Low = <50% of students with participation score of 3–4 1 = Moderate = 50–74% of students with participation score of 3–4 2 = High = 75% of students in grade or more with participation score of 3–4
Student Participation in on-line forums in *one science and one technology class* per grade	Teacher records for completion of five forums for Science		For Science: 0 = No forum completion 1 = Less than 3 forums 2 = 3–5 forums or more -PLUS- For Technology: 0 = No forum completion 1 = Less than 3 forums 2 = 3–5 forums or more	0 = Low = <50% of students participated in 3+ online forums in both science and technology class 1 = Moderate = 50–74% of students participated in 3+ on-line forums for both science and technology class 2 = High = 75% of students in grade participated in 3+ online forums in both science and technology class

(Continued)

Table 4.4 (Continued)

	Source	Schedule	Score	Grade-level Score (*Same students in 2 classes per grade*)
Component 2 = Classroom/Grade Implementation Fidelity				
Curriculum components completed by teacher in *one science* and *one technology class*	End-of-year checklist for each class	June	For Science: 0 = 0–33% of components 1 = 34–66% of components 2 = 67–100% of components –PLUS– For Technology: 0 = 0–33% of components 1 = 34–66% of components 2 = 67–100% of components	0 = Low = <50% of teachers complete 67% of curriculum components in both science and technology classes 2 = Moderate = 50–74% of teachers complete 67+% of curriculum in both of science and technology classes 4 = High = 75% of teachers complete 67+% of curriculum in both science and technology classes

Grade-level Implementation Fidelity Calculations

Overall Score

Grade-level score for grade participation

Range = 0–16 for each grade
0 = low participation = total score 0–4
1 = medium participation = total score of 5–9
2 = high participation high participation = total score of 10–16

School-level implementation score for grade implementation

0 = Low School-level implementation = <50% of grades with high implementation
1 = Moderate School-level implementation = 51–75% of grades with high implementation
2 = High School-level implementation = >65% of grades with high implementation

Sample Implementation Fidelity Calculations

Sample-level student fidelity threshold

Implemented "with fidelity" = 65% of schools with high student participation in Academy activities and teacher completion of curriculum components (score = 2)

Table 4.5 Digital Academy Implementation Fidelity Scoring and Calculations: Program Implementation Fidelity

Component 3 = Program Responsibility	Source of Data	Schedule	Scoring of Level of Implementation
Year 1			
Underrepresented groups in programs	Registration	June	0 = 0–25% of students from disadvantaged/underrepresented groups 1 = 25–50% of students from disadvantaged/underrepresented groups 2 = 51–100% of students from disadvantaged/underrepresented groups
Expected number of students in program	Registration	June	0 = 0–33% of expected number of students participating in program 1 = 34–66% of expected number of students participating in program 2 = 67–100% of expected number of students participating in program
Calculation and Threshold			
Total score Sample threshold for fidelity of implementation			Range = 0–4 Program is implemented "with fidelity" if program reaches goals for number, types of students in the program (total >2)
Years 2 and 3			
Quality Summer Institute Professional development provided to HS teachers	Daily schedule compared to rubric rating workshop **content** and **time-on-task**.	July	PD provided on inquiry and 21st century skills: 0 = not provided, 1 = provided inquiry Quality of each PD session: 0 = Average score of 2.5/4 or above on 5 components for <60% of sessions 1 = Average score of 2.5/4 on 5 components for 60% or more of sessions Total Possible 2

(Continued)

Table 4.5 (Continued)

Component 3 = Program Responsibility	Source of Data	Schedule	Scoring of Level of Implementation
Make Up Session offered for Summer Institute	Attendance	August	0 = not provided, 1 = provided
Two (2) hour coaching sessions offered per teacher	Attendance	January and May	0 = 0–33% of teachers provided 2 coaching sessions 1 = 34–66% of teachers provided two coaching sessions 2 = More than 67% of teachers provided two coaching sessions
Reflection Session	Attendance	June	0 = not provided, 1 = provided

Calculations

Overall Professional Development			Range = 0–6 0 = low implementation of PD = total score of 0–2 1 = medium implementation of PD = total score of 3–4 2 = high implementation of PD = total score of 5–6
Underrepresented groups in programs			0 = 0–24% of students from disadvantaged/underrepresented groups 1 = 25–50% of students from disadvantaged/underrepresented groups 2= 51–100% of students from disadvantaged/underrepresented groups
Expected number of students in program			0 = 0–33% of expected number of students participating in program 1 = 34–66% of expected number of students participating in program 2 = 67–100% of expected number of students participating in program

Threshold

Sample Threshold for Program Responsibility Fidelity of Implementation			Range = 0–6 Program is implemented "with fidelity" if goals for number, types of students are met >4 (out of 6)

Year 4

Quality Summer Session Professional development provided to HS teachers	Daily schedule compared to rubric rating workshop **content** and **time-on-task**.	July	PD provided on inquiry and 21st century skills: 0 = not provided, 1 = provided inquiry Quality of each PD session: 0 = Average score of 1–2 (Pre-Inquiry or Developing Inquiry) on five rubric components for all sessions 1 = Average score of 3 or 4 (Proficient Inquiry or Exemplary Inquiry) on five rubric components for all sessions. Total Possible 2
Make Up Session offered for Summer Session	Attendance	August	0 = not provided, 1 = provided
Two (2) hour coaching sessions offered to each teacher each year	Attendance	January and May	0 = 0–33% of teachers provided 2 coaching sessions 1 = 34–66% of teachers provided two coaching sessions 2 = More than 67% of teachers provided two coaching sessions
Reflection Session	Attendance	June	0 = not provided, 1 = provided

Calculations

Overall Professional Development			Range = 0–6 0 = low implementation of PD = total score of 0–2 1 = medium implementation of PD = total score of 3–4 2 = high implementation of PD = total score of 5–6
Underrepresented groups in programs			0 = 0–25% of students from disadvantaged/underrepresented groups 1 = 25–50% of students from disadvantaged/underrepresented groups 2 = 51–100% of students from disadvantaged/underrepresented groups

(Continued)

Table 4.5 (Continued)

Component 3 = Program Responsibility	Source of Data	Schedule	Scoring of Level of Implementation
Expected number of students in program			0 = 0–33% of expected number of students participating in program
			1 = 34–66% of expected number of students participating in program
			2 = 67–100% of expected number of students participating in program
6 courses articulated as planned	Articulation letters from	End of final year	*For each course:* 0 = course not articulated, 1 = course articulated
			Range 0–6
8 courses in 12 schools implemented as planned	COT Course schedules	End of final year	*For each course:* 0 = course not implemented, 1 = course implemented
			Range 0–8
Threshold			
Sample threshold for Program Responsibility Fidelity of Implementation			Range 0–20
			Program is implemented "with fidelity" if program components are implemented at a high level (>13 (out of 20)

Table 4.6 2011–2013 STEM21 Digital Academy Implementation Fidelity

	Thresholds for 2011–2012	2011–2012 Implemented with fidelity	Thresholds for 2012–2013	2012–2013 Implemented with fidelity
Teacher PD Fidelity	65% of schools with high teacher participation	80% High Fidelity. Above threshold. "Yes"	65% of schools with high scores for teacher participation	66% High Fidelity. Above threshold. "Yes"
Grade-level Implementation Fidelity	65% of schools with high classroom fidelity	71% High Fidelity: Above Threshold "Yes"	65% of schools with high scores classroom fidelity	66% High Fidelity. Above threshold. "Yes"
Program Fidelity	Program has score >2 out of 4	Score = 4 Above Threshold "Yes"	Program has score >4 out of 6	Score = 6 Above Threshold "Yes"

member of this triad brings a unique understanding and perspective on program activities and has limitations related to their role in and knowledge of program and research activities. The ability of these partners to work together to develop a shared understanding of the program, the impact of data collection on program implementation, and the impact of necessary program changes on research design and implementation, while ensuring that data collection meets the needs of a small and growing program, is critical to success.

Role of Communication in Maintaining Research-Based Partnerships

The majority of educational administrators and teachers are practitioners by training and commitment. These individuals face constant challenges and con-flicting priorities related to their responsibilities prior to data collection. As data collection and research begin to be incorporated into daily activities, the need to put time and effort into these "other" activities can create friction and resistance. Our experience has shown that this resistance can be seen in organization and program leadership, program staff, and in school and district participants.

Our experience has identified the need to continuously strive, both inter-nally and externally, to inform leadership and practitioners of what research is being conducted, why it is being conducted, and how the results will benefit their schools, districts, and organizations. The means in which this communi-cation may happen can be expected to vary by stakeholder group (internal leadership, internal staff, external leadership, and external staff) and is necessary on a continuous basis. It is particularly important that as program or data collection changes are made, and requirements and expectations of stakeholders are altered, the reasons for these alterations are clearly shared.

Identifying How and When to Incorporate Program Changes into Data Collection

In a growing and changing program, the conceptualization of the program model and setting and calculating corresponding fidelity measures is an ongoing and iterative process (Darrow, et al., 2013; James Bell Associates, 2009). As a result, plans to measure implementation fidelity may need revision. As in the case of the Digital Academy, these changes may result in measures of fidelity that differ by year, increasing the difficulty in tracking levels of fidelity over time. In addition, these changes create challenges for studies wishing to calculate student-level, multi-year fidelity scores that align with the impact analysis. In this study, the decision was made to adapt the fidelity measures to program changes that occurred after the first program year as both the program director and the evaluation team believed the changes in the program activities could be expected to have a major impact on expected outcomes. This decision was supported by yearly outcome data analysis to identify which schools were having more impact on student outcomes and which cohort was performing better than the other in each year. These changes are appropriate and expected when a program is in the development phase.

Assigning Appropriate Weights to Fidelity Measures

Any educational program is impacted by situations and changes not within the control of the program developer. As an example, a school district may reassign classroom teachers based on their own needs, teachers may leave the position for personal or professional reasons, weather-related issues may impact attendance, and school district policies and procedures may impact program implementation in any particular school. These changes can impact both program outcomes and implementation fidelity and are not within the control of the program director.

   This challenge can create difficulty when assigning a weight to a particular measure that is not completely within the control of the program. The question emerges, "how can we weight this measure in a manner that is fair to the program and is also accurate within the research setting?" In the case of the Digital Academy, we faced this challenge when participating schools hired teachers to teach Academy classes just before the school year began but after the completion of the Summer Institute. Through no fault of the teachers or the program, these individuals were forced to attend a 6-hour make-up session instead of a 28-hour Summer Institute required of first-year teachers. Our evaluation team needed to decide how to weight attendance at the full session verses attendance at the make-up session. In our case, the decision was made to weight them equally with the expectation that a teacher would receive more intensive and individualized professional development at the make-up session, hopefully sufficient to equalize the learning which occurred and therefore make an equal weight appropriate. These challenges emerged frequently, and, in our experience, decisions needed to be made with little and insufficient data available.

Informing Program Development

In our experience, it is critical that there be consistent interactions between the program director and the evaluation team. We have discovered that the key and first point of evaluation contact with the program director and program team is the internal evaluator. This individual often has physical proximity to both the program director and the program staff, making it conducive to act as a conduit of information between evaluators and program staff. We have found it to be crucial for the internal evaluator to have constant interactions, not only with the program director, but with the program team. The Academy internal evaluator attends program staff meetings on a regular basis, goes to the majority of schools to conduct interviews and focus groups, and attends the Innovation Expo and student meetings whenever possible. Our evaluation team has found that this close interaction with program activities provides the evaluator with a deep understanding of program needs and can result in the ability to create improvements in both the evaluation and data collection process.

Close interaction between the internal partners (the program director and the internal evaluator) and the external evaluator is also critical. The Academy evaluation team initiated these conversations through quarterly, or more frequently, telephone conferences. Our team, however, found the use of telephone and e-mail communication alone to be insufficient for good evaluation planning and enhancement of the use of data to inform program development. In many cases, face-to-face discussion was required to successfully clarify the underlying causes of a challenge and therefore to successfully resolve the issue. As a result, our evaluation team now holds face-to-face meetings on a quarterly basis. These conversations are extremely valuable for keeping the data collection process on track and for supporting the incorporation of results of data collection in ongoing program development and implementation.

Analysis of implementation fidelity is, by definition, analysis of what is happening as the program is being implemented. As such, the potential impact on classroom teachers can be large. Fidelity data collection, for Academy teachers, requires that each teacher complete particular activities and provide particular sources of data at particular times. During the first year of "experimentation" with the data collection process, it became obvious that for data collection to work, teachers need to be completely on board at all levels with the data collection process. They need to understand the use of the data in program development, and not in teacher evaluation, and therefore the need to be as unbiased and accurate as possible. As a result, intensive training on the collection and role of implementation fidelity data was incorporated into the Summer Institute professional development session. We also expected that training on data collection would improve our reporting consistency, data quality and response rate as participants could be expected to understand the questions being asked similarly and to feel more accountable to the outcome.

The ability of our evaluation team to measure implementation fidelity began with a clearly defined program model. Clear identification of the Academy's four primary program components (blended learning, the use of the portfolio, attendance at experiential education, and completion of Unit Performance Assessments) influenced our ability to describe and explain the model to other researchers and program staff. It also helped us to identify appropriate data collection instruments to use for measuring implementation fidelity.

Last, the collection of implementation fidelity data allowed program staff to identify and ascertain what specific aspects of the program are not being implemented as expected. This knowledge was used to identify additional program support or recommend changes in the implementation process. Similarly, access to clear and specific data related to implementation has allowed program staff to clearly identify teachers, school, and program staff who are not performing as intended and to use this information to either support these individuals as needed to allow them to implement more successfully, to revise the program if needed, or to replace poor performers with individuals willing and able to implement the program as required. This ability has greatly enhanced program success at ensuring that activities are implemented throughout participating schools, as intended.

Working with Program Developers

The importance of working in close partnership with program developers cannot be overemphasized. The Digital Academy is fortunate to have a program director with expertise in measurement and evaluation. This expertise has allowed the program director to provide input and insight into both the evaluation and the program aspects of implementation as needed and has been invaluable to the success of the Digital Academy and related data-collection activities.

Our evaluation team is extremely cognizant of the importance of this knowledge on the part of our program director. As a result, we highly recommend that all program developers obtain at least a working knowledge of evaluation and measurement prior to, or in parallel with, the initiation of intensive research or data-collection activities. This knowledge can be gained through local, state, or national workshops or webinars, by sitting in on a few relevant classes at the local college or by attending an evaluation or research training held nationally. The Evaluator's Institute (TEI, 2013), for example, operated by George Washington University, provides annual trainings in multiple locations to beginning researchers and program staff. In addition, the American Evaluation Association (AEA, 2013) and the American Educational Research Association (AERA, 2013) provide pre-conference workshops on a regular basis designed to meet the needs of programmers and beginning researchers.

As with the success of any partnership, consistent and frequent interaction between parties is critical and generally includes phone conversations, quarterly meetings, and collaborative discussion of research options. The role of the internal evaluator is critical in supporting interaction with the program development, and physical proximity allows close interaction and more intimate knowledge of program activities.

The program evaluator should support program staff in a number of ways. Program staff are immersed in the day-to-day aspects of running a program and, for most of them, the collection of data is perceived as an unwelcome, and generally unasked for, addition to an already heavy workload. The impact of data collection on program workload is real and must be respected by the evaluation team at all times. Support can be expressed in a number of ways, including clear communication with program staff of both the reasons and need for data collection and the expected impacts of data collection on program quality and growth. Similarly, to minimize the influence on staff workload, data collection must be as efficient, effective, and simple as possible to allow program staff to incorporate data collection into their day-to-day activities without undue stress or effort.

Program staff may also need support and input to develop strategies to encourage participation in the data collection process by teachers and schools. It is important that evaluators provide input and suggestions to encourage participation. These ideas could include the use of incentives for data completion, incorporation of results into a teacher's program planning, or the collaborative discussion of results by teachers involved in the same process and course.

Last, our evaluation team has learned that the collection of data related to implementation fidelity, particularly at the teacher or classroom level, can easily be perceived to be a threat to teachers and their administrators. These individuals are often under tremendous pressure from state officials and national results-based accountability efforts. It can be expected, therefore, that if a teacher or administrator perceives the collection of data related to classroom activities to have the potential to be used against the teacher or administrator, that individual might bias results or resist data collection efforts to avoid potential repercussions. In our case, for instance, we needed to clearly articulate the relationship between low fidelity scores (i.e., students in a classroom do not complete the portfolio) and potential implications on the teacher or school while maintaining the data confidentiality that is critical for obtaining valid information from teachers and school staff.

To ensure the comfort of school staff and support data collection efforts, the evaluator must take steps to work with the program staff, attend school programs, address implementation weaknesses on the part of teachers or schools with support as opposed to criticism, simplify the evaluation process, and adapt methodologies and experimental designs to make it work for the program. As part of this process, we have found that evaluation discussions, trainings, and data results need to be incorporated into organizational improvement activities, staff training, and professional development to both school and program staff as needed to ensure smooth implementation and adequate and accurate data collection.

Overall, we have found that the assessment of implementation fidelity has been a challenging and extremely worthwhile experience. The process of implementing rigorous assessment of implementation fidelity, has helped us improve our program, developed our research capacity, and strengthened our awareness, and that of our stakeholders, of the relationship between research and program development. We have found the overall process to be invaluable. Although the i3 funding which initiated our experience with quantitative evaluation of implementation fidelity will end this year, we are expecting to continue the collection of implementation fidelity data in upcoming years and are committed to the use of results to understand and improve our program.

References

American Evaluation Association (AEA) (2013). Washington, DC. Retrieved from http://www.eval.org

American Educational Research Association (AERA) (2013). Washington, DC. Retrieved from http://www.aera.net

Blase, K. & Fixsen, D. (2013). *Stages of implementation analysis: Where are we?* Chapel Hill, NC: National Implementation Research Network: The State Implementation & Scaling-up of Evidence-based Practices Center (SISEP).

Century, J., Cassata, A., Rudnick, M., & Freeman, C. (2012). Measuring enactment of innovations and the factors that affect implementation and sustainability: Moving toward common language and shared conceptual understanding. *The Journal of Behavioral Health Services & Research, 39,* 343–361.

Century, J., Freeman, C., Rudnick, M. (2008). A framework for measuring and accumulating knowledge about fidelity of implementation of science instructional materials. Annual meeting of the National Association for Research in Science Teaching. Baltimore.

Creswell, J. W. (2009). *Research design: Qualitative, quantitative and mixed methods approaches* (3rd ed.). Thousand Oaks, CA: Sage.

Darrow, C. L., Goodson, B. D., & Caven, M. (2013). Challenges in measuring implementation fidelity of educational programs in development. Association for Education Finance and Policy Annual Meeting. New Orleans, LA.

Fixsen, D., Naoom, S. F., Blase, K. A., Friedman, R. M., & Wallace, F. (2005). Implementation research: A synthesis of the literature. *The National Implementation Research Network* (FMHI Publication #231). Tampa, FL: University of South Florida, Louis de la Parte Florida Mental Health Institute.

Goodson, B. D. & Darrow, C. (2013). Methods in developing systematic measures of implementation fidelity in evaluation research. Annual meeting of the Association for Education Finance and Policy. New Orleans, LA.

James Bell Associates. (2009). Evaluation brief: Measuring implementation fidelity. Arlington, VA: Author.

Joyce, B., & Showers, B. (2002). *Student achievement through staff development* (3rd ed.). Alexandria, VA: Association for Supervision and Curriculum Development.

Kitsen, A., Havey, G., & McCormack, B. (1998). Enabling the implementation of evidence based practice: A conceptual framework. *Quality in Health Care, 7*(3), 149–158.

LaBanca, F., Worwood, M., Schauss, S., LaSala, J., & Donn, J. (2013). Blended instruction: Exploring student-centered pedagogical strategies to promote a technology-enhanced learning environment. Litchfield, CT: EDUCATION CONNECTION.

Macallair, D., & Males, M. (2004). A failure of good intentions: An analysis of juvenile justice reform in San Francisco during the 1990s. *Review of Policy Research, 21*(1), 63–78.

Morariu, J., Athanasiades, K., & Emery, A. (2012). *State of evaluation, 2012: Evaluation practice and capacity in the nonprofit sector.* Research Report #soe2012. Washington, DC: Innovation Network.

Oh, Y. J., Lorentson, M., Jia, Y., Sibuma, B., Snellback, M., & LaBanca, B. (2014). Blended instruction: Measuring the impact of a technology-enhanced student-centered learning environment on underserved student engagement, 21st century inquiry skill acquisition, and science achievement. Quincy, MA: Nellie Mae Education Foundation.

Rossie, P. H., Lipsen, M. W., & Freeman, H. (2004). *Evaluation: A systematic approach* (7th ed.). Thousand Oaks, CA: Sage.

Shapley, K. S., Sheehan, D., Maloney, C., & Caranikas-Walker, F. (2010). Evaluating the implementation fidelity of technology immersion and its relationship with student achievement. *Journal of Technology, Learning and Assessment, 9*(4). Retrieved from http://ejournals.bc.edu/ojs/index.php/jtla/article/view/1609/1460

Survey Monkey, Inc. (2014). Palo Alto, CA: Author. Retrieved from www.surveymonkey.com

The Evaluator's Institute (2013). George Washington University, Washington, DC: Author. Retrieved from http://tei.gwu.edu/

W. K. Kellogg Foundation. (2004). Logic model development guide (pp. 1–71). Retrieved from http://www.wkkf.org/knowledge-center/resources/2006/02/wk-kellogg-foundation-logic-model-development-guide.aspx

5

THE EMINTS PROFESSIONAL DEVELOPMENT PROGRAM AND THE JOURNEY TOWARD GREATER PROGRAM FIDELITY

Lorie F. Kaplan, Christine E. Terry, and Monica M. Beglau

Introduction to the eMINTS National Center and the eMINTS Comprehensive Professional Development Program

The convergence of the Common Core State Standards (CCSS), the ubiquity of technology in the lives of students, and the national call for students who are better prepared in the areas of science, technology, engineering, and mathematics has created an unprecedented urgency to fully integrate technology into education and to do it well. The eMINTS National Center is dedicated to supporting teachers and teacher preparation programs around the globe as they transform education through the powerful intersection of inquiry-based learning and technology. We began as a pilot project designed and implemented through a partnership between the Missouri Department of Elementary and Secondary Education (DESE), the Missouri Department of Higher Education (DHE), and the University of Missouri (UM). The pilot rapidly developed into a full-fledged program guided by the same partners. The eMINTS National Center is currently an independent program that is part of the University of Missouri-Columbia (UM-C) College of Education.

We present our story here with the hope that the insights gained, lessons learned, and economies of scale achieved across the program's 16-year history will be of interest to both program evaluators and to program developers/implementers in similar settings. We learned about, operationalized, and refined program evaluation and program fidelity measures as we implemented our program. We came to understand the different purposes of program evaluation including providing accountability to stakeholders, documenting the impact of program interventions, and identifying areas for program improvement. We learned about program fidelity, how to scale the program's reach while maintaining fidelity, and how to allow for the flexibility requested to meet local needs without sacrificing program fidelity. Working with multiple program evaluation teams has also provided us with background to offer ideas that may increase the effectiveness of similar teams.

Over the past 16 years we developed a variety of professional development (PD) offerings, including those delivered through face-to-face, blended, and online models. Our flagship program, the eMINTS Comprehensive Professional Development (Comp PD) Program is the most intensive of our programs and is the program used to detail our work with evaluation and fidelity in this chapter.

Comp PD demands the most dedication from teachers, is supported by the greatest depth of research and evaluation, and, we believe, has the greatest potential to impact teaching and learning in positive ways. The goal of Comp PD is to transform classrooms into highly engaging, technology-rich, student-centered learning communities where students are engaged in solving authentic, real-world problems; collaborating with other students, teachers and individuals outside of the classroom on projects; and becoming savvy consumers of information as well as producers of new knowledge. In short, students become 21st Century learners. To this end, we have designed Comp PD to develop 21st Century teachers who are technologically and pedagogically fluent and are prepared to make instructional decisions about how, when, and why to integrate technology effectively into their instruction.

We ask a great deal of teachers who commit to participating in Comp PD and to becoming eMINTS teachers. We challenge them to learn a variety of new technology tools, many of which are completely new to their use in an educational context *and* we ask them to integrate these tools into their classrooms while implementing teaching practices that are significantly different from those they experienced as students. In addition, participating teachers and their students face the scrutiny of peers, administrators, parents, and program evaluators who hope to see the best returns in terms of teacher effectiveness and improved student achievement for the significant investment of scarce resources required. Comp PD has been implemented in nine states including more than 500 school buildings in Missouri alone, in eight teacher education programs in Missouri, and in schools in Australia.

The enormity of the task we present to our teachers in Comp PD requires commensurate intensive and multidimensional support from their districts in the form of a technology-rich classroom, ongoing and intensive PD, regular in-classroom coaching, and participation in a learning network of other eMINTS teachers and graduates of the program. Key district stakeholders must be educated about and invested in Comp PD goals. Over the years we have developed additional training and support for school administrators, technology coordinators, and special educators. The following sections provide additional detail about the ways training and support are provided to teachers in Comp PD as well as preliminary information about how each element has been involved in aspects related to program evaluation and fidelity.

Technology-rich Classroom

Teachers in Comp PD teach in classrooms that are required to be equipped with a suite of technology appropriate to the content they teach and the developmental level of their students. In recent years, we have moved from a strict list of equipment specifications to a focus on functionality. eMINTS classrooms may use mobile technology such as tablets, netbooks or laptops, or they may use desktops. Classrooms also include interactive whiteboards and data projectors, access to a printer, and productivity software. While the computing devices have changed, the emphasis on the importance of technology tools and software that are designed to function as mind tools, "knowledge construction tools that students learn *with* not *from*" (Jonassen, Carr, & Yueh, 1998, p. 24), has remained consistent. We also require that the resources be installed in a specific sequence within specific timeline parameters. Technology resources must be located within the classroom so that they are available throughout all learning experiences for students and teachers. We have developed measures to document the installation and functionality levels of classroom technology resources.

Ongoing Professional Development

During the 2 years of the Comp PD Program, teachers participate in 2–3 PD sessions each month. These face-to-face sessions typically last 3.5 to 4 hours each, are held in geographically central locations, and total more than 200 hours collectively by the end of the 2-year period. PD sessions are led by certified trainers who not only model uses of technology in inquiry-based instruction during the sessions but also provide in-classroom coaching and mentoring for participants. Trainers are called "eMINTS Instructional Specialists (eISs)." The University of Missouri employs some eISs while others are staff members of their local districts or teacher preparation programs. eISs are provided with specialized training and support for their roles as PD providers and in-classroom coaches through the eMINTS train-the-trainer program described in a later section. Materials developed by eMINTS staff using a specific scope and sequence guide the PD sessions. PD sessions are designed to model the teaching practices we want teachers to use in their own classrooms. eISs actively engage teachers in reflecting on and making decisions about their professional practice and give them new experiences using technology to achieve educational and personal professional development goals. Teachers experience professional learning in the same way we believe the classrooms where their students learn should be structured, giving teachers new insight into the benefits of strategies such as cooperative learning, inquiry-based learning, and community building. With support from our evaluation and fidelity teams, we have developed and validated measures to assess the content of PD sessions and the activities eISs engage in during PD sessions (Martin, Strother, Weatherholt, & Dechaume, 2008).

Classroom Coaching Visits

In-classroom coaching has been a part of the Comp PD program from its inception. eISs visit program teachers in their classrooms at least monthly using coaching methods and techniques that have been standardized across the program. During these visits eISs act as coaches, mentors, and advocates using Costa and Garmston's (2002) Cognitive Coaching methodology. eISs may model an instructional practice, observe a lesson and follow-up with a coaching conversation, assist in lesson development, or occasionally assist with troubleshooting classroom technology resources. The goal of our coaching visits is to help teachers transfer their learning from PD sessions into their classroom practice. Teachers and eISs work together to determine the activities and goals for each visit. We have developed logs to document the duration and content of classroom coaching visits to provide data our evaluation and fidelity teams can use to analyze the effectiveness of the visits in changing teacher practices (Martin, et al., 2008).

Administrators and Technology Coordinator Programs

Finally the work of teachers in Comp PD is also supported through PD for key players in their system of support. Administrators in schools implementing Comp PD begin with a visit to the classroom of an established eMINTS teacher who has successfully completed Comp PD. Throughout the program administrators participate in an online community that has been designed for them and is facilitated by eMINTS staff. Administrators complete collegial walkthroughs of the classrooms in their schools where teachers are participating in Comp PD. The walkthroughs are done following a day of face-to-face PD conducted by eMINTS staff. Administrators and eMINTS supervisory staff use a list of the typical characteristics or "look fors" they might expect to see as teachers progress through Comp PD on the walkthroughs. The characteristics or "look fors" were developed by eMINTS staff with input from practicing administrators in schools where Comp PD had resulted in the successful eMINTS classroom implementations and from findings reported by Office of Social and Economic Data Analysis (OSEDA) about the relationships between principal leadership styles and successful eMINTS classroom implementations (Tharp, 2006). The walkthroughs provide time for conversation between eMINTS staff and school administrators. Questions and concerns provide formative data that can be addressed informally with the intent of improving the support system for teachers. The ultimate goal of the administrator training is to help school leaders understand how they can actively support teachers in Comp PD, how to avoid unintentionally undermining teachers' efforts to change instructional strategies and to use technology, and to provide opportunities to proactively correct concerns.

We also work hard to build relationships with the technology coordinators in each school implementing Comp PD. Schools commit to providing classrooms of teachers in Comp PD with a suite of technology including devices for teachers and students on a schedule set by eMINTS. Meeting technology deployment deadlines and supporting the technology once it is in the classroom can add an unanticipated burden to typically already overworked technology coordinators. We try to ease the burden on these key district personnel by providing webinars, email support, and regular classroom check-ins from our eISs to uncover issues that can be easily resolved by the eIS or teacher without requiring the technology coordinator's involvement. For example, the eIS might help the teacher learn how to troubleshoot problems encountered in using speakers attached to the interactive whiteboard. We have developed communication systems within our staffing patterns to gather data about how technical support is being provided to teachers. Early awareness of technical support issues is used to assist in the development of plans designed to alleviate problems before they threaten the quality of program implementation.

History of Comp PD and the Multimedia Interactive Networked Technologies (MINTs)

MINTs Pilot Project

Beginning in summer 1997, DESE, DHE, and UM secured grant funds from the Southwest Bell Foundation. The collaborators used the grant funds to form an innovative partnership exploring how emerging technologies might be used to help the state meet its goal of improving education for all Missouri students. Thirteen elementary classrooms in six St. Louis area school districts were selected and equipped with high-speed Internet access and in-classroom technology resources. The technology was paired with intensive PD and in-classroom support.

This pilot project was called the Multimedia Interactive Networked Technologies (MINTs) project, and as an exploratory project that lasted through spring of 1999, had a well-defined set of technology resources but lacked a precise PD intervention or classroom coaching model. With only 13 teachers to serve, staff could develop and deliver PD sessions using a just-in-time model. Classroom coaching visits were also just-in-time and without a set schedule or technique. During the first year of the project, both the PD and classroom visits focused primarily on helping teachers learn the technical skills associated with using the project equipment and software.

From the beginning we knew that technology and technical training alone were not enough to obtain the improvements in student achievement and teacher effectiveness that we hoped were possible. We were still not sure what pedagogical model we wanted to incorporate into the program during the MINTs pilot. The influence of the College of Education at UM-C pushed us more towards "open" or "inquiry-based" models where student exploration and experimentation were valued as opposed to models that focused on "closed" or "direct" instruction where the teacher was the main source of knowledge and information (Brooks & Brooks, 1999).

From the very beginning, the partners involved in the MINTs project understood the importance of program evaluation. OSEDA was involved in all major project planning activities and conducted the MINTs evaluation beginning in summer 1997 and concluding in spring 1999. OSEDA developed a quasi-experimental program evaluation design focused on connecting technology uses and improved teacher practices with gains in student achievement, which was a relatively new concept in education at the time.

Evaluators collected data to measure changes in teacher attitudes and teaching style through classroom observations, unstructured conversations with teachers, weekly journals submitted by teachers, and focus groups related to specific program features. The OSEDA report suggested that MINTs classrooms were more collaborative, student-centered learning environments where both teachers and students exhibited higher levels of technology fluency than in typical traditional classrooms. "It's a new way of educating students—a way that engaged them in their education by making resources available in a learning environment that fosters cooperation, collaboration and life-skill development" (Bickford, Hammer, McGinty, McKinley, & Mitchell, 2000, p. 1).

Evaluators measured student achievement using the state's standardized test at the time, the Missouri Mastery Achievement Test (MMAT). The evaluators reported statistically significant academic improvement for students in the MINTs classrooms compared to students in non-MINTs classrooms across all participating grade levels in both mathematics and language arts (Bickford, et al., 2000). The preliminary dissemination of these findings in the early summer of 1999 was even more significant given the timing of their release prior to the concepts of "data-driven decision-making" and "scientifically-based research" that rose to popularity beginning in early 2001–2002.

In addition to studying project outcomes for teachers and students, OSEDA evaluators examined and documented the processes of the pilot's implementation—the processes used to set up the MINTs project, how the equipment was chosen, how school districts were selected, how teachers were selected and prepared, and how project staff supported project teachers (Bickford, et al., 2000).

Another important outcome of the OSEDA program evaluation process of the MINTs project was the establishment of the relationship between program evaluation and program implementation. Our early understanding of the relationship led to our commitment to using program evaluation findings to change and improve program implementation, both short-term immediate changes and longer-term, more thoughtful changes.

Since the scale of the project was relatively small (13 teachers in six school districts in geographically centric locations), it was possible to use qualitative data such as teacher journals and teacher focus group findings to make rapid changes to the project's direction as it occurred. For example, MINTs pilot teachers reported ongoing frustration with finding time to complete Internet searches for appropriate material that their students could use to conduct classroom research projects. In response, a resource called "eThemes" was developed by program staff within just a few weeks' time. The eThemes resource is a searchable database of child-safe Internet resources organized by grade level, topic (theme), and educational standard that teachers can use to quickly locate resources they could integrate into their lessons and classroom presentations. eThemes resources are based on teaching topics requested by teachers participating in Comp PD. More than 1,200 unique eThemes resources have been developed. eThemes has endured and continues today as a free resource available to anyone via web browser (eMINTS, 2014).

The longer-term, more thoughtful changes based on program evaluation are described in the following section that details how the MINTs project became eMINTS.

Birth of New Statewide eMINTS Program

Encouraged by the positive findings of the MINTs pilot project (Bickford, et al., 2000), the Missouri Commissioner for Education serving at the time scaled up the project by launching the eMINTS Program (later known as eMINTS Comp PD). The Commissioner approved the use of funds to implement eMINTS as a statewide initiative beginning with the 1999–2000 school year, serving 88 teachers in 44 school districts around the state. School districts essentially volunteered to participate in the program or were recruited by their participating peers. Each district then selected one school where two classrooms, typically one third- and one fourth-grade classroom, would act as model high-technology classrooms for the district. Program partners provided funding to support the acquisition of most of the technology resources and to deliver the PD sessions and classroom coaching visits. Participating districts agreed to provide funds to secure the remaining technology resources and to compensate teachers for out-of-contract time spent in PD.

Like the MINTs pilot, the quasi-experimental eMINTS program evaluation design created by OSEDA focused on connecting technology use and improved teaching practices to gains in student achievement. The evaluation design examined changes in teaching practices and teacher effectiveness through data collected during classroom observations and structured teacher focus groups.

Improvements in student achievement were measured using the new Missouri Assessment Program (MAP) that was replacing the MMAT in spring 2000. Student achievement data from the MAP were collected in communication arts (reading and language arts) and science for third-grade students and in mathematics and social studies for fourth-grade students. In addition, data related to student attitudes towards school were collected using instruments developed for Missouri's school accreditation process known as the Missouri School Improvement Program (MSIP). Whenever possible, the non-eMINTS students in the same building and grade level served as the comparison group, a convenience sampling that helped reduce costs.

OSEDA program evaluations from 2002 through 2005 used a similar methodology and reported positive findings for changes in teacher effectiveness and student performance across several different grade levels in several different content areas (Office of Social and Economic Data Analysis [OSEDA], 2002, 2003a, 2004, 2005).

The growth of the program from MINTs to eMINTS required a more systematic approach due to the number of schools and teachers to be involved as well as their geographic scatter across the state. Based on findings from the MINTs evaluations, teacher focus groups, and feedback from staff implementing the program, we identified the specific variables we felt we could control and measure. We specified the technology resources to be placed in each classroom, the scope and sequence of PD topics, and the classroom coaching visits to form the support systems we felt would be instrumental to success for the newly expanded eMINTS program.

The specific list of technology resources we developed for the classroom included the same resources that were used in the MINTs project: an interactive whiteboard and data projector; a laptop for the teacher; a teacher computer workstation with a printer, scanner and digital camera; video conferencing equipment; one computer for every two students; high-speed Internet connectivity; and software limited primarily to productivity software (e.g., MS Office). It was at this point that we also specified the timeline districts would use when deploying the resources in the classroom.

We decided that PD sessions would take place in regional cohorts and would be paired with in-classroom coaching visits from the eIS hired to provide PD to the cohort. The duration of PD would be ongoing over 2 years. The 2-year time span was determined based on the initial MINTs evaluation findings based on teachers' self-reports, which suggested that at least 2 years of PD support was required to make the instructional changes envisioned by the program developers (Bickford, et al., 2000). We also began developing standard PD materials to be used by all eISs delivering PD. Materials development was guided by the principles of adult learning or andragogy, and addressed both technology and teaching strategies based on a commitment to the four elements of the evolving eMINTS Instructional Model: high-quality lesson design, inquiry-based teaching, development of a community of learners, and learning powered by technology. The evolving instructional model incorporating both technology and constructivist-based teaching strategies (Brooks and Brooks, 1999; Burns, Heath, & Dimock, 1998) would later form the basis for our fidelity measures related to PD sessions.

It was at the end of the first year of the statewide launch of Comp PD that we learned of the work of Dr. Bernie Dodge at San Diego State University. Dr. Dodge was developing a method for organizing instruction called "WebQuests" that use inquiry-based methodologies, are web-based and technology-enhanced, and are structured to encourage higher-order thinking and cooperative learning (Dodge, 1997). The WebQuest concept fit perfectly with our eMINTS Instructional Model and was immediately incorporated into Comp PD. Teachers would eventually be required to develop a WebQuest for inclusion in the portfolio that we began using as a measure of teacher change and effectiveness in our program fidelity work (Martin, et al., 2008).

The in-classroom coaching visits initially implemented in Comp PD were less structured in terms of content than our PD sessions but were intended to occur at least monthly and to be associated in some way with what teachers were learning in their PD sessions. Since the eMINTS Program classroom technology resources were initially provided and installed through a central purchasing arrangement not controlled by the participating districts, early classroom visits often devolved to the provision of technical support such as installing software programs and setting up hardware such as printers or scanners. During the early years of eMINTS, many participating districts did not have adequate technology coordinator support or the individuals in such positions lacked the knowledge and skills needed. The development of logs for classroom coaching visits did not occur until we worked with our program fidelity team (Martin, et al., 2008).

Formative Assessment Measures

Taking the program statewide meant hiring individuals to serve as eISs who lived near the participating schools and worked out of their homes. To assist in the supervision of these regional eISs, we developed in-house surveys designed to directly solicit anonymous teacher feedback on the PD experience delivered by the eISs assigned to geographically based cohort groups. Participants complete these participant feedback surveys at the close of each semester in Comp PD, for a total of four times over the 2-year program. This survey takes approximately 15–20 minutes to administer and is divided into two main parts: (1) feedback on the overall Comp PD program, including schedules, materials, etc.; and (2) feedback on teachers' experiences with their eIS during PD sessions and classroom coaching visits. Supervisory eMINTS staff members routinely review survey results from each geographic cohort with the eIS assigned to the cohort to discuss how the teachers in the cohort groups are responding to the PD sessions and classroom visits the eIS delivers. eISs make changes for the upcoming semester to better accommodate teachers' learning preferences or to provide re-teaching of concepts for which teachers indicate they need assistance. Within the first 2 years of the collection of the survey data, program leadership made the decision to isolate the use of the survey results to formative program evaluation as opposed to using results as part of the employee performance review. The decision to use the survey results for strictly formative purposes was based on the discovery that survey items did not include questions about overall Comp PD implementation (e.g., whether the teacher was receiving adequate technical support, the school administrator supported the program). We learned that teachers often rated the PD sessions or materials lower as a means of expressing their frustrations with the support they were receiving or with overall eMINTS implementation processes in their district. Additional survey questions were added to probe for program support and implementation issues. When support or implementation issues were noted, program leadership devised methods to engage with the appropriate school personnel for resolution.

The overall statewide survey results were used to inform the sequencing of the PD session topics, the number of sessions devoted to particular topics, and how examples and illustrations used in the PD materials were structured. These surveys are still used today to uncover issues and inform program adjustments as we strive to ensure a high-quality implementation.

Program Growth Drives Need for Program Fidelity Measures

The growth of the eMINTS program was further spurred by changes in national education policy, including Public Law PL 107–110, better known as No Child Left Behind (NCLB), enacted in 2001. Under NCLB each state received Title II.D Enhancing Education Through Technology (EETT) funds to implement technology integration programs in their schools. Programs funded through EETT were required to have evidence of program effectiveness in terms of positive impacts on student achievement and to allocate at least 25 percent of their funds for professional development. In 2001, we were one of a handful of technology programs with the required levels of PD and preliminary evidence of effectiveness in both changing teaching practices and improving student performance to meet NCLB/EETT requirements.

In summer 2002, we were asked to present our findings from our first student evaluation study showing positive gains in communication arts and science for students in third grade and for mathematics and social studies for students in fourth grade (OSEDA, 2002) to a newly organized national policy and advocacy group called the State Education Technology Directors Association (SETDA). This group is comprised of the individuals responsible for oversight of instructional technology in each state educational agency (SEA) and other national instructional technology advocates and leaders. The group was looking for ways to address the new NCLB/EETT regulations defining scientifically based research. As a result of the presentation, several state education agencies, with Utah being the first to move forward, contacted us to indicate an interest in replicating Comp PD via competitive local education agency (LEA) grants funded by Title II.D.

Around this same time, we began developing a train-the-trainer model to support Missouri districts in growing and sustaining their existing eMINTS implementations and in building long-term capacity for eMINTS to grow within the districts. This new program, called Professional Development for Educational Technology Specialists (PD4ETS) trained district staff to become eISs and deliver Comp PD. PD4ETS helps district staff to develop the skills needed to become an eIS for their own teachers. Participants also develop the skills and understanding they need to serve as key players in their district's implementation of Comp PD. Participants in PD4ETS learn how to use all eMINTS PD materials, how to work effectively with adult learners based on the principles of andragogy, how to develop skills as an instructional technology coach, and to become the primary liaison between the district and the eMINTS National Center. Learning to serve as a liaison was critical to the success of out-of-state eMINTS implementations funded by Title II.D. LEA grants.

Although program evaluation and feedback had been a part of the eMINTS Program from its inception, rapid growth in Missouri and an expansion to other states motivated us to look for ways to develop a better understanding of program fidelity. Yet another push for a stronger, more systematic focus on fidelity came from members of the eMINTS Advisory Board executive council. One member in particular encouraged us to look beyond the positive findings of academic achievement noted after the 2 years of PD. To replicate our success consistently, we needed to know the answers to questions such as, "What benchmarks along the way will help us to know the program is being implemented in a way that's going to get similar results? How are we going to turn around an implementation or a program that is not going well and how will we know that it's not going well?"

While we had some feedback from teacher surveys and staff observations in classrooms, most of our internal formative evaluation data were not collected or analyzed systematically. Furthermore, implementations located geographically outside of Missouri added even more challenges for collecting, analyzing, and using fidelity data since all of our staff members were located in Missouri.

We knew we would need an evaluation design that would help lead us to a standardization of the intervention we called Comp PD. This standardization would build on the early program implementation fidelity efforts, a way of making sure that despite the growth of the program, every participating teacher would have a similar experience. We determined which pieces of the program could be standardized including the technology resources provided in the classroom; the duration, scope and sequence of the PD; and the duration and content of classroom coaching visits. With the expansion to Utah, we realized that we also needed to better understand how to balance the flexibility needed to contextualize the program in new locations and the consistency of implementation needed to realize the same results found in Missouri. We had a starting point based on findings from an OSEDA report (Hagar & Tharp, 2005) with preliminary data to suggest that PD4ETS participants could have the same positive outcomes in terms of teacher effectiveness and student performance as eMINTS staff.

The need to answer these critical questions about balancing fidelity with flexibility prompted the eMINTS executive committee to open a Request for Proposal (RFP) for an independent evaluation focused on program fidelity. The Center for Children and Technology at the Educational Development Center (EDC) was selected to design and conduct the evaluation. Senior research staff at EDC wrote the evaluation design to study the fidelity of two key components of Comp PD: the content of PD sessions and how they were conducted and the classroom coaching visits (Martin, et al., 2008).

The goal of the study was to help us understand relationships between the fidelity of delivery for Comp PD and classroom coaching visits and student and teacher outcomes. More specifically, we wanted to learn which components of the PD and classroom coaching visits seemed to be the most important for achieving the expected outcomes of increased teacher effectiveness leading to improved student achievement. In addition, we wanted to learn if there were any differences between the relationships outlined above depending on who delivered the PD and classroom coaching visits: eISs who were employees of eMINTS and eISs who had successfully completed our train-the-trainer program, PD4ETS.

eMINTS and EDC staff collaborated to develop two observation instruments called "the checklist" and "the snapshot" that defined the desirable characteristics of an eMINTS PD session. The checklist was used by trained observers to record the types of activities and components included in a given PD session. Observers were also trained to use the snapshot tool every 15 minutes during a PD session to record activities at a single point in time giving us frequency and trend data about PD session activities and the strategies used by eISs to facilitate those sessions.

Until this study, we had not systematically examined classroom coaching visits conducted by eISs. To help us understand the relationship between classroom visit activities and teacher and student outcomes, eISs completed logs that recorded how often they visited teachers, the length of each visit, and the types of activities they carried out during each classroom visit. In addition, eISs completed a narrative with a detailed description of each classroom coaching visit.

The findings from PD data collection tools and the classroom coaching visit logs were analyzed as they related to both teacher effectiveness and student achievement. Teacher portfolios that included ratings for a lesson plan, a Web-Quest (an inquiry-based technology-rich teaching unit), and a teacher website were used as proxies for teacher effectiveness. MAP achievement scores were used as a proxy for student achievement (Martin, et al., 2008).

The evaluators confirmed that both eISs who were eMINTS staff and eISs who had completed our PD4ETS program implemented Comp PD with similarly high levels of fidelity and that there was a significant, positive correlation between PD fidelity and teacher mastery scores on the lesson plans teachers submitted in their portfolios (Martin, et al., 2008). A positive trend between PD fidelity and the WebQuests teachers submitted was also noted. The evaluators found a significant, positive correlation between the amount of time teachers spent on lesson planning during classroom visits with their eIS and the portfolio lesson plan scores. In the analyses of student achievement, evaluators found that students whose teachers scored higher on the lesson plan component of their portfolio achieved at higher levels on the MAP tests. Further analyses reported that improved student achievement tended to persist across time, meaning that teachers with higher lesson plan portfolio scores created classroom environments where students continued to achieve at higher levels even in the years following the teachers' completion of Comp PD (Martin, Strother, & Reitzes, 2009).

From these studies we learned that maintaining a high level of program fidelity was critical for ensuring that the goals we set for teachers through our PD are mastered. We also confirmed our belief that classroom coaching visits is a key component of Comp PD, especially when the visits focus on helping teachers prepare higher quality lessons for their students.

The 2008 EDC fidelity study not only laid the foundation for our program revisions and improvements from that point forward, but it also helped us to carefully guide the expansion of our program through our train-the-trainer program, PD4ETS. For example, we entered into a formal agreement with the Center for Cognitive Coaching to prepare eMINTS staff members to become certified Cognitive Coaching (CC) trainers. Having certified CC trainers on staff allowed us to implement CC techniques more fully and with greater fidelity into both Comp PD and PD4ETS. EDC's fidelity findings strengthened our previous research identifying critical pieces in the chain of evidence from program implementation to teacher practices, and ultimately student achievement (Martin, Strother, Beglau, Bates, & Reitzes, 2010).

Lessons Learned

Evaluations Should Inform Program Decisions

In the early development phases of Comp PD, we learned that careful process documentation allowed us to identify and verify critical aspects of the intervention (such as checking to ensure that critical technology installation targets are being met and monitoring the technical support available to teachers), and to pinpoint areas for improvement. Additionally, one portion of early evaluation studies of Comp PD uncovered key characteristics of an effective eIS (OSEDA, 2001a). This information informed the development of PD4ETS (train-the-trainer program), staff development decisions, and staff hiring decisions. EDC's analyses also helped us strengthen our foci on preserving certain aspects of Comp PD, such as the classroom coaching visits, the importance of modeling teaching strategies in PD sessions, and helping teachers understand how effective lesson design affects student outcomes (Martin, et al., 2008).

Evaluation Findings Should Be Shared With Program Participants

Another example of evaluation impacting Comp PD relates to the administrator's role in supporting the program. In one early study, the OSEDA team examined various principal leadership styles in schools that were expanding the number of eMINTS Comp PD classrooms (Tharp, 2006). OSEDA established a typology of leadership styles and was able to find relationships between principal leadership styles and teacher instructional practices which ultimately impacted student outcomes. The findings suggested that principals who exhibited a more collaborative style of leadership (compared to more regulatory or disconnected styles), encouraged more teachers to adopt the teaching styles promoted by Comp PD in their classrooms. The study findings not only informed our work with administrators by reinforcing the importance of administrator support for teachers participating in Comp PD but were also shared in detail with participating administrators. The findings helped us justify the investment needed to provide adequate PD for administrators and helped administrators see their role in a new light. It also helped us focus our attention on helping supervisory eMINTS staff who worked with administrators understand how to foster more collaborative leadership styles in schools implementing Comp PD.

Over the 16-year life of the MINTs Project and eMINTS Program, we have learned a number of lessons about working with evaluators, both from positive and negative experiences. To most effectively tackle challenges that arise, evaluators should be included as early as possible in the program planning process, and communication and collaboration must continue through implementation.

Involving Evaluators in the Program Planning Process

Since the MINTs pilot, an evaluation design has been in place to document how the program was implemented and gather feedback on the impact the program was making in those first six schools. Having OSEDA involved from the beginning ensured that any data collected was a natural part of the pilot's implementation and teachers knew that providing feedback was an expected part of their participation.

Probably the most important lesson is that including evaluators in the program planning process allows for a better fit between the program and the evaluation. These early discussions allow for accommodation of the needs of data collection, ensuring that the metrics built into the program are available for program staff to learn from. For example, in our Investing in Innovation (i3) project, it was particularly important for both program implementers and evaluators to be at the table when determining the scope of the project (which grade levels, number of schools to include, etc.). This discussion and joint decision-making ensured that not only were the essential parts of Comp PD included but also that the implementation (e.g., number of sites, teachers, students, subjects, etc.) would yield meaningful data and allow for sufficient power for planned analyses. The team planning also allows evaluators to design research/evaluation that extends what we already know and relies on existing knowledge to create efficiencies and improve the rigor and relevance of the evaluation.

In turn, program implementers also play an important role in the evaluation process. When working with all the evaluation and fidelity teams, we have been instrumental in assisting with the data collection tools and verifying the validity of assumptions from evaluators. eMINTS staff collaborated with the EDC fidelity team on the iterative process of developing the snapshot and checklist tools to help identify the key behaviors for instrument development. We found this process very helpful to ensure that the program implementers agreed that the correct aspects were being measured as these PD session observation instruments were developed and refined.

Working Together to Find Efficiencies

Shared decision-making and the meaningful involvement of evaluation/fidelity team members with program implementers also allows for finding places to enhance efficiencies, such as using information for dual purposes, to eliminate burdening participants with too many data collection requirements. Working together helps prevent duplicate requests for information for both program management and evaluative purposes. Evaluators can review what existing information is collected to see if that would meet their needs or may only need to be slightly modified, rather than asking participants to provide something entirely new.

On the other hand, we also have learned to be mindful of the unintended consequences and possible negative impact of coordination on the project implementation. For example, early in the implementation of Comp PD, we developed a tool called the "Hallmarks of an Effective eMINTS Classroom," a scoring guide that outlined what an eMINTS classroom might look like as teachers move from the beginnings of their journeys to becoming proficient and experienced eMINTS teachers. Teachers would rate themselves and discuss their self-evaluation with their eIS, who helped them set some specific goals for areas they wanted to focus on during the year. Early evaluators felt that this tool could be used to rate teacher progress over time by having the eIS collect and report their ratings of teachers. However, this put the eIS in the position of evaluator of teachers' performance rather than as a supportive coach, which undermined the trust that is essential in the coaching relationship and threatened to compromise the effectiveness of the eIS's ability to help the teacher. After a brief period of having eISs collect Hallmarks data, we determined that, while it was convenient for eISs to do this job since they were already visiting those eMINTS classrooms, it was detrimental to the success of the implementation; therefore, this practice was quickly discontinued.

Educating Evaluators About the Program

Another lesson we learned was the importance of educating evaluation research staff about Comp PD so that they could accurately collect data on program outcomes. Comp PD is a complex, multifaceted program intervention, and it takes time for individuals who have primarily university research backgrounds to learn and understand all program specifics and intricacies. In some cases, we had difficulty effectively conveying what to "look for" in an eMINTS classroom to those researchers. It has helped us to work with evaluation team members who have had more experience evaluating education projects, studied similar types of PD programs, or have classroom teaching experience. It has also helped to have eMINTS staff more involved in the development of standardized methods for training observers to ensure inter-rater reliability.

Mitigating Unintended Evaluation Impacts

Other lessons learned have included how to manage negative responses from Comp PD participants following their interactions with evaluation team members. For example, during some classroom observations in early years of Comp PD, teachers became angered when some observers did not give teachers adequate notice before arriving or did not show up for scheduled visits and had not notified teachers they were not coming. While this behavior was problematic for the evaluation team, it was also a problem for eMINTS staff implementing Comp PD. Teachers did not distinguish between eMINTS staff and evaluation staff, and their negative experiences with evaluation staff left them with negative feelings about Comp PD, which, in turn, negatively impacted their participation in Comp PD. We helped OSEDA establish more specific communication processes with schools and teachers to ensure that evaluation staff properly communicated their schedules and any changes that occurred.

We have also found that required evaluation activities may also have a negative impact on participant attitudes about Comp PD, particularly if participants perceive that the data collection requirements are overly burdensome or intrusive. For example, it was challenging to get teachers to complete lengthy online surveys. As a solution, we worked with the evaluation team to shorten the survey where possible without compromising survey validity and also provided some time during PD sessions for teachers to complete the survey.

Maintaining Ongoing Communication

As issues come up with program implementation, it is important to consider the impact solutions might have on data collection and overall evaluation and to try to make programmatically effective decisions that do not undermine the ability of the evaluators to do what they need to do. For example, at one point during the i3 project, feedback from field staff indicated they were spending excessive amounts of time on data collection, often duplicating the same information in different places. Before final decisions were made by program leaders about how to solve the problem, we consulted our evaluation team to develop solutions that would ensure critical data would still be collected.

Coordinating Communication with Participants

Another important lesson learned from working with evaluators is the importance of coordinating interactions with and requests of program participants. Establishing clear lines of responsibility, especially when data used in program management is also used in the evaluation, help ensure that program participants know what to do. For example, we already collected the teacher portfolio items as a requirement for eMINTS certification. Those portfolios were also used for fidelity measurements in several evaluation projects, including the i3 Validation Project. Deciding who would send instructions to teachers regarding their responsibilities and who would perform necessary follow-up is important to ensure that teachers and their administrators have one reliable source of information.

Another way that we have found careful coordination to be helpful in making both the program implementation and evaluation successful is to have program staff assist with communication regarding evaluation requirements with participants where appropriate. For example, in the i3 project, eMINTS staff work closely with all of our evaluators to help improve response rates on return of consent forms from participating schools. eMINTS staff can follow up in person when school representatives are not responding to evaluator requests for information regarding contact people or school calendars, etc. Since our staff members are in the schools frequently, it makes sense for us to find ways to minimize communication costs so that evaluators do not have to travel to resolve these kinds of situations.

Challenges

Funding Evaluation Studies

Well-designed and implemented program evaluation and fidelity studies are expensive. Finding the funds to do the most rigorous evaluation studies has often been a challenge. Having Title II.D funding available helped in that it required approximately 5 percent of each competitive grant be set aside for project evaluation. The requirement provided for moderately rigorous evaluations at the LEA level but did little to help aggregate findings at the SEA level. When we established the need for the more rigorous fidelity metrics, we were unsuccessful in our attempts to secure grant funding and had to use internal savings to go forward.

Evaluation costs and funding limitations also impact decisions about how to establish measures of outcomes. For example, while observations are a highly reliable and preferred way to measure the levels of implementation of eMINTS teaching strategies in the classroom, they are extremely expensive and time-consuming (OSEDA, 2003b,c). This limitation led to the need to develop a proxy for observations. We created and validated a teacher portfolio process that contains the three elements described in the section on the EDC study: a lesson plan, a WebQuest, and a teacher website (Martin, et al., 2008). We now use the portfolio process as a method for both "certifying" teachers as having successfully completed Comp PD and as an internal measure for tracking program effectiveness in changing teacher practice.

The Future of eMINTS Scaling and Fidelity

eMINTS National Center Goals

Building on Lessons From i3

One of the key goals of the Center is to take the lessons learned from our past experience with evaluation/fidelity work and the extensive i3 Validation project to help inform our work going forward. One particular aspect of Comp PD that we are examining is the impact of adding a third year of support and PD to the traditional 2-year Comp PD. We partnered with Intel Teach to provide teachers with a blended (partly online and partly face-to-face) PD experience that also included additional classroom coaching visits. Teachers completed the Intel Project-based Approaches (PBA) online course and attended three face-to-face PD sessions based on Intel's Thinking with Technology materials. In the study, we are comparing teacher and student outcomes from the groups that completed the traditional 2-year Comp PD to the group that also completed the additional third year, and the control or "business as usual" group. If this third year of support and material is found to significantly improve the outcomes of improved teacher effectiveness and student performance, we will certainly want to consider making that third year a permanent part of Comp PD. The additional year of PD may take the form of a third year of PD or it may be framed as a "refresher" course that teachers complete within 2 to 3 years of the completion of Comp PD to help maintain the changes in practice that Comp PD promotes. We may also use the additional year of PD to evolve a portion of Comp PD into a more "blended" model with some of the PD occurring face-to-face and some occurring in online settings.

Keeping Up With Changes in Technology

Although eMINTS is truly focused on teaching and learning, technology is a core component of the eMINTS Instructional Model. Our participants look to us to help them make the connection between new technologies and effective teaching and learning. One of our primary challenges within Comp PD is to routinely update PD materials so that links are live, online projects and tools mentioned are still active, and are relevant to a variety of content areas and grade levels. We also have to be aware of new technologies available to students outside of school and help teachers make connections between the new technology and high-quality instructional practices. While the underlying philosophy and goal for relevant, constructivist-based learning of an eMINTS classroom does not change with new technology, educators often need help making the connections between a new device, online tool, social media, and so forth, and how the technology can be used most effectively for meeting learning objectives.

Strengthening Sustainability

Another key goal of the eMINTS National Center is to find ways to sustain our program over time and across distances by supporting schools and teachers implementing the Comp PD. We have been successful using the train-the-trainer model (PD4ETS) to establish and continue supporting an "eMINTS champion" in schools and districts. We would like to do a better job of building an active and robust online eMINTS community to continue supporting these individuals. We also continue seeking new ways to regularly update the skills and knowledge of teachers who have completed Comp PD. We currently provide several online webinars each school year and invite district eISs and teachers who have completed Comp PD to our annual conference to learn about changes and updates to our program and materials. We need to continue to create targeted PD experiences to help revitalize and refresh teachers who have successfully completed Comp PD to allow them to find new ways of engaging students and using new technology long after their Comp PD experience is complete.

Scaling and Fidelity in the Future

Scaling Considerations

We have successfully scaled Comp PD in several settings over the last 16 years. Missouri districts around the state were given opportunities to apply for grants from state and federal funds to implement the program. Moving from the small MINTs pilot to a statewide implementation required us to standardize a number of pieces of the program to ensure teachers in different regions of the state were getting similar levels of support. When we scaled beyond Missouri, we decided to rely on a train-the-trainer model of implementation and created the PD4ETS program. This change forced us to become further removed from the actual classroom implementation and required that we develop checkpoints to ensure that district eISs were implementing Comp PD with fidelity. District eISs are currently required to submit schedules at the beginning of each school year that outlines their PD schedules for Comp PD groups along with requests for approval for any variations on the regular schedule provided by the Center. In addition, throughout the year, district eISs are required to submit records of their classroom coaching visits to ensure that they are meeting the basic requirements of the program implementation. Studies conducted by EDC on the efficacy of PD4ETS are cited earlier (Martin, et al., 2008). Reports from other states such as Utah (Elder & Greever-Rice, 2007), Alabama (Beglau, 2010), and Delaware (Beglau, 2011) that have implemented eMINTS using the train-the-trainer model show gains in teacher effectiveness and in student academic performance similar to that achieved in Missouri. However, we believe that more rigorous research is needed to measure the fidelity of the PD4ETS program itself. At this time, we do not have strong information about what pieces of the PD4ETS program are most highly correlated with better teacher and student outcomes as we do with Comp PD. This information would be invaluable for program implementers in making decisions about where to use limited resources and in deciding which parts of the program can be adapted without compromising fidelity.

Adaptation and Contextualization

Another goal we have for the program is to expand to other contexts, including other regions in the world. Expansion to New South Wales, Australia, required adjustments to our materials, especially unit plan examples, to contextualize the materials for this new group. We partnered with the participants to collaboratively develop adapted materials for the Australian teachers who would be implementing Comp PD teaching strategies in their classrooms. As we look for ways of expanding into other parts of the world, we have to consider how materials can continue to be adapted for eISs and teachers in new countries and contexts while maintaining program fidelity. Comp PD materials are currently maintained only in English and would need to be translated into other languages and contextualized for implementation in many countries. Successful expansion will require strong partnerships with individuals who are intimately familiar with a variety of aspects of the target country—the culture, educational policy climate, the structure of the education system, and so on—to preserve the integrity and intent of Comp PD while allowing for the appropriate types of adaptation to succeed in the new contexts. Additional fidelity checkpoints and measures may need to be developed to ensure that key aspects of the program are still being implemented with and that similar critical teaching and learning outcomes are being achieved.

Another intriguing adaptation the Center is considering involves moving parts or all of Comp PD to an asynchronous online model. Since so much of Comp PD relies on the interactions within the community of learners formed by the eISs and participants, considering moving to an online environment brings a whole new set of challenges. The importance of face-to-face classroom coaching visits to the successful implementation of Comp PD would also have to be carefully adapted in an online version of the program.

Conclusion

Evaluation and continuous improvement have always been a critical part of the design of PD at the eMINTS National Center. Our goal is to transform teaching and learning through the integration of technology and inquiry-based teaching strategies as outlined in our instructional model. We want to support teachers as they unleash their students' potential to become skilled problem solvers, creative thinkers, collaborative team members, and knowledge creators. By focusing on the lessons learned through extensive program evaluation and especially program fidelity measures of Comp PD, we are able to replicate the essential pieces needed to achieve similar positive results while adapting where necessary to the new contexts. We are confident that we can continue our role of bringing high-quality PD that changes teaching and improves learning for students to new national and international audiences while leading educators in the best and highest uses of new emerging technologies in support of all learners.

References

Beglau, M. (2010). *eMINTS in Delaware 2008–2010 program evaluation report: An analysis of program impact on participating teachers and students.* Columbia, MO: eMINTS National Center and Assessment Resource Center.

Beglau, M. (2011). *Baldwin County Public Schools eMINTS program implementation evaluation report: An analysis of program impact on participating teachers and students (2008–2010).* Columbia, MO: eMINTS National Center and Assessment Resource Center.

Bickford, A., Hammer, B., McGinty, P., McKinley, P., & Mitchell, S. (2000). MINTs Project evaluation report, February 11. University of Missouri, Columbia, MO: Office of Social and Economic Data Analysis (OSEDA), 1–35.

Brooks, J. G., & Brooks, M. G. (1999) *In search of understanding: The case for constructivist classrooms.* Alexandria, VA: ASCD Press.

Burns, M., Heath, M., & Dimock, V. (1998). Constructivism and technology: On the road to student-centered learning. TAP into Learning. 1(1). Retrieved May 1, 2010, from http://www.sedl.org/pubs/tapinto/v1n1.pdf

Costa, A. L., & Garmston, R. J. (2002). *Cognitive coaching: A foundation for renaissance schools* (2nd ed.). Norwood, MA: Christopher-Gordon.

Dodge, B. ([1995, May 5] 1997). Some thoughts about WebQuests. Retrieved August 1, 2007, from http://webquest.sdsu.edu/about_webquests.html

Elder, B., & Greever-Rice, T. (2007). *eMINTS4Utah: Final report.* Columbia, MO: Office of Social and Economic Data Analysis.

eMINTS. (2014). eThemes. Retrieved February 22, 2014, from http://ethemes.missouri.edu.

Hagar, D. R., & Tharp, S. (2005). *Professional development of eMINTS teachers: A comparison of delivery methodology between eMINTS staff and PD4ETS participants.* Columbia, MO: eMINTS National Center.

Jonassen, D. H., Carr, C., & Yueh, H. P. (1998). Computers as mindtools for engaging learners in critical thinking. *TechTrends, 43*(2), 24–32.

Martin, W., Strother, S., Beglau, M., Bates, L., & Reitzes, T. (2010). Connecting instructional technology professional development to teacher and student outcomes. *Journal of Research on Technology in Education, 43*(1), 53–74.

Martin, W., Strother, S., & Reitzes, T. (2009). *eMINTS 2009 Program Evaluation Report: An analysis of the persistence of program impact on student achievement.* New York: Education Development Center, Center for Children and Technology.

Martin, W., Strother, S., Weatherholt, T., & Dechaume, M. (2008). *eMINTS program evaluation report: An investigation of program fidelity and its impact on teacher mastery and student achievement.* New York: EDC Center for Children and Technology.

Office of Social and Economic Data Analysis (OSEDA). (2001a). *Final results from the eMINTS teacher survey.* Columbia, MO: Author.

Office of Social and Economic Data Analysis (OSEDA). (2001b). *A general typology of eMINTS lessons.* Columbia, MO: Author.

Office of Social and Economic Data Analysis (OSEDA). (2002). *Analysis of 2001 MAP results for eMINTS students.* Columbia, MO: Author.

Office of Social and Economic Data Analysis (OSEDA). (2003a). *Analysis of 2002 MAP results for eMINTS students.* Columbia, MO: Author.

Office of Social and Economic Data Analysis (OSEDA). (2003b). *Assessing instructional practices in eMINTS classrooms.* Columbia, MO: Author.

Office of Social and Economic Data Analysis (OSEDA). (2003c). *Classroom climate, instructional practices and effective behavior management in eMINTS expansion classrooms.* Columbia, MO: Author.

Office of Social and Economic Data Analysis (OSEDA). (2004). *Analysis of 2003 MAP results for eMINTS students.* Columbia, MO: Author.

Office of Social and Economic Data Analysis (OSEDA). (2005). *Analysis of 2004 MAP results for eMINTS students.* Columbia, MO: Author.

Tharp, S. (2006). Principals exhibiting student-centered leadership correlates with positive school climate indicators in Title I eMINTS schools and higher MAP math scores in Title I eMINTS classrooms. University of Missouri, Columbia, MO: Office of Social and Economic Data Analysis.

6

PLACING EVALUATION AT THE CORE

How Evaluation Supported Scale Up of the eMINTS Comprehensive Program

W. Christopher Brandt, Coby V. Meyers, and Ayrin Molefe

The eMINTS National Center places evaluation at the heart of eMINTS Comprehensive, the Center's flagship program. Evaluation is woven throughout all the elements of the eMINTS Comprehensive instructional model. For example, eMINTS instructors help teachers learn about all types of assessment and evaluation for themselves and their students. Instructors emphasize the importance of using data systematically to track school and classroom outcomes and differentiate instruction for individual students. Internal evaluation activities are responsible for the program's evolution. eMINTS instructors gather data using a common set of instruments (e.g., instructor observations, teacher surveys, classroom observations, school checklists, etc.) within each of their school sites. They use results to inform ongoing improvement. External evaluations establish an ever-growing evidence base to validate the program's efficacy. Annual evaluations are conducted to examine the relationship between program implementation and key student outcomes.

Growing the eMINTS Comp Program

In 1999, eMINTS National Center staff began implementing the eMINTS Comp program with a handful of teachers and schools in central Missouri. By 2009, eMINTS Comp was being implemented in partner schools across six U.S. states and Australia. eMINTS Comp's growth was impressive. The National Center's ability to successfully manage the program's growth was perhaps even more impressive.

The National Center implemented at least five strategies to increase their internal capacity and manage the eMINTS program's growth. First, they hired new staff to support implementation in a growing number of schools. Second, they rolled out a "train the trainer" program to certify eMINTS instructional specialists (eISs) and develop a cadre of eMINTS trainers outside of Missouri. Third, they adopted an online learning management system to support ongoing communication between teachers and eMINTS eIS trainers, manage assignment, and facilitate a virtual learning community. Fourth, they developed tools and processes for evaluating instructional specialists who delivered training in a variety of contexts and diverse locations. And finally, they leveraged word of mouth advertising with more systematic approaches to market their portfolio of services, which included eMINTS Comp and a variety of online and blended learning teacher professional development programs.

Maintaining a Persistent Focus on Evaluation

In addition to strategies for building internal capacity, the National Center maintained a persistent focus on evaluation and implementation fidelity. This proved to be critically important for improving program elements, establishing the program's efficacy, and maintaining its integrity during this growth period. How did they use evaluation and fidelity research to do this? Primarily, they relied on three strategies.

First, the Center collected formative data to inform program improvements. eMINTS instructional specialists collected data from teachers via formal surveys and informal feedback after each training and coaching session. The Center analyzed the data collectively and used results to improve the eMINTS instructional model, the instructional content, and the quality of interactions between the individual training and coaching sessions. They also relied on independent summative evaluations to establish evidence that the program was efficacious and improved teaching and learning. The Center contracted with an independent evaluation group to conduct a quasi-experimental evaluation, which compared student outcomes in eMINTS and non-eMINTS classrooms using state standardized performance measures. The independent evaluators consistently found that students enrolled in eMINTS classrooms significantly outperformed students enrolled in similar non-eMINTS classrooms. Evaluators reported the strongest impacts in mathematics and language arts; smaller and somewhat less consistent impacts were also reported in science and social studies across these years. And the National Center's focus on eMINTS Comp implementation fidelity strengthened the program's integrity over time. Since its inception in 1999, the center prioritized the collection and use of fidelity data to maintain program quality and ensure consistent implementation across classrooms and school sites. As the program grew outside of Missouri to schools in other states, and eventually other countries, the Center needed a common set of tools and processes to systematically maintain program quality and consistency across a variety of contexts. In 2008, the Center worked with an external organization to develop and validate a set of tools to monitor program fidelity. The Center now uses these tools to ensure consistent and high-quality program implementation across instructors and a large, growing, and diverse group of school sites.

Establishing Evidence of the eMINTS Comp Program's Effectiveness

From 1999 to 2009, at least seven eMINTS Comprehensive evaluation reports were written. Every report found that eMINTS rolled out the program as planned, and the program improved teacher practice and student achievement. But even with 10 years of progress and a mounting evidence base on the program's efficacy, gaps remained. The Center needed to validate their fidelity measures and strengthen the evidence of the program's effectiveness by addressing three limitations. First, expert reviewers validated the content of one eMINTS fidelity measure; a rubric that assesses eMINTS teachers' lesson plans. But prior studies had not established the predictive validity of the rubric by linking results to key teacher and student outcomes. Although the quality of lesson plans appear to be correlated with student achievement, it was unclear whether teachers' use of the eMINTS lesson planning process, one of four eMINTS Comp program components, actually influenced changes in student achievement (Martin, Strother, Weatherholt, & Dechaume, 2008). Second, prior evaluation studies had limited rigor. Evaluations used matched comparison groups and did not establish group equivalence at baseline (i.e., before the study began). Non-equivalent comparison groups at baseline left open the possibility that positive findings might be due to factors other than the eMINTS program. In addition, although eMINTS offered their Comprehensive program in K-12 classrooms, prior evaluation findings pertained only to students in grades three through five. Third, the relationship between eMINTS Comp and short- and long-term outcomes remained unknown. The Center wanted to know, "after we train teachers, do they use the prescribed instructional practices? And if so, do those practices, in turn, influence long-term increases in student achievement?"

The eMINTS National Center navigated challenges commonly faced by developing programs. As a new decade approached, Center staff were on the brink of new challenges that, if successfully addressed, would promote eMINTS Comp's scale up. But conquering these challenges would not be easy.

The eMINTS Funding Conundrum

In 2009, the National Center faced an imminent challenge to secure additional funding. They needed funding to support the eMINTS program's scale up within and outside of Missouri. Within Missouri, eMINTS schools traditionally relied on Title II funds to support program-related technology purchases. In 2010, however, Missouri no longer approved using Title II for eMINTS Comp. The Center saw this as a setback for scaling up the program in Missouri. Many partner schools relied on Title II funding to support the eMINTS program. And although the number of schools implementing eMINTS Comp outside of Missouri had increased substantially over the previous 10 years, the program's bread and butter was found in Missouri school districts. In 2010, the vast majority of eMINTS schools were located in the National Center's home state. Missouri's new Title II restrictions would undoubtedly reduce future eMINTS participation. Moreover, the National Center believed that growth outside of Missouri would be difficult if federal or state funding was not available to offset what was at the time eMINTS program's high implementation costs. Without a consistent funding stream, schools would find it difficult to adopt or sustain the program. The National Center explored alternative funding sources such as Title I to support school participation. This search for alternative funding became part of the Center's long-term sustainability plan.

In the short term, however, the National Center needed to find a way to address the void in Title II funds and continue to grow the program. The Center began looking into alternative funding sources that would support eMINTS implementation in a new cohort of schools and districts. At this same time, the U.S. Department of Education launched a new federal "Investing in Innovation" program.

Identifying a Strategy for Short-Term Program Scale Up

The eMINTS National Center saw the i3 program as the ideal mechanism through which to continue scaling up the eMINTS Comp program in the short term. If the Center won, they could support the program in several Missouri schools and keep their growing cadre of instructional specialists employed. The grant would also allow the National Center to advance their research and evaluation agenda, by establishing causal evidence of the program's effectiveness in previously untested school settings: rural Missouri middle schools. And the grant would provide resources to support a rigorous randomized control trial, which is considered the gold standard for establishing causal evidence of a program's effectiveness. A randomized trial was essential for strengthening the program's evidence base.

Partnering to Pursue Grant Funding

During the summer of 2009, the eMINTS National Center approached Learning Point Associates (LPA)—an organization that merged with the American Institutes for Research (AIR) in 2010—about partnering to submit an i3 grant. They wanted the grant to accomplish four goals: scale up the eMINTS program in Missouri, extend the program's reach in rural areas, strengthen the program's evidence of effectiveness, and expand the applicability of evaluation findings beyond grades three to five. As the proposed evaluators, a team of us at LPA worked with eMINTS to design an evaluation that accomplished these goals. To meet evaluation requirements specified under the i3 validation grant, external evaluators needed to design a rigorous study that would have potential for establishing a causal link between the program and its intended outcomes. Additionally, the evaluation needed to carefully measure the extent to which the program was delivered to schools and teachers as planned and implemented within the schools by principals, teachers, and technology staff as intended. This is what we set out to do for the eMINTS National Center.

The eMINTS i3 Evaluation Design

The eMINTS Comp program is based on four underlying research-based components: inquiry-based learning, high-quality lesson design, community of learners, and technology integration. The program provides teachers with approximately 240 hours of professional development (PD) spanning 2 years and support that includes monthly classroom visits. eMINTS added a third year of professional development to the traditional 2-year eMINTS Comp program, relying on the Intel Teach Program to build on what teachers learn during the first 2 years of eMINTS Comp. The purpose of this third year of training is to combine additional professional development and Intel's suite of web-based teaching tools to expand teachers' use of inquiry-based learning.

The eMINTS Validation Study used a 3-year cluster randomized design that randomly assigned 60 high-poverty rural Missouri middle schools to one of three groups in fall 2010. Schools assigned to Group 1 receive the traditional eMINTS 2-year professional development program in 2011–12 and 2012–13. Group 2 schools receive eMINTS 2-year professional development in Years 1 and 2 plus a third year of professional development designed with Intel in 2013–14. Group 3 schools conduct business as usual (BAU), with no exposure to the eMINTS or Intel professional development in the first 3 years of the study, although they will receive eMINTS professional development once data collection is complete. Table 6.1 illustrates the random assignment of schools and treatment conditions.

To remove extraneous variation due to differences in grade configuration, randomization was blocked by the grade range in each school (Block 1: PK–8 schools; Block 2: 5–8, 6–8, 7–8 schools; Block 3: 6–12, 7–12 schools). Note that although

Table 6.1 Random Assignment of Schools to Treatment Conditions

Summer 2010	Fall 2010		2011–12	2012–13	2013–14
Qualify 60 schools for project*	Random assignment of N=60 schools	*Group 1* eMINTS N=20	eMINTS Yr 1	eMINTS Yr 2	No PD
		Group 2 eMINTS+Intel N=20	eMINTS Yr 1	eMINTS Yr 2	eMINTS +Intel Teach
		Group 3 Control N=20	BAU	BAU	BAU

the schools were randomized into three groups, the steps to determine implementation fidelity presented in this chapter are effectively limited to only two groups because the treatment groups are combined in the first 2 years of the evaluation.

Key evaluation objectives include: (1) employing experimental methods to rigorously examine the program's impact on teacher practice and student achievement, particularly for middle school students in rural settings; (2) examining impacts of a third year of professional development, using Intel Teach Elements courses and tools, on teacher and student outcomes; and (3) expanding the applicability of evaluation results to middle school students in high-poverty rural schools.

The study includes 191 teachers and 3,610 students in 60 high-poverty rural schools throughout Missouri. The study examines implementation and impacts annually on teachers and students across three years of eMINTS Comprehensive implementation.

The study includes three main research questions:[1]

1. What is the impact of the eMINTS Comprehensive program on seventh- and eighth-grade students' mathematics and communication arts performance?
2. What is the impact of the eMINTS Comprehensive program on seventh- and eighth-grade students' 21st century skills, which include communication, technology literacy, and critical thinking?
3. Does eMINTS plus a third year of professional development supported by the Intel Teach program result in a greater impact on seventh- and eighth-grade students' performance than is seen in traditional eMINTS Comprehensive and control schools?

National Evaluation of i3 Implementation Fidelity Criteria

The Institute of Education Sciences (IES)—the research arm of the Department of Education—sponsored a National Evaluation of i3 (NEi3). NEi3's goals are twofold: provide technical assistance to support rigorous, independent evaluations of all i3 grant-funded projects and systematically report on the progress of and findings from these independent evaluations. The NEi3 evaluation focuses on implementation fidelity and outcomes. In part, NEi3 seeks to answer the question: "Were i3-funded interventions implemented with high fidelity and did these interventions produce the intended improvements in student outcomes?"

Our research design incorporated methods to meet the National Evaluation i3 (NEi3) standards for high-quality implementation studies. The NEi3 standards established minimum criteria for reliably and systematically assessing and reporting high-quality implementation of i3 grant-funded projects. NEi3 encouraged i3 grant evaluators to go further than the NEi3 standards and develop more comprehensive fidelity systems and implementation studies. But the minimum systematic criteria allowed the NEi3 research team to report implementation fidelity findings across i3 grants. These minimum criteria included:

1. Evaluator provides a logic model for the intervention.
2. Logic model identifies all key components of the intervention.
3. Logic model identifies the mediators through which the intervention is expected to have its intended outcomes.
4. Logic model identifies the student outcome(s) that the intervention is designed to improve.
5. Evaluator periodically measures implementation fidelity.
6. Fidelity is measured separately for each key component of the intervention.
7. Fidelity measures cover the entire sample (or an approved subsample of sites).
8. Evaluator specifies thresholds for determining whether for the entire sample the key components of the intervention were implemented with fidelity.
9. Evaluator assesses and reports for the entire sample whether each key component was implemented with fidelity or not implemented with fidelity.

Aligning the eMINTS Evaluation Design with National Evaluation of i3 Standards

With the NEi3 criteria in mind, the implementation fidelity component of the eMINTS Comp evaluation focused on: (1) the delivery of core eMINTS Comp program resources and activities by the eMINTS National Center; and (2) the implementation of eMINTS Comp resources and core instructional activities received by eMINTS teachers. We asked:

1. Did eMINTS staff deliver the eMINTS Comprehensive Program as designed?
2. To what extent did schools implement the eMINTS Comprehensive Program as Planned?

During the first 2 years of eMINTS implementation, our fidelity analysis focused on program implementation in the treatment schools and the extent to which eMINTS staff and teachers, school leaders, and technology coordinators who participated in eMINTS Comp implemented core components of the program as planned, and schools implemented the necessary technology infrastructure and technology support elements. In other words, we sought to describe "what happened" as eMINTS staff delivered the eMINTS program components, and as principals, teachers, and district personnel attempted to implement these program components. We did not attempt to explain potential variation in the extent to which schools and teachers implemented various components of the program.

Methodology: Seven Steps to Determine Program-Level Fidelity

The remainder of this chapter details the steps we took to measure and report on implementation fidelity according to the NEi3 standards. Detailing the steps of this process benefits evaluators by helping them to think through possible ways of establishing rules for and determining levels of fidelity achieved. In addition, this work provides program developers with a clearer path to identify core program components and developing instruments for their individual and collective measurement. We conclude the chapter with a discussion of design limitations, fidelity measurement challenges, and how we addressed these challenges.

In most instances of program development, there are two fundamental channels of information flow to consider with regards to implementation fidelity. The first is simply identifying whether or not the provider is adequately delivering their services. The focus of this paper is not on the delivery of services because it is typically easy to determine. And in this evaluation, eMINTS delivered the appropriate equipment and professional development services at high levels (for more information, see Brandt, Meyers, & Molefe, 2013).

We instead focus on the second aspect of implementation fidelity that is substantially more difficult to report. Specifically, we lay out our steps for addressing the following research question: To what extent did schools implement the eMINTS Comprehensive Program in Year 1? This question deemphasizes the delivery of the program while emphasizing its receipt. In other words, did schools and teachers do their part to adhere to program and training guidelines?

Step 1: Identifying and Defining the Core Components of the Program

Understanding the program and how it is supposed to work is the first step in any evaluation. Before developing the evaluation design (which included measuring program fidelity and key teacher and student outcomes), we needed a better understanding of the program's core components and how they worked to achieve desired outcomes. Before submitting our i3 proposal, the evaluation team spent one full day working with eMINTS staff to understand the eMINTS Comp program and identify and define its core components. We then translated what we learned into a program description, and used the program description to develop a logic model and a change model. The logic model outlines the resources, processes, teacher outputs, and expected student outcomes to be realized as a result of implementing the eMINTS Comprehensive and eMINTS+Intel programs. The change model describes constructs, or core underlying changes in teacher and student behaviors, that are expected to change as a result of implementing the eMINTS Comp program (Nelson, Cordray, Hulleman, Darrow, & Sommer, 2012). Although a draft description and set of models were developed shortly after our one-day session, the process of finalizing the models took several months and involved multiple iterations. The final eMINTS Comp description, model of change and logic model are described below.

eMINTS Comp Program Description

Equipment Requirements

To be properly implemented for this evaluation, eMINTS classrooms had to first meet minimum hardware, software, Internet and equipment connectivity requirements. An official eMINTS Comprehensive classroom for this evaluation includes an interactive whiteboard (e.g., SMART Board), LCD projector, teacher laptop, camera, printer/scanner, and at least a 1:1 ratio of students to computers. Specific Internet and equipment connectivity requirements must be met in an eMINTS classroom to ensure proper instructional functionality. Connectivity requirements may be met using either wired or wireless connectivity configurations or may be a combination of the two. In addition to Internet connectivity, the following setup requirements must be met to achieve minimum instructional functionality:

- A teacher laptop/workstation must connect to a classroom interactive whiteboard.
- A teacher laptop/workstation image must appear on the teacher monitor and interactive whiteboard simultaneously.
- Students must be able to display their work on the interactive whiteboard through a shared folder system or server.

Schoolwide Professional Development

eMINTS Comp is an intensive program that consists of training for school principals, district and school technology coordinators, and classroom teachers. Before the start of the school year, a certified eMINTS instructional specialist is assigned to a collection of schools according to the instructional specialist's geographic location to provide formal and individualized training to principals and teachers. Along with these training responsibilities, the instructional specialist facilitates the development of a school-based leadership team within each school to support implementation and ensure that the required technology infrastructure and equipment functionality is maintained in eMINTS classrooms.

The instructional specialists train principals and technology specialists to monitor and support eMINTS teachers' instructional improvements. Specifically, during a one-day face-to-face training session early in the school year, the instructional specialist introduces principals to constructivist theories underlying the eMINTS model and their implications for classroom teaching and learning. They introduce principals to an observation rubric for rating eMINTS teachers' instructional performance according to eMINTS standards. During the winter and spring of each school year, the instructional specialist or other certified eMINTS consultant returns to conduct a school walk-through with the principal to support implementation and to help the school integrate eMINTS with other school initiatives. During the 2 years, principals receive about 12 hours of training. They also receive a monthly newsletter with information about important elements of the eMINTS model and how they are applied in schools and class-rooms. School technology coordinators are trained to understand eMINTS pedagogy and how technology is intended to support instruction. A certified eMINTS consultant conducts two 2-hour online sessions with coordinators (4 hours total) during each school year to introduce technology coordinators to eMINTS pedagogy and train them on equipment maintenance.

Teachers receive about 240 hours of professional development over 2 years to design high-quality inquiry-based lesson plans, implement inquiry-based learning strategies, build community among teachers and students, and integrate technology into classroom instruction. The instructional specialist works with his or her assigned schools and teachers throughout the year to secure dates and times to conduct formal training sessions. During the first year of training, teachers receive 126 hours of formal training in 26 sessions that are held throughout the school year. Training sessions typically take place in a computer lab in a central location and last between 4 and 6.5 hours each. The first-year curriculum focuses on understanding constructivist pedagogy, community-building strategies (including interaction and interdependence), inquiry-based learning strategies, technology integration, and introducing authentic learning experiences into the classroom. At the end of the first training year, teachers spend up to 12 additional hours developing a classroom website with the help of the instructional specialist. During the second year of training, the specialist conducts 88 hours of training in 20 sessions throughout the school year. The Year 2 curriculum focuses on classroom management, website enhancement, assessment, interdisciplinary teaching and learning, and development of multimedia and online projects. One session is reserved for teachers to travel to an eMINTS school and observe a certified eMINTS teacher. During both training years, the specialist supplements these formal training sessions with 9–10 on-site and individualized coaching sessions (about 14 hours total) and within-building communities of practice where teaching staff meet to share ideas, collaborate on online project development, and deepen their existing understanding of concepts embedded in the eMINTS training. Finally, eMINTS provides teachers with written curricula and just-in-time learning opportunities via online courses to help teachers improve their practice over time.

Intel Teach Program Description

As mentioned earlier, eMINTS and the Intel Corporation recently partnered to establish a third year of professional development for eMINTS teachers to augment the current eMINTS Comprehensive program. This combined program, referred to as "eMINTS+Intel," provides a third year of professional development using the Intel Teach courses and online tools to further enhance teachers' technology integration skills and provide a specific set of online resources for teachers to support the four eMINTS components.

The third year of Intel Teach Elements combines 30 hours of online course instruction with 12 hours of face-to-face professional development. The Elements training is designed to help teachers use a set of online tools to implement project-based instructional approaches. The eMINTS instructional specialists who provide Year 1 and Year 2 professional development to their assigned schools facilitate the online course to the same schools. Throughout the course, teachers consider their own teaching practice and the ways that technology supports project-based approaches. The training focuses on: (1) principles of project-based learning; (2) steps of project design; (3) integrating assessment throughout a project; (4) developing a project timeline and implementation plan; and (5) guiding learning through questioning, collaboration, self-direction, and reflection. In addition to the face-to-face and online professional development sessions, teachers receive four or five in-classroom coaching visits throughout the year. Coaching visits from the eMINTS instructional specialist last approximately 1 hour.

eMINTS+Intel Model of Change and Logic Model

Figure 6.1 describes the model of change underlying the eMINTS Comprehensive and eMINTS+Intel programs. In the eMINTS Comprehensive program, the technology resources combined with intensive teacher professional development and schoolwide support is intended to transform teachers' classroom lesson planning and instruction. Through intensive professional development and one-on-one support, teachers learn how to develop high-quality lesson plans and integrate technology in their classroom instruction, in order to promote inquiry-based lessons and collaborative classroom communities. These instructional changes should, in turn, influence students' engagement in school and improve students' 21st century skills (i.e., critical thinking, communication, technology literacy) and achievement on annual state-administered assessments.

The third year of Intel Teach professional development is expected to accelerate outcomes for teachers and students by providing teachers with additional

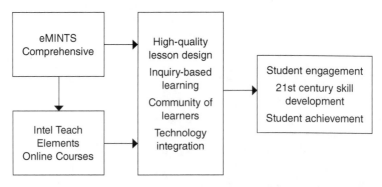

FIGURE 6.1 eMINTS Comprehensive + Intel Teach Elements Model of Change

professional development and web-based tools to build on what they learned during the first 2 years of the program.

Figure 6.2 provides a more detailed logic model, which diagrams the resources, processes, teacher outputs, and expected student outcomes to be realized as a result of implementing the eMINTS Comprehensive and eMINTS+Intel programs. Building-level inputs include improvements to the school's technology equipment and infrastructure such as computers, SMART Boards, digital cameras, scanners, LCD projectors, advanced software programs for teachers and students, and technology support and bandwidth.

The eMINTS theory holds that school conditions should improve teachers' classroom practice when

- schools are provided with up-to-date technology and a high-performing technological infrastructure
- principals are trained to understand constructivist pedagogy and its potential for accelerating students' learning
- principals support and monitor eMINTS classroom improvements over time
- technology specialists are available in the school to support technology use and conduct regular equipment maintenance
- school decision making occurs regularly through professional learning communities involving teachers, school leadership, and outside consultants (e.g., the instructional specialist).

With adequate conditions in place at the school level, classroom practice should improve when teachers

- understand the benefits of constructivist pedagogy for accelerating students' learning
- learn to design standards-based lessons, implement inquiry-based learning strategies, build collaborative classroom communities, and infuse technology into their instruction
- receive individualized support from a specialist to reinforce what they learn in formal professional development sessions
- participate in a professional learning community to share ideas and receive feedback from their colleagues
- receive support and accountability from their school leadership (via walk-throughs and ongoing feedback).

With intensive and differentiated professional development grounded in constructivist pedagogy, an adequate technology infrastructure to engage teachers and students, support to understand and apply new strategies in their classrooms, and accountability from colleagues and school leadership, teachers should gradually improve the extent to which their lesson plans are aligned to standards and

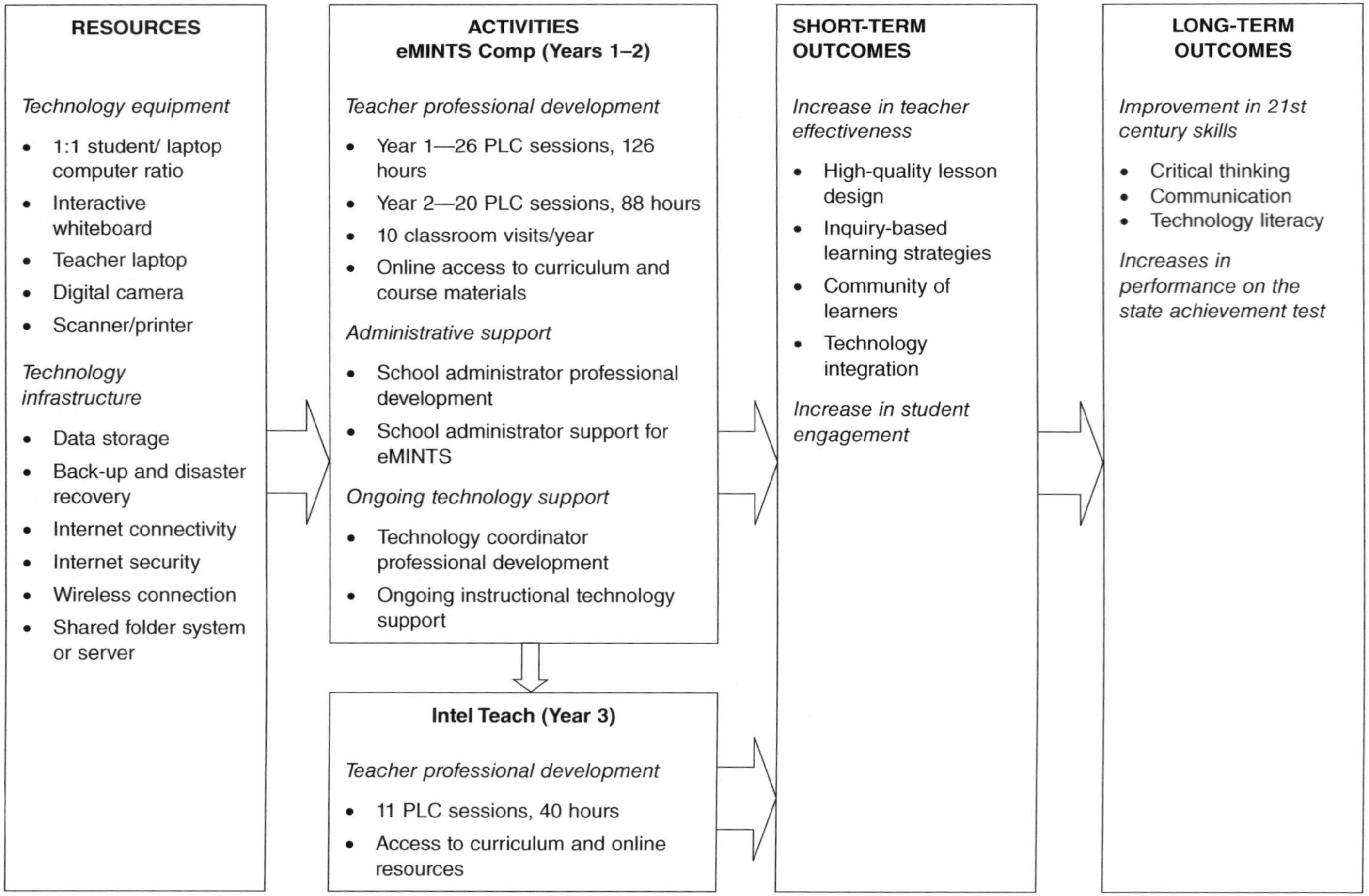

RESOURCES

Technology equipment
- 1:1 student/ laptop computer ratio
- Interactive whiteboard
- Teacher laptop
- Digital camera
- Scanner/printer

Technology infrastructure
- Data storage
- Back-up and disaster recovery
- Internet connectivity
- Internet security
- Wireless connection
- Shared folder system or server

ACTIVITIES
eMINTS Comp (Years 1–2)

Teacher professional development
- Year 1—26 PLC sessions, 126 hours
- Year 2—20 PLC sessions, 88 hours
- 10 classroom visits/year
- Online access to curriculum and course materials

Administrative support
- School administrator professional development
- School administrator support for eMINTS

Ongoing technology support
- Technology coordinator professional development
- Ongoing instructional technology support

Intel Teach (Year 3)

Teacher professional development
- 11 PLC sessions, 40 hours
- Access to curriculum and online resources

SHORT-TERM OUTCOMES

Increase in teacher effectiveness
- High-quality lesson design
- Inquiry-based learning strategies
- Community of learners
- Technology integration

Increase in student engagement

LONG-TERM OUTCOMES

Improvement in 21st century skills
- Critical thinking
- Communication
- Technology literacy

Increases in performance on the state achievement test

FIGURE 6.2 Logic Model for eMINTS Comprehensive+Intel

grounded in assessment, incorporate more inquiry-based learning strategies in their instruction, strengthen relationships with students, improve their own technology literacy, and facilitate a vibrant classroom community of learners.

As schools and teachers gradually develop and demonstrate these characteristics, students should demonstrate

- improvement in academic orientation in school
- improvement in 21st century skill development such as communication, technology literacy, and critical thinking
- improvement in achievement as measured by statewide achievement tests.

Integration of eMINTS Comprehensive and Intel Teach Programs

As mentioned in the section above, the theory supporting the eMINTS+Intel model holds that a third year of professional development should accelerate the changes observed in teachers' practices and students' achievement over and above the traditional 2-year eMINTS model. This occurs primarily through professional development to reinforce concepts in standards-based lesson design, inquiry-based learning strategies and assessment, and technology integration.

The core components of a program are those components that developers determine are its foundational elements. Although the program can be considered implemented if low levels of receipt are demonstrated for one or more of these components, complete disregard for any one suggests a lack of commitment. Thus, in this evaluation, program developers and evaluators made presentations and held additional communications with participating schools to clearly explain expectations. In addition, a memorandum of understanding was signed by the administrator of each school formally recognizing eMINTS' five core components: technology infrastructure, technology use,[2] teacher professional development, administrative support, and ongoing technology support. The various communications also made clear for schools program developers expectations regarding each component. Those core expectations for each program component are illustrated in the Figure 6.2 logic model. For example, primary teacher professional development activities in Year 1 included 26 professional learning community meetings led by trained eMINTS staff and 10 classroom observations by eMINTS staff.

Step 2: Identifying Data Sources to Measure Core Components

Once each component was identified, we then identified data sources to measure each component. We began by working with eMINTS to determine what relevant data they were already collecting for their records that could also be used for fidelity measurement purposes. eMINTS had a sophisticated system for collecting teacher and administrator professional development attendance data because most of the sessions occurred outside of the typical school day, so districts required the information to provide stipends. The eMINTS attendance records for teachers recorded arrival and departure at quarter-hour segments. This data provided us with a good foundation for measuring fidelity related to teacher professional development attendance.

In other cases, however, eMINTS either did not collect data or the data collected would not translate into implementation fidelity measurement. For example, eMINTS conducted a baseline audit of all study schools to ensure that school's technology infrastructure met minimum technology capability requirements. Although the information was useful for baseline comparisons of technology readiness, information about whether or not schools made necessary, on-time upgrades in their infrastructure were not recorded. In those cases, we developed survey items to collect this information. Overall, we surveyed students, teachers, and technology coordinators.

Step 3: Determining the Relative Importance of Each Component

We then worked with the eMINTS National Center to determine the relative importance of each component and assign weights to each. As the developer, eMINTS made all decisions about how to weigh the components. As evaluators, we discussed the potential impacts of weighting decisions; that is, the more weight assigned to a particular component results in that component having increased impact on fidelity analyses. Although weighting decisions were somewhat arbitrary, they were made by the developers based on their program model. Not surprisingly, eMINTS gave substantially more priority to teacher professional development. All decisions were made prior to data analysis.

Step 4: Developing Component Indexes

Next we developed component indexes by identifying sub-components and criteria for minimum levels of implementation; establishing a measure for each sub-component; and combining sub-component measures to create a component index. Table 6.2 illustrates how we created an index for the component Technology Use.

Three sub-components were identified with eMINTS as the most critical aspects of technology use for treatment schools: student laptop use, teacher laptop use, and interactive whiteboard use. We then developed criteria for minimum levels of technology use for each sub-component. In each case, adequate implementation translated into teachers reporting the use of technology equipment at least once per week. Teacher survey responses on items aligned with each sub-component were the sources of data, as illustrated in Table 6.3. Each response option was assigned a value, 1–5, with increasing value indicating more technology usage.

Table 6.2 Component Development: Technology Use

Sub-Component	Criteria	Measure	Variable Definition	Index
Students' laptop use	Teacher reports students using laptops at least once/week	Teacher Survey Q5.6b = stulap_use (code "never or almost never"=1, "3–6 sessions per year"=2, "1–3 sessions per month"=3, "1–3 sessions per week"=4, "almost every or every session"=5)	If stulap_use>=4, then X1=1; otherwise X1=0	Teacher_use = (X1+X2+X3)/3
Teacher laptop use	Teacher reports using laptop at least once/week	Teacher Survey Q5.6a = tchlap_use (code "never or almost never"=1, "3–6 sessions per year"=2, "1–3 sessions per month"=3, "1–3 sessions per week"=4, "almost every or every session"=5)	If tchlap_use>=4, then X2=1; otherwise X2=0	
Interactive whiteboard use	Teacher reports using whiteboard at least once/week	Teacher Survey Q5.6g = whtbd_use (code "never or almost never"=1, "3–6 sessions per year"=2, "1–3 sessions per month"=3, "1–3 sessions per week"=4, "almost every or every session"=5)	If whtbd_use>=4, then X3=1; otherwise X3=0	

Table 6.3 Subcomponents and Response Options

How often do you use the following when teaching your target class?	Never or almost never	3–6 sessions per year	1–3 sessions per month	1–3 sessions per week	Almost every or every session
a. Teacher computer (desktop or laptop)	Value = 1	Value = 2	Value = 3	Value = 4	Value = 5
b. Student classroom computers					
c. Interactive whiteboard (e.g., SMART Board)					

The measure and corresponding values are also represented in Table 6.2, where descriptions of each measure are provided to establish a quantified variable definition. As the variable definition indicates, teachers either did or did not use (or report student use) the various sources of technology available to them to an adequate extent. Finally, teacher responses for sub-components were then averaged for an overall index of teacher technology use.

For two of the five program components, multiple data sources were used to measure them. In these cases, separate indexes were developed for each data source. Then the data sources were averaged to arrive at an overall program component index. Figure 6.3 illustrates this. Consider Ongoing Tech Support as an example, where technology coordinator attendance of training sessions and teacher survey responses about school technology support are the data sources. An index for each is determined and the average of the two is the fidelity score for that program component.

Step 5: Finalizing Plans With Program Developer

Once all of the previous steps were completed, we met again with the program developer to review all of the decisions. Specifically, we asked the program developer the following:

- Did we include the right components?
- Are we using the right data sources and measures?
- Are the components weighted correctly?
- Are index values appropriate and useful for understanding implementation levels?
- Do our component indexes measure implementation accurately?

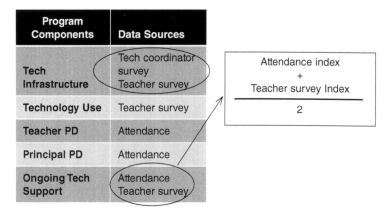

FIGURE 6.3 Combining Indexes When Using Multiple Data Sources to Measure a Single Component

Although we had been working with the program developer throughout the process, this conversation allowed them to respond to the overall plan for measuring fidelity and reconsider each component as separate parts of the whole. Some important changes were made, including the currently constructed component of technology use, which was previously conceptualized as technology access. Thus, instead of measuring the component based on school technology audits (i.e., does the school have the technology necessary?), we focused on measuring levels of technology use.

In addition, we worked with the program developers to establish school-level criteria for high, moderate, and low levels of implementation for each component and overall fidelity scores. As illustrated in Table 6.4, these cut points varied by program component. These differences were primarily the result of various response options and data sources.

Step 6: Aggregating Individual Scores to the School-Level

We then calculated component-level and overall fidelity scores for each school. From an evaluative perspective, this is a logical step toward establishing overall implementation fidelity across schools. It also creates a potential mediating variable that enables analysis of teacher instructional practices and student achievement by level of program implementation per school. In addition, this identification provides the program developer with practical information. The scores aid the program developers in identifying schools and program components for which the program is being implemented at high or low levels. Table 6.5 demonstrates some school-level results.

Step 7: Determining Overall Level of Implementation Fidelity

The cut points established for school-level fidelity, at the program component and overall levels, remain the same for determining overall levels of implementation fidelity. Then we averaged the implementation scores across schools with each school weighted equally. The resulting fidelity scores for program components and overall implementation indicate the extent to which the eMINTS

Table 6.4 Cut Points by Program Component

	Technology Infrastructure	Technology Equipment	Teacher Training	Administrative Support	Ongoing Technology Support	Overall Fidelity Score
Cut Points	High >.74	High >.66	High >.89	High >.67	High >.79	High >.79
	Mod. .50–.74	Mod. .34–.66	Mod. .8–.89	Mod. .34–.67	Mod. .60–.79	Mod. .60–.79
	Low <.50	Low <=.33	Low <.80	Low <.34	Low <.60	Low <.60

Table 6.5 Reporting Aggregated Individual Scores to the School Level

Cut Points	Technology Infrastructure	Technology Equipment	Teacher Training	Administrative Support	Ongoing Technology Support	Overall School Fidelity Score	Overall School Fidelity Level
	High >.74	High >.66	High >.89	High >.67	High >.79	High >.79	High
	Mod. .50–.74	Mod. .34–.66	Mod. .8–.89	Mod. .34–.67	Mod. .60–.79	Mod. .60–.79	Moderate
	Low <.50	Low <=.33	Low <.80	Low <.34	Low <.60	Low <.60	Low
	Score Weight = 15%	Score Weight = 10%	Score Weight = 45%	Score Weight = 20%	Score Weight = 10%	Score Weight = 100%	
Treatment School ID							
1	.75	.67	.93	1.00	.58	.86	High
2	1.00	.83	.91	1.00	.48	.90	High
3	1.00	1.00	.92	1.00	.90	.95	High
4	.67	.67	.93	1.00	.70	.84	High
5	.92	.81	.92	1.00	.48	.88	High
6	1.00	.67	.95	1.00	.60	.91	High
8	1.00	.67	.95	.67	.50	.84	High
9	.92	.78	.91	1.00	.63	.89	High
10	.75	1.00	.92	1.00	.64	.89	High

program was implemented across all schools. The overall fidelity score was "high," as were four of the five program components. These results suggest that reporting the information at the program component level is practically important. Ongoing technology support was barely moderate, suggesting to the program developer that voluntary technology coordinator training sessions were not well attended, which could eventually adversely affect teachers' ability to enact critical instructional components in their classrooms. If teachers do not receive the technology support that they need, they may stop using the equipment.

Study Constraints and Design Limitations

When designing the evaluation, we had to make some difficult decisions about how to allocate a finite amount of resources to address our evaluation questions. Resources included staff time and budget for developing and validating our fidelity measures, collecting multiple sources of data for triangulation, and addressing fidelity questions vs. questions on teacher and student outcomes. As with any evaluation or research study, these decisions resulted in data and analytic limitations, which affected the level of certainty about our fidelity estimates. The major limitations in our fidelity estimates rested in three areas: our ability to triangulate with multiple data sources, consistency of our index metrics, and the empirical rigor of our measures.

Data Triangulation Limitations

During the first year of eMINTS implementation, each of our five component fidelity scores were based on only one or two data sources. This limited our ability to substantiate findings from any one individual source. For example, using only teacher surveys meant that we relied solely on individual teachers' perceptions of their personal use and integration of technology into classroom instruction. Although helpful, prior survey research suggests that results of self-perception data tends to be inflated (Epley and Dunning, 2006). That is, teachers likely reported using technology in their instruction more than they actually did. We collected observation data on teachers' use of technology, which we plan to retroactively incorporate into the technology use component metric to obtain a more reliable component estimate. However, our budget limited us to conducting classroom observations once per year, so our observation estimates of teachers' technology use are likely to be unstable.

Inconsistent Data Metrics

A second limitation was that each of the five individual eMINTS component scores were not calculated using the same measuring stick. To illustrate, schools' fidelity scores on several components were based in part on attendance records at eMINTS training sessions. eMINTS teachers were required to attend well over 30 training and coaching sessions each year. Administrators were asked to attend up to three training sessions per year. The large number of teacher training opportunities compared to that of administrators resulted in high levels of variability across schools on the final teacher professional development component score across schools. On the contrary, final scores on the administrator support component varied much less. As a result, our ability to differentiate between schools' implementation performance was much more limited with administrative support than with teacher professional development. It also affected our ability to interpret schools' overall fidelity scores, since more information was available to inform teacher professional development than administrative support.

Lack of Empirical Measures of Fidelity

Measuring implementation of the eMINTS Comp and eMINTS+Intel programs is still in its early stages. The National Center worked with other partners in recent years to develop and validate training observation measures and improve the delivery of their training to schools; however, these fidelity measures focused on training delivery and provided limited utility for measuring schools' participation and receipt of core eMINTS Comp training components. The i3 grant evaluation represents their first attempt at identifying the intervention's core components and sub-components, weighting each component's relative importance in achieving desired outcomes for students, and developing measures and indices of school participation and receipt of services. Constructs represented by surveys, logs and observation items, while based on existing measures, had not been empirically validated until after the first year of implementation. With data from the first year of eMINTS implementation now in hand, we spent part of Year 2 examining the psychometric properties of our surveys, logs and refining our measures.

Improving eMINTS' Implementation Fidelity Measurement

After completing 2 full years of implementation, we have been able to examine and refine our implementation measures. However, much is still left to be done to improve implementation fidelity measurement of the eMINTS Comp program. First, the indices, components, and component weights used in our fidelity analysis still need to be validated. Second, we need to validate the established cut scores for distinguishing between high, moderate and low implementing schools. Various sensitivity analyses are necessary to examine the reliability and stability of our fidelity estimates. To date, the program component weights and criteria for cut points are not yet empirically based but have been determined jointly with program developer expectations. Third, we need to explore how different methods for indexing fidelity might affect implementation outcomes. For example, how do scores change when new measures and more comprehensive approaches for indexing individual components are incorporated into our fidelity analysis? What are the implications of different approaches of measuring eMINTS Comp implementation on final school fidelity scores? Is there an optimal method for indexing implementation? Finally, through other funding sources, we hope to co-develop a rating tool with the eMINTS National Center that can be used to reliably measure implementation fidelity. Ideally, the rating tool would be used by a certified eMINTS instructional specialist to periodically monitor school implementation, identify strengths and weaknesses, and provide targeted support to school staff. To ensure the tool's validity, analyses would need to establish relationships between core implementation components in the rating tool and short- and long-term outcomes.

In future years, we also plan extend our fidelity analysis beyond minimum NEi3 criteria to address the influence of variation in implementation on student outcomes. We will do this by including treatment differentiation in our definition of treatment fidelity (Cordray & Pion, 2006; Waltz, Addis, Koerner, & Jacobson, 1993). Treatment differentiation suggests that the underlying constructs embedded in the treatment should be stronger or different from the counterfactual condition. Measuring this differentiation requires a parallel "fidelity" assessment of programmatic components in both conditions (Hulleman & Cordray, 2009). This assessment is referred to as the achieved relative strength of the contrast (Cordray & Jacobs, 2005), or the difference between the treatment as implemented and the control as implemented (Hulleman & Cordray, 2009). To assess the achieved relative strength of the intervention, we will compare implementation in the eMINTS+Intel Teach schools to the eMINTS-only schools and control or "business as usual" schools during the third and final year of eMINTS implementation. This comparison will be conducted using indices derived from the same measures used as teacher outcomes and intermediate student outcomes (e.g., academic orientation and 21st century skills).

Conclusions

Although there were clear limitations to our methods, the steps explicated in this chapter provide evaluators with a straightforward way to consider measuring implementation. It also provides program developers with an understanding of what is required of them in conceptualizing how the implementation of their program should be measured. What are the most important aspects or components? Are there instruments in place to measure those important aspects? How do we define satisfactory implementation? We worked closely with the eMINTS National Center to address these and other essential questions related to measuring implementation fidelity of the eMINTS Comp and eMINTS Comp+Intel Teach programs.

The most critical time to engage with National Center staff was during the first year of our grant, before implementation began. We spent over 10 months working directly with National Center staff on a bi-weekly basis. Our conversations focused on recruitment, IRB approval, and evaluation planning. The evaluation team took the lead in developing, revising, and refining the program description, logic model and change model. We vetted the descriptions, models and implementation measures with Center staff to make sure that our measures (surveys, observations, and logs) were capturing the full range of core program implementation activities. Center staff also provided feedback on the items we used to represent key constructs associated with the eMINTS instructional model (e.g., inquiry-based learning, technology integration). We were also able to identify measures already developed by the eMINTS National Center, which proved to be useful tools for measuring fidelity.

Acknowledgements

This research was supported by a grant from the Office of Innovation and Improvement (OII), U.S. Department of Education (U396B100038). The findings and opinions expressed are those of the authors and do not represent the position or policies of the U.S. Department of Education.

Notes

1. Confirmatory research questions are the main questions this study is designed to address. This study was designed using an experimental design to provide rigorous estimates of the causal effects of the eMINTS and eMINTS+Intel Teacher Program.
2. Note the switch in perspective from developer delivery—"equipment"—to participant receipt—"use"—where simply having the equipment is not enough to warrant fidelity for participants.

References

Brandt, C., Meyers, C., & Molefe, A. (2013). *The impact of eMINTS professional development on teacher instruction and student achievement: Year 1 report*. (Unpublished report). Washington, DC: American Institutes for Research.

Cordray, D. S., & Jacobs, N. (2005). *Treatment fidelity and core components in school-based ATOD prevention programs*. Paper presented at the annual meeting of the Society for Prevention Research, Washington, DC.

Cordray, D. S., & Pion, G. M. (2006). Treatment strength and integrity: Models and methods. In R. R. Bootzin & P. E. McKnight (Eds.), *Strengthening research methodology: Psychological measurement and evaluation* (pp. 103–124). Washington, DC: American Psychological Association.

Epley, N., & Dunning, D. (2006). The Mixed Blessings of Self Knowledge in Behavioral Prediction: Enhanced Discrimination but Exacerbated Bias. *Personality and Social Psychology Bulletin, 32*(5), 641–655.

Hulleman, C., & Cordray, D. (2009). Moving from the lab to the field: The role of fidelity and achieved relative intervention strength. *Journal of Research on Educational Effectiveness, 2*, 88–110.

Martin, W., Strother, S., Weatherholt, T., & Dechaume, M. (2008). *eMINTS Program evaluation report: An investigation of program fidelity and its impact on teacher mastery and student achievement.* New York: Education Development Center, Center for Children and Technology.

Nelson, M. C., Cordray, D. S., Hulleman, C. S., Darrow, C. L., & Sommer, E. C. (2012). A procedure for assessing intervention fidelity in experiments testing educational and behavioral interventions. *The Journal of Behavioral Health Services & Research, 39*(4), 374–396.

Waltz, J., Addis, M. E., Koerner, K., & Jacobson, N. S. (1993). Testing the integrity of a psychotherapy protocol: Assessment of adherence and competence. *Journal of Consulting and Clinical Psychology, 61,* 620–630.

7

SUCCESS FOR ALL DESIGN AND IMPLEMENTATION OF WHOLE SCHOOL REFORM AT SCALE[1]

Robert E. Slavin and Nancy A. Madden

Despite the constant public outcry about the crisis in American education, every community has one or more outstanding and often widely recognized public schools. Some of these appear to succeed because they serve children of wealthy, well-educated parents, or because they can screen out unmotivated or low achieving students. However, there are also schools that serve disadvantaged and minority children in inner city or rural locations and, year after year, produce outstanding achievement outcomes. Such schools play a crucial role in reminding us that the problems of our school system have little to do with the capabilities of children; they provide our best evidence that all children can learn. Yet the success of these lighthouse schools does not spread very far. Excellence can be demonstrated in individual schools but rarely in whole districts or communities. An outstanding elementary school benefits about 500 children, on average. Yet there are millions of children who are placed at risk by ineffective responses to such factors as economic disadvantage, limited English proficiency, or learning difficulties. How can we make excellence the norm rather than the exception, especially in schools serving many at-risk children? How can effective practices based on research and on the experiences of outstanding schools be effectively implemented every day by hundreds of thousands of teachers? How can we monitor the quality of implementation of effective practices in large numbers of schools that are widely dispersed?

Success for All was designed in an attempt to answer these questions. Born in one Baltimore school in 1987, Success for All is used (as of fall 2013) in about 1,000 schools in 40 states, plus schools in Britain and Canada. More than two million children have attended Success for All schools. These schools are highly diverse. They are in most of the largest urban districts, but also hundreds of rural districts, inner suburban districts, and Indian reservations. Most are Title I schoolwide projects with many children qualifying for free lunches. Success for All is by far the largest research-based, whole-school reform model ever to exist. It is the first model to demonstrate that techniques shown to be effective in rigorous research can be replicated on a substantial scale with fidelity and continued effectiveness.

The purpose of this chapter is to describe Success for All, its rationale and research base, and to describe the process used to focus on and continuously improve the quality of implementation at each individual school.

What Is Success for All?

Most children enter kindergarten with enthusiasm, intelligence, creativity, and an expectation that they will succeed. The first goal of school reform should be to ensure that every child, regardless of home background, home language, or learning style, achieves the success that he or she so confidently expected in kindergarten, that all children maintain their motivation, enthusiasm, and optimism because they are objectively succeeding at the school's tasks. Any reform that does less than this is hollow and self-defeating.

What does it mean to succeed in the elementary grades? The elementary school's definition of success, and therefore the parents' and children's definition as well, is overwhelmingly success in reading. Very few children who are reading adequately are retained, assigned to special education, or given long-term remedial services. Other subjects are important, of course, but reading and language arts form the core of what school success means in the early grades.

When children fail to read well in the early grades, they begin a downward progression. In first grade, some children begin to notice that they are not reading adequately. They may fail first grade or be assigned to long-term remediation. As they proceed through the elementary and middle grades, many students begin to see that they are failing at their most important task in life. When this happens, things begin to unravel. Failing students begin to have poor motivation and poor self-expectations, which lead to continued poor achievement, in a declining spiral that ultimately leads to despair, delinquency, and dropout (see Alexander, Entwisle, & Kabbani, 2001; Juel, 1988; Lesnick, George, Smithgall, & Gwynne, 2010).

Remediating learning deficits after they are already well established is extremely difficult. Children who have already failed to learn to read, for example, are now anxious about reading, and doubt their ability to learn it. Their motivation to read may be low. They may ultimately learn to read but it will always be a chore, not a pleasure. Clearly, the time to provide additional help to children who are at risk is early, when children are still motivated and confident and when any learning deficits are relatively small and remediable. The most important goal in educational programming for students at risk of school failure is to try to make certain that we do not squander the greatest resource we have: the enthusiasm and positive self-expectations of young children themselves.

In practical terms, what this perspective implies is that schools, and especially Title I, special education, and other services for at-risk children, must be shifted from an emphasis on remediation to an emphasis on prevention and early intervention (Barr & Parrett, 2001; Snow, Burns, & Griffin, 1998). Prevention means providing developmentally appropriate preschool and kindergarten programs so that students will enter first grade ready to succeed (Berrueta-Clement, Schweinhart, Barnett, Epstein, Weikart, 1984; Ramey & Ramey, 1992), and it means providing regular classroom teachers with effective instructional programs, curricula, and professional development to enable them to ensure that most students are successful the first time they are taught (Waxman, Padrón, & Arnold, 2001). Early intervention means that supplementary instructional services are provided early in students' schooling and that they are intensive enough to bring at-risk students quickly to a level at which they can profit from good-quality classroom instruction.

Success for All is built around the idea that every child can and must succeed in the early grades, no matter what this takes. The idea behind the program is to use everything we know about effective instruction for students at risk to direct all aspects of school and classroom organization toward the goal of preventing academic deficits from appearing in the first place; recognizing and intensively intervening with any deficits that do appear; and providing students with a rich and full curriculum to enable them to build on their firm foundation in basic skills. The commitment of Success for All is to do whatever it takes to see that every child becomes a skilled, strategic, and enthusiastic reader by the end of the elementary grades and beyond.

Usual practices in elementary schools do not support the principle of prevention and early intervention (Vaughn, Bos, & Schumm, 2007). Starting in first grade, a certain number of students begin to fall behind, and over the course of time these students are assigned to remedial programs (such as Title I) or to special education, or are simply retained.

Our society's tacit assumption is that those students who fall by the wayside are defective in some way. Perhaps they have learning disabilities, or low IQs, or poor motivation, or parents who are unsupportive of school learning, or other problems. Too many educators assume that since most students do succeed with standard instruction in the early grades, there must be something wrong with those who do not.

Success for All is built around a completely different set of assumptions. The most important assumption is that every child can learn. Some children need more help than others and may need different approaches than those needed by others, but one way or another virtually every child can become a successful reader.

The first requirement for the success of every child is *prevention*. This means providing excellent preschool and kindergarten programs, improving curriculum, instruction, and classroom management throughout the grades, assessing students frequently to make sure they are making adequate progress, and establishing cooperative relationships with parents so they can support students' learning at home.

Top-quality curriculum and instruction from age 4 on will ensure the success of most students, but not all of them. The next requirement for the success of all students is intensive early intervention. This means small group or, if necessary, one-to-one tutoring for primary-grade students having reading problems. It means being able to work with parents and social service agencies to be sure that all students attend school, have medical services or eyeglasses if they need them, have help with behavior problems, and so on.

The most important idea in Success for All is that the school must relentlessly stick with every child until that child is succeeding. If prevention is not enough the child may need tutoring. If this is not enough he or she may need help with behavior or attendance or eyeglasses. If this is not enough he or she may need a modified approach to reading or other subjects. The school does not merely provide services to children, it constantly assesses the results of the services it provides and keeps varying or adding services until every child is successful.

Overview of Success for All Components

Success for All is a schoolwide reform model, not just a classroom instructional program. It has somewhat different components at different sites, depending on the school's needs and resources available to implement the program. However, there is a common set of elements characteristic of all. These elements are summarized in Box 7.1, and then explained in more detail.

BOX 7.1 MAJOR ELEMENTS OF SUCCESS FOR ALL

Success for All is a schoolwide program for students in grades pre-K to eight which organizes resources to attempt to ensure that virtually every student will reach the third grade on time with adequate basic skills and build on this basis throughout the elementary grades, that no student will be allowed to "fall between the cracks." The main elements of the program are as follows:

A Schoolwide Curriculum

During reading periods, students are regrouped across age lines so that each reading class contains students all at one reading level. Use of tutors as reading teachers during reading time reduces the size of most reading

Preschool and Kindergarten

The comprehensive, theme-based, preschool and kindergarten programs in Success for All cover all domains of learning, with a particular focus on language and literacy.

(Continued)

(Continued)

classes to about 20. The reading program in grades K–1 emphasizes language and comprehension skills, phonics, sound blending, and use of shared stories that students read to one another in pairs. The shared stories combine teacher-read material with phonetically regular student material to teach decoding and comprehension in the context of meaningful, engaging stories. In grades 2–8, students use novels or basal readers, but not workbooks. This program emphasizes cooperative learning and partner reading activities, comprehension strategies such as summarization and clarification built around narrative and expository texts, writing, and direct instruction in reading comprehension skills. At all levels, students are required to read books of their own choice for 20 minutes at home each evening. Cooperative learning programs in writing/language arts are used in grades 1–6.

Tutors

In grades 1–3, specially trained certified teachers and paraprofessionals work one-to-one with any students who are failing to keep up with their classmates in reading. Tutorial instruction is closely coordinated with regular classroom instruction. It takes place 20 minutes daily during times other than reading periods.

Quarterly Assessments

Students in grades 1–8 are assessed every quarter to determine whether they are making adequate progress in reading. This information is used to suggest alternate teaching strategies in the regular classroom, changes in reading group placement, provision of tutoring services, or other means of meeting students' needs.

Solutions Team

A Solutions Team works in each school to help support families in ensuring the success of their children, focusing on parent education, parent involvement, attendance, and student behavior. This team is composed of existing or additional staff such as parent liaisons, social workers, counselors, and vice principals.

Facilitator

A program facilitator works with teachers to help them implement the reading program, manages the quarterly assessments, assists the Solutions Team, makes sure that all staff are communicating with each other, and helps the staff as a whole make certain that every child is making adequate progress.

Reading Program

Success for All uses a reading curriculum based on research and effective practices in beginning reading (e.g., Adams, 1990), and an appropriate use of cooperative learning (Slavin, 1995, 2013).

Reading teachers at every grade level begin the reading time by reading children's literature to students and engaging them in a discussion of the story to enhance their understanding of the story, listening and speaking vocabulary, and knowledge of story structure. In kindergarten and first grade, the program emphasizes development of basic language skills with the use of Story Telling and Retelling (STaR), which involves the students in listening to, retelling, and dramatizing children's literature. Big books as well as oral and written composing activities allow students to develop concepts of print as they also develop knowledge of story structure. Specific oral language experiences are used to further develop receptive and expressive language.

Reading Roots (Madden, Goins, & Hybl, 2003) is introduced in the second semester of kindergarten. This K-1 beginning reading program uses as its base a series of phonetically regular but meaningful and interesting minibooks and emphasizes repeated oral reading to partners as well as to the teacher. The minibooks begin with a set of "shared stories," in which part of a story is written in small type (read by the teacher) and part is written in large type (read by the students). The student portion uses a phonetically controlled vocabulary. Taken together, the teacher and student portions create interesting, worthwhile stories. Over time, the teacher portion diminishes and the student portion lengthens, until students are reading the entire book. This scaffolding allows students to read interesting literature when they only know a few letter sounds.

Letters and letter sounds are introduced in an active, engaging set of activities that begins with oral language and moves into written symbols. Individual sounds are integrated into a context of words, sentences, and stories. Instruction is provided in story structure, specific comprehension skills, metacognitive strategies for self-assessment and self-correction, and integration of reading and writing.

Spanish bilingual programs use an adaptation of Reading Roots called Lee Conmigo ("Read With Me"). Lee Conmigo uses the same instructional strategies as Reading Roots, but is built around shared stories written in Spanish; they then transition to English in about second grade, depending on local policies.

When students reach the second grade reading level, they use a program called Reading Wings (Madden et al., 2009), an adaptation of Cooperative Integrated Reading and Composition (CIRC) (Stevens, Madden, Slavin, & Farnish, 1987). Reading Wings uses cooperative learning activities built around story structure, prediction, summarization, vocabulary building, decoding practice, and story-related writing. Students engage in partner reading and structured discussion of stories or novels, and work toward mastery of the vocabulary and content of the story in teams. Story-related writing is also shared within teams. Cooperative learning both increases students' motivation and engages students in cognitive activities known to contribute to reading comprehension, such as elaboration, summarization, and rephrasing. Research on CIRC has found it to significantly increase students' reading comprehension and language skills (Stevens et al., 1987).

In addition to these story-related activities, teachers provide direct instruction in reading comprehension skills, such as clarification, graphic organizers, and summarization (Pressley & Woloshyn, 1995) and students practice these skills in their teams. Classroom libraries of trade books at students' reading levels are provided for each teacher, and students read books of their choice for homework for 20 minutes each night. Home readings are shared twice a week during "book club" sessions.

Materials to support Reading Wings through the eighth grade level (and beyond) are built around children's literature and around the most widely used basal series and anthologies. Supportive materials have been developed for more than 100 novels for children and for most current basal series (e.g., Houghton Mifflin, Scott Foresman, Harcourt, Macmillan, Open Court).

Beginning in the second semester of program implementation, Success for All schools usually implement a writing/language arts program based primarily on cooperative learning principles (see Madden, Slavin, Logan, & Cheung, 2011).

Video for Students

Success for All uses a great deal of video content to enliven lessons at all grade levels, to strengthen key skills, and to model effective cooperative learning skills, metacognitive strategies, social-emotional skills, and other desired behaviors. Videos are always brief, usually 30 seconds to 2 minutes, and are shown on interactive whiteboards or projected from computers or tablets. Evaluations of the use of these "embedded multimedia" strategies in first grade found that they significantly enhanced program outcomes (Chambers, Cheung, Madden, Slavin, & Gifford, 2006; Chambers et al., 2008).

Animated Alphabet

A series of humorous cartoons introduces letter sounds and key words linked by a story. For example, the sound /b/ is represented by "bat" and "ball," and the story shows a boy repeatedly hitting a ball against a wall, each time producing the 'b' sound, until the ball flies into a bird's nest. The Animated Alphabet is used in kindergarten and first grade.

The Sound and the Furry

A series of puppet skits introduces sound blending strategies. For example, a furry monster sees a sign that says, "Watch out for stick." He carefully sounds out "stick," and then finds out that there is glue on the stick, so when he picks it up, he's in big trouble. The Sound and the Furry is used in grades K–1.

Word Plays

In grades K–1, children read decodable stories. The Word Plays are live action skits that introduce the vocabulary in the stories.

Backgrounders

In grades 2–8, students usually read novels or factual books to build comprehension, vocabulary, and fluency. To facilitate their motivation and background knowledge, we have recently introduced "backgrounders" for each book. A backgrounder may be a brief video giving the historical or scientific background for a story. For example, if children are about to read a story set in the Great Depression, they might first see a backgrounder on that time period. Others show appealing characters who set a purpose for reading and give enticing clues about what the students will read. For example, one character, Shirleylock Holmes, introduces anything with a mystery theme. Lurleen LaVoyage introduces books involving travel or far-away places, and other characters equally engage students with books, much as movie trailers motivate people to see movies. Backgrounders exist for each of 132 books used in grades 2–5, plus many books in middle school.

Strategy Videos

Numerous videos model for children specific learning strategies. These include cooperative learning, clarification, prediction, summarization and graphic organizers. One series of videos involves a writing team, "The Write-On Dudes," learning to use a writing process approach and then apply it to many writing genres. This series also includes animations modeling grammar and punctuation.

Regrouping

Students in grades 1 and up are regrouped for reading. The students are assigned to heterogeneous, age-grouped classes most of the day, but during a regular 90-minute reading period they are regrouped by reading performance levels into reading classes of students all at the same level. For example, a reading class taught at the 2–1 level might contain first-, second-, and third-grade students all reading at the same level. The reading classes are smaller than homerooms because tutors and other certificated staff (such as librarians or art teachers) teach reading during this common reading period.

Regrouping allows teachers to teach the whole reading class without having to break the class into reading groups. This greatly reduces the time spent in seatwork and increases direct instruction time, eliminating workbooks or other follow-up activities which are needed in classes that have multiple reading groups. The regrouping is a form of the Joplin Plan, which has been found to increase reading achievement in the elementary grades (Slavin, 1987).

Goal Setting and Progress Monitoring

At the beginning of the school year and at the end of each quarter, school staff members come together to review progress and set goals. Formative assessments on text comprehension, vocabulary development, phonics and word reading skills, writing, and fluency are collected during lesson activities and reviewed in conjunction with formal assessments of reading progress administered quarterly. The formal assessments are aligned with Common Core State Standards or other state objectives. The results of the assessments are used to determine who is to receive tutoring, to change students' reading group assignments, to suggest other adaptations in students' programs, and to identify students who need other types of assistance, such as family interventions or screening for vision and hearing problems. In addition, teacher teams review implementation progress and set specific targets to improve implementation of elements of the program that will help accelerate student academic progress (Success for All Foundation, 2012).

A major addition to Success for All's whole-school, data-driven approach is Member Center, a computerized data management system. Teachers, facilitators, and other staff enter student assessment data into Member Center, which then suggests placements in reading groups, forms cooperative teams, and identifies individual children who are in need of attention. Data on attendance is also monitored, and data on students receiving additional services (such as tutoring or family support) are kept in an integrated file, so all staff involved can easily see data from others involved with the same child. Data from Member Center forms a key focus of conversations within schools and between school staff and Success for All (SFA) coaches.

Reading Tutors

Tutors are used in Success for All to promote students' success in reading. Most tutors are paraprofessionals, but teachers may work with students experiencing the greatest difficulties. Tutors work in small groups (up to six) or one-on-one with students who are having difficulties keeping up with their reading groups. Specially designed computer software helps tutors assess student progress and provide exactly the right content to each child. The tutoring occurs in 20-minute sessions during times other than reading or math periods.

In general, tutors support students' success in the regular reading curriculum, rather than teaching different objectives. For example, the tutor generally works with a student on the same story and concepts being read and taught in the regular reading class. However, tutors seek to identify learning problems and use different strategies to teach the same skills. Schools may have several tutors depending on school size, need for tutoring, and other factors. Reading teachers and tutors use brief computerized forms to communicate about students' specific problems and needs and meet at regular times to coordinate their approaches with individual children.

Initial decisions about reading group placement and the need for tutoring are based on informal reading inventories that the tutors give to each child. Subsequent reading group placements and tutoring assignments are made based on curriculum-based assessments given every quarter, which include teacher judgments as well as more formal assessments. First-graders receive priority for tutoring, on the assumption that the primary function of the tutors is to help all students be successful in reading the first time, before they fail and become remedial readers.

Preschool and Kindergarten

Most Success for All schools provide a half-day preschool and/or a full-day kindergarten for eligible students. The preschool and kindergarten programs focus on providing a balanced and developmentally appropriate learning experience for young children. The curriculum emphasizes the development and use of language. It provides a balance of academic readiness and non-academic music, art, and movement activities in a series of thematic units. Readiness activities include use of language development activities and Story Telling and Retelling (STaR), in which students retell stories read by the teachers. Reading instruction begins during the second semester of kindergarten.

Recently, we have introduced "Home Links" in preschool and kindergarten. These consist of video content from Sesame Street and other sources that follow up the themes, skills, and concepts introduced each day. A narrated story is included in each "Home Links" program. Parents usually watch with the children and learn what the children are doing in school, so they can support their learning at home.

Schoolwide Solutions Teams

Many elements beyond the classroom affect children's success in school. To insure success, the school must attend to such factors as attendance, readiness to learn, and parent and community involvement. Strategies for improvement in each of these areas are incorporated into Success for All through the development of five teams of school staff members called Schoolwide Solutions teams that focus on attendance, parent involvement, intervention for struggling students, development of a positive school culture, and community involvement (Success for All Foundation, 2013).

Parents are an essential part of the formula for success in Success for All. The Parent Involvement team works to make families feel comfortable in the school and become active supporters of their child's education as well as providing specific services. The Parent Involvement team consists of the Title I parent liaison, vice-principal (if any), counselor (if any), and any other appropriate staff already present in the school. The team works towards building good relations with parents and increasing their involvement in the school, conducting "welcome" visits for new families, and organizing parenting skills workshops. Most schools use a program called "Raising Readers" in which parents are given strategies to use in reading with their own children. The Parent Involvement team also encourages and trains parents and other community members to fulfill numerous volunteer roles within the school, ranging from providing a listening ear for emerging readers to helping in the school cafeteria.

The Cooperative Culture team focuses on developing a positive school culture and helps introduce a social skills development program called "Getting Along Together," which gives students peaceful strategies for resolving interpersonal conflicts and helps children with issues such as managing frustration, active listening, dealing with shyness, and cooperating with others. Books and video help reinforce the Getting Along Together skills.

The Intervention team helps teachers and parents solve challenging problems of student learning or behavior that require strategies beyond the classroom. The Intervention team is strongly integrated into the academic program of the school. It receives referrals from teachers and tutors regarding children who are not making adequate academic progress, and thereby constitutes an additional stage of intervention for students in need above and beyond that provided by the classroom teacher or tutor. Staff are called upon to provide assistance when students seem to be working at less than their full potential because of problems at home. Families of students who are not receiving adequate sleep or nutrition, need glasses, are not attending school regularly, or are exhibiting serious behavior problems, may receive assistance. The team pulls together a child's teacher, parent, and counseling resources to build a joint solution that all will support.

The Attendance team is responsible for insuring that students are in school on time, so that they can participate in instruction. A variety of strategies are defined, starting with a system for tracking attendance efficiently. Team members may contact parents whose children are frequently absent to see what resources can be provided to assist the family in getting their child to school.

Program Facilitator

A program facilitator works at each school to oversee (with the principal) the operation of the Success for All model. This position typically comes from the school's existing Title I budget. The facilitator helps plan the Success for All program, helps the principal with scheduling, and visits classes and tutoring sessions frequently to help teachers and tutors with individual problems. He or she works directly with the teachers on implementation of the curriculum, classroom management, and other issues, helps teachers and tutors deal with any behavior problems or other special problems, and coordinates the activities of the Solutions Team with those of the instructional staff. Facilitators use a coaching model called Goal Focused Implementation Support, which focuses on the measurable outcomes of teachers' instruction, such as performance on frequent assessments, student engagement in lessons, and effective uses of cooperative learning (see Success for All Foundation, 2013).

Professional Development

Professional development for all school staff is extensive. Teachers and school leaders receive detailed guides supplemented by introductory workshops at the beginning of the school year. Classroom observations, discussion, and data reviews provide a basis for coaching that is provided throughout the year. This includes an overall introduction for all staff to the goals and schoolwide elements of SFA, followed by breakout sessions on the program elements individual staff members will be responsible for: Curiosity Corner (pre-K), KinderCorner, Reading Roots (beginning reading), Reading Wings (upper elementary and middle school), tutoring, and Solutions Team. All trainings make extensive use of simulations, video modeling, and opportunities for participant engagement.

Teachers meet together during the course of the year in "component teams" to support each other in developing their expertise in implementation. A wide range of tutorials and media-based resources, many provided online, offer "just-in-time" support to assist teachers in addressing their school-specific goals and issues in implementation. Throughout the year, facilitators help guide the component teams and Success for All coaches provide brief presentations on such topics as classroom management, instructional pace, and cooperative learning. The staff development model used in Success for All emphasizes relatively brief initial training with extensive classroom follow-up, coaching, and group discussion.

Special Education

Every effort is made to deal with students' learning problems within the context of the regular classroom, as supplemented by tutors and the Solutions Team. Tutors evaluate students' strengths and weaknesses and develop strategies to teach in the most effective way. In some schools, special education teachers work as tutors and reading teachers with students identified as learning disabled as well as other students experiencing learning problems who are at risk for special education placement. One major goal of Success for All is to keep students with learning problems out of special education if at all possible, and to serve any students who do qualify for special education in a way that does not disrupt their regular classroom experience (see Slavin, 1996).

Model Program Implementation

The components of Success for All need to be implemented with care, precision, and appropriate adaptions to the needs and resources of individual schools, teachers, and children. They need to be coordinated with each other so that strengths are maximized, problems are prevented, and the whole school works as an efficient system to ensure that all children achieve their full potential. The school should be able to learn from and use the crystalized experiences of Success for

All schools that have come before it while using distributed leadership teams within the school to interpret the manuals, materials, software, and professional development provided by Success for All to meet the particular needs of this particular school. The school staff needs to become a cohesive learning organization, in which all members of the staff feel empowered and capable of contributing ideas to overall plans and then carrying out designated parts of the plan with energy and intelligence.

Roles of Success for All Foundation Coaches and School Leadership

The interplay between Success for All coaches and the building principal and facilitator is core to the program's success. When schools first adopt SFA, their principal and facilitator participate in a week-long New Leaders Conference, usually the summer before starting implementation. New principals and facilitators taking roles in existing SFA schools also participate in these intensive introductions to all aspects of SFA.

During the New Leaders Conference and during the on-site training for staff, SFA coaches begin to form relationships with the principal and facilitator. The SFA coach visits new schools about once a month, but is in email or telephone contact much more frequently.

The goal of the SFA coach is to transfer responsibility for quality implementation from SFA to the building principal and facilitator and then to distributed leadership teams. Initially, SFA coaches visit teachers' classes and give teachers individual and group feedback to model these processes for the building facilitator. As time goes on this continues, but the emphasis moves to using school visits to empower the staff and leadership to solve its own problems. SFA coaches and central office staff (such as Help Desk) remain involved indefinitely, but gradually reduce time in the school.

Goal-Focused Leadership

From the outset, Success for All helps schools embrace a focus on setting and achieving goals at all levels, from individual students to classes to the school as a whole. These goals are specific (e.g., improve the percentage of students reading at grade level from 63 percent to 70 percent by March) and they establish strategies, timelines, responsibilities, and resources. Short-term goals are established as steps toward achieving agreed-upon annual goals, such as achieving AYP. Progress toward goals is closely monitored, usually using Member Center to track progress. Principals, facilitators, and distributed teacher leaders are asked to focus their energies on whatever advances the school toward its key goals.

As school staffs set long-term goals and mileposts along the way, they create and modify plans and reallocate resources to ensure that key goals are being met.

Regular data reviews focus on thoughtful reflection on a range of data indicating progress or barriers, with a conscious limitation of focus on no more data than the school can meaningfully interpret and use in its intervention planning. These data answer questions about which children are succeeding and which are not, what skills or dispositions they may be lacking, why they may be struggling, and how the school can address the root causes of the children's difficulties. Part of this discussion involves data from "snapshots" on the completeness of implementation of research-proven program elements, one indicator of the degree to which the school is building capability to meet its agreed-upon goals.

Data Exchange and Feedback

Throughout the goal-focused leadership process, data are regularly exchanged among facilitators, principals, and staff within each school and between the school staff and SFA staff. SFA coaches provide feedback to school staff, drawing on their experiences in many other SFA schools struggling with similar issues, and principals, facilitators, and teachers within the school provide supportive feedback to each other and exchange ideas about how to use the tools and measures provided by SFA to advance on the desired outcomes.

Progressive Improvement

No low-achieving school turns itself around in a month. All need to set long-term goals that express high aspirations for all children, but then to break these down into steps, so that progress can be celebrated before the final goal is achieved. However, setting progress goals short of the ultimate goal cannot become an excuse for low expectations ("at least we're doing better than we used to"). Instead, short-term goals are carefully watched, and if the school plateaus at a level that indicates progress but not enough to get to its full aspirations for its children, this is an indication of a problem to be solved.

The Success for All approach to building implementation quality has three stages—preparation, startup, and continuous improvement. First, we insure that the school is ready for implementation—that they as a community want to implement a set of strategies that will improve the achievement of their students, and that Success for All is the model they wish to select. An "awareness" process that involves review of research findings and visits to Success for All schools, a presentation to the school, and a vote by school staff forms the first stage of the implementation.

The second stage is immersion in professional development, written materials, technology supports, and video models to guide teachers and school leaders in beginning implementation. Feedback from implementation fidelity studies and discussions with teachers indicated that more detailed instructional guidance and descriptions of effective practices leads to higher quality implementation. To respond to this information, we have refined our teacher's guides and school leadership guides, added video for students to classroom presentations to demonstrate to them the cooperative learning process, and added video and discussion guides for teachers to use collaboratively to refine implementation fidelity. The integration of professional development and detailed written and video guidance has proven very powerful in getting schools off to a strong start in implementing research-proven practices with high fidelity.

The third stage is the ongoing process of continuous improvement and maintenance of implementation fidelity that continues as long as Success for All is in use in a school. This is the stage at which ongoing measures of both student achievement and implementation fidelity are critical. Ultimately, the progress of a school toward meeting its goals is determined by its outcomes for children on measures of reading achievement. Success for All tracks and reports student progress in reading at the school level quarterly using a tool called the Grade Summary Form. This form summarizes the number of students in each grade reading below, at, or above the expected level for the grade (see Figure 7.1). It provides a transparent view of reading success for all members of the school community, against which goals are set and instructional performance is measured, which in turn creates a sense of urgency and focus. The presence of an accurate Grade Summary Form is one of the foundational measures of implementation of Success for All. Initially, the Grade Summary Form was assembled by hand by the school's facilitator from paper records provided by teachers. The online data management tool now available to Success for All schools makes the process easier by summarizing data on student progress across reading groups and homeroom groups, and allowing easy entry of mastery levels. The Grade Summary Form is then created automatically as an interactive document as well as a printable form. It provides a drilldown feature that allows for review of groups of students, and a progress report on each individual student over time.

Assessment of fidelity of other aspects of program implementation has proved more difficult to measure. The history of our efforts and our current approach to describing implementation are described in the next section.

Measuring Implementation Fidelity

During our 26 years of implementing Success for All, we have utilized a variety of strategies to measure implementation quality for two purposes. First, we need to provide our school leaders and teachers with feedback that will guide them toward continuous improvement in the quality of implementation. If school staff members do not have a metric for how they are doing, they will not have the information they need to improve. Our second purpose has been to use the information to guide our own continuous improvement. We have wanted to know whether the research-proven strategies that our model is based on are being implemented, and to improve the model and thereby increase impact on

K–8 Grade Summary Form English/Mastery Level* | Four Assessments

School Name: Sally Francis Academy School Year 2011/2012

Assessment					
Date Assessment Began	Baseline	02-Sep	01 Nov	15-Jan	30-Mar	10-Jun
Instructional Day Number**	Baseline	3	45	87	127	175
Grading Period	Baseline	1st	1st	2nd	2nd	3rd	3rd	4th	4th

Main grid (mastery-level columns):

G	GP	MND	K1	K2	K3	RR 1-5	RR 6-10	RR 11-15	RR 16-20	RR 21-25	RR 26-31	RR 32-37	RR 38-42	RR 43-48 (RE 1)	RW 2-1	RW 2-2	RW 3-1 (RE 2-3)	RW 3-2	RW 4-1 (RE 4)	RW 4-2	RW 5-1 (RE 5)	RW 5-2	6+	T	%GL
K	1	26	32																					58	55%
K	2	9	9	39																				57	68%
K	3	1	5	9	48																			63	76%
K	4			7	56																			63	89%
1	B		3	5		9	3	17	13	10	3													56	59%
1	1		8	3		3	9	11	12	4	9	15	6	8										61	45%
1	2		1	3		1	3	4	2	12	7	6	13	27										59	59%
1	3			1		1	2	2	1	4	3	10	10	27										59	68%
1	4							1	1				10	39	10									59	83%
2	B						1	3	1	3	9	3	11	34	8									73	58%
2	1							1	1	4	3	4	6	23	20	9								71	73%
2	2							1	1		2	3	2	13	28	11	24							70	75%
2	3							2		1		3	1	10	17	24	12	12						71	75%
2	4											1	1	2	11	33	10	12						71	77%
3	B								1	1	4	2	3	3	11	28	20	6						59	64%
3	1									2	2	1	1	1	12	20	17	6	8					61	70%
3	2													1	4	12	18	13	13					61	72%
3	3													1	3	14	21	13	15	11				64	73%
3	4					1									10	6	22	22	15	11				64	75%
4	B		3									1	1		5	10	7	25	12	1				62	52%
4	1												1	1	1	4	9	8	22	14	2			60	61%
4	2														1	11	10	20	13	1			56	63%
4	3											1				2	4	23	22	2			53	79%
4	4																	8	24	15			61	89%
5	B												1	1	3	2	7	24	25	8			61	64%
5	1									1		2	2	4	10	19						61	72%
5	2												3	4	22	22	23				60	75%
5	3													2	3	7	24	24			60	80%
5	4															8	24	35	3		59	86%

Elementary Summary

GP	Total Students	Total Students at or Above Grade Level	Total Percentage at or Above Grade Level
B	311	184	59%
1	311	202	64%
2	312	215	69%
3	310	232	75%
4	306	250	82%

Kindergarten students are excluded from the above summary.

G = Grade   GP = Grading Period   MND = Mastery Not Determined   T = Total Number of Students   %GL = Percentage of Students at Grade Level

* Mastery level: Level at which students can read independently. See facilitator guide or online resources for more information about using mastery to determine placement levels.

** Counting from the first day of school, calculate how many completed school days have occurred.

© 2013 Success for All Foundation

(SfAF)

FIGURE 7.1 Grade summary form

© 2013 Success for All Foundation.

student achievement. The tools needed to achieve both purposes are the same, though the use of the information is different.

Measuring implementation of a comprehensive schoolwide program is challenging. The process requires compromises between thoroughness and cost in time as well as dollars. Our initial effort focused on assessing classroom instructional processes as the critical tip of the iceberg that would indicate adequate implementation. To maximize efficiency we identified a set of readily observable artifacts that would be evident in classrooms that were implementing Success for All instructional processes but not in those maintaining traditional instructional patterns. We developed brief checklists for classrooms that noted whether the classroom was organized for cooperative learning, whether schedules and resources for lesson components such as active instruction and teamwork were posted, whether signals for team discussion and class attention were in use, and so on.

This method was an adequate first step. Observations were able to be completed quickly in the course of classroom visits that were already part of the routine for Success for All coaches. Reliability of the metrics was high. However, this method focused schools on fairly superficial indicators of implementation. We found schools working hard to put these specific indicators in place, but not necessarily implementing the intended instructional processes with high quality. It is possible to set up a classroom to facilitate cooperative learning, but to still not utilize effective forms of cooperative learning. In addition, we had not included some schoolwide elements of implementation such as implementation of tutoring or increasing attendance and parent involvement, and schools began to assume that these areas were of less importance.

Our second attempt was more comprehensive, and included collection of evidence about schoolwide structures. We attempted to include indicators of level of quality of implementation of both classroom instructional processes and schoolwide structures. A revised reporting tool was developed that allowed coaches to note quality in terms of mechanical, routine, and refined implementation. This approach provided better information about the depth of implementation. Coaches felt that their reports better discriminated between high and low implementers. Three weaknesses to this approach became evident, however. Of greatest importance was that reliability of ratings between coaches was less strong than on the simpler checklist. In addition, coaches were less comfortable sharing their rating with school staff members, because they were not sure how to explain them with confidence. Finally, coaches felt that accurate reporting took more time than they had.

Up to this point, we had been depending solely on direct observations by Success for All staff. We decided to involve school staff members in the process of assessing implementation quality for two reasons. First, greater transparency about the goals of implementation quality assessment would improve school partners' knowledge of the program. Second, school staff members have more time for observation of all aspects of implementation and should be able to report with greater knowledge of actual day-to-day practice.

This approach led to the tool currently used to monitor implementation quality that we call the Snapshot.

Snapshot

The Snapshot is designed to be an overview document for school leaders and Success for All coaches to describe the status of implementation in their building. SFA coaches work with building facilitators to fill out Snapshots during their visits. Ratings are the product of observations, discussions among school staff and the SFA coach, informal interviews with students, and review of "artifacts" of implementation such as data recorded during lessons and assessments completed by students. The ratings are not completely "independent." Ultimately, however, completing the Snapshot is the responsibility of the coach, who must complete an official report that is submitted to their supervisor, and be able to support the ratings with evidence. Between visits, school facilitators use items from the Snapshot to monitor implementation throughout the quarter.

The Snapshot consists of four parts.

- The Status section summarizes the basic data on achievement, attendance, tardiness, and discipline for each quarter and provides the history from previous years.
- The Schoolwide Structures section summarizes presence of fundamental structures such as regrouping for reading instruction, a facilitator, the leadership team, quarterly assessments for reading, attendance strategies, parent involvement strategies, an intervention team, tutoring, and regular teacher team meetings to support implementation. Schoolwide Structures are rated every quarter as in place or not in place. Items rated in Schoolwide Structures include:
  - An accurate Grade Summary Form is maintained for every grading period.
  - Attendance plans are complete and effectively implemented. At least 95 percent of children are in school on time every day.
  - Cross-grade regrouping is used each grading period in all grades except pre-K and kindergarten.
  - Capacity exists to tutor 30 percent of first-grade students, 20 percent of second-grade students, and 10 percent of third-grade students.
  - Success Network meetings are held at the start of school and quarterly to review schoolwide progress toward achievement goals and Leading for Success team reports.
- *Instructional Processes:* This section of the Snapshot provides an overview of implementation quality for key instructional elements and indicates what proportion of teachers in each component (e.g., KinderCorner, Reading Roots, Reading Wings) are implementing these instructional elements with high quality. Verification can be done by observation or artifacts such as team

scoresheets, facilitator observation records, videos, audio recordings, transcripts of instruction, or records of student responses. Both SFA coaches and school personnel are involved in verification. Items selected by school staff and coaches are rated each quarter and all items are rated once or twice each year. Sample items are shown below.

- o   Teachers facilitate partner and team discussion (and student interaction in labs) by circulating, questioning, redirecting, and challenging students to increase the depth of discussion and ensure individual progress.
- o   Following Team Talk or other team study discussion, teachers conduct a class discussion in which students are randomly selected to report for their teams; rubrics are used to evaluate responses, and team points are awarded.
- o   Teachers calculate team scores that include academic achievement points in every instructional cycle and celebrate team success in every cycle.
- o   Teachers use team scores to help students set goals for improvement, and students receive points for meeting goals.

- •   *Student Engagement:* This section looks at the quality of implementation from a student perspective. In a program like SFA that stresses cooperative learning as the vehicle for instruction, high-level student engagement is essential for program results. This section describes students' demonstration of critical behaviors that indicate high levels of engagement in cooperative learning. Again, ratings are done by the proportion of classrooms in each component that are showing strong levels of student engagement in those areas. Items selected by school staff and coaches are rated each quarter and all items are rated once or twice each year. Sample items rated are shown below.

- o   Student talk equals or exceeds teacher talk. (Each student should be engaged in partner/team discussion as a speaker or active listener during half of class time.)
- o   Teams are engaged in highly challenging discussions, in which students explain and offer evidence from the text to support their answers.
- o   Students value team scores and work daily to ensure that team members are prepared to successfully report for the team during Random Reporter and to succeed on tests.
- o   Students use win–win decision-making skills to solve problems that arise through the use of the Peace Path, conflict stoppers, and Think It Through sheets.

Snapshot Guidelines

After the first year of piloting, it became clear that not only did coaches have a different understanding of the expectations for rating a Snapshot item as being in place in the school or in an individual classroom, but that greater specificity was needed to make the intent of each item clear to school staff members who needed to understand the Snapshot better to guide their improvement. In order to create a set of expectations that could be rated reliably by school partners and SFA coaching staff members, specific indicators were identified for each item on the Snapshot. A few examples of the specifications for items are shown below.

- An accurate Grade Summary Form is maintained for every grading period.

    o The Grade Summary Form is completed within two weeks of the end of the grading period and is made available to the SFA coach.
    o Every student's reading performance is reviewed by the teacher, the facilitator, and other colleagues or school leaders when appropriate and possible.
    o Mastery is determined for every student based on formal and informal measures.
    o Procedures are in place to apply mastery determination consistently and to verify the accuracy of mastery-level entry into the Member Center. If the school does not use the Member Center, calculations are checked and verified.

- Teams are engaged in highly challenging discussions, in which students explain and offer evidence from the text to support their answers, or, for writing, students offer thoughtful responses during the revision process.

    o All students are engaged in highly challenging discussions with team-mates most of the time.
    o Students challenge one another to explain their thinking.
    o Students require one another to provide evidence from the text.
    o Students extend discussion with questions and offer thoughtful responses to one another.
    o With minimal teacher prompting, students successfully use discussion to extend their comprehension or to revise their writing.

With the clarity provided by these indicators, understanding of expectations is high and agreement on ratings across coaches and between school staff members and coaches is high.

Success of the Snapshot

The Snapshot has been in use for about 5 years in Success for All schools. It has been well received by school partners as well as staff, as it provides a clear path to continuing growth in quality of implementation. Both the specificity and the transparency have deepened discussions about how to get to the levels of implementation where success for students is sustained at high levels. The availability of this kind of information is not without its dangers. In districts with a group of schools implementing Success for All, it is tempting to make comparisons across schools rather than to look at growth within a school, as is intended. However, the tool has been highly effective in providing information that has enabled our schools and coaches to work collaboratively to improve implementation and with it, their students' achievement. While the Snapshot is not a simple document, we have found that when it is presented as a basic tool at the beginning of implementation and when its use is supported by professional development workshops and ongoing coaching in schools, it meets the needs it was developed to address.

Continuous Improvement of the Snapshot

The Snapshot has not been a static document over its first 5 years. As feedback from schools and coaches has been received, and as data have been summarized and reviewed, updates to increase clarity of items and to correct indicators have been made to the guidelines. A few additional items have been added as coaches realized some expectations were not clearly expressed. Each change has been designed to improve the quality of communication around the quality of implementation.

Conclusion

None of the elements of Success for All is completely new or unique. All are based on well-established principles of learning and rigorous instructional research. What is most distinctive is that in Success for All, school staffs commit to a schoolwide, coordinated, and proactive plan for putting proven practices into action every day to create concrete success for all children. Every child can complete elementary school a confident, strategic, and joyful learner and can maintain the enthusiasm and positive self-expectations they had when they came to school. The purpose of Success for All is to introduce and maintain high-fidelity implementations of proven approaches to see that this vision can become a practical reality in every school.

Note

1. Portions of this chapter are adapted from Slavin, R. E., Madden, N. A., Chambers, B., & Haxby, B. (2009). *Two million children: Success for All*. Thousand Oaks, CA: Corwin.

References

Adams, M. J. (1990). *Beginning to read: Thinking and learning about print*. Cambridge, MA: MIT Press.

Alexander, K., Entwisle, D., & Kabbani, N. (2001). The dropout process in life course perspective: Early risk factors at home and school. *Teachers College Record, 103*, 760–822.

Barr, R. D., & Parrett, W. H. (2001). *Hope fulfilled for at-risk and violent youth: K-12 programs that work* (2nd ed.). Boston: Allyn & Bacon.

Berrueta-Clement, J. R., Schweinhart, L. J., Barnett, W. S., Epstein, A. S., & Weikart, D. P. (1984). *Changed Lives.* Ypsilanti, MI: High/Scope.

Chambers, B., Cheung, A., Madden, N., Slavin, R. E., & Gifford, R. (2006). Achievement effects of embedded multimedia in a Success for All reading program. *Journal of Educational Psychology, 98*(1), 232–237.

Chambers, B., Slavin, R. E., Madden, N. A., Abrami, P. C., Tucker, B., J., Cheung, A., & Gifford, R. (2008). Technology infusion in Success for All: Reading outcomes for first graders. *Elementary School Journal, 109*(1), 1–15.

Juel, C. (1988). Learning to read and write: A longitudinal study of 54 children from first through fourth grades. *Journal of Educational Psychology, 80*, 437–447.

Lesnick, J., Goerge, R., Smithgall, C., & Gwynne, J. (2010). *Reading on grade level in third grade: How is it related to high school performance and college enrollment?* Chicago: Chapin Hall at the University of Chicago.

Madden, N. A., Goins, K., & Hybl, L. (2003). *Reading Roots teacher's manual* (2nd ed.). Baltimore: Success for All Foundation.

Madden, N. A., Conway, K., & Fitchet, W. et al. (2009). *Reading Wings teacher's manual* (2nd ed.). Baltimore: Success for All Foundation.

Madden, N. A., Slavin, R. E., Logan, M., & Cheung, A. (2011). Effects of cooperative writing with embedded multimedia: A randomized experiment. *Effective Education, 3*(1), 1–9.

Pressley, M., & Woloshyn, V. (1995). *Cognitive strategy instruction that really improves children's academic performance* (2nd ed.). Cambridge, MA: Brookline.

Ramey, C. T., & Ramey, S. L. (1992). *At risk does not mean doomed.* Birmingham: Civitan International Research Center, University of Alabama.

Slavin, R. E. (1987). Ability grouping and student achievement in elementary schools: A best-evidence synthesis. *Review of Educational Research, 57*, 347–350.

Slavin, R. E. (1995). *Cooperative learning: Theory, research, and practice* (2nd ed.). Boston: Allyn & Bacon.

Slavin, R. E. (1996). Neverstreaming: Preventing learning disabilities. *Educational Leadership, 53*(5), 4–7.

Slavin, R. E. (2013). Overcoming the four barriers to evidence-based education. *Education Week, 32*(29), 24.

Slavin, R. E., Madden, N. A., Chambers, B., & Haxby, B. (2009). *Two million children: Success for All.* Thousand Oaks, CA: Corwin.

Snow, C. E., Burns, S. M., & Griffin, P. (Eds.). (1998). *Preventing reading difficulties in young children.* Washington, DC: National Academy Press.

Stevens, R. J., Madden, N. A., Slavin, R. E., & Farnish, A. M. (1987). Cooperative Integrated Reading and Composition: Two field experiments. *Reading Research Quarterly, 22*, 433–454.

Success for All Foundation (2012). *Leading for Success principal's guide.* Baltimore: Author.

Success for All Foundation (2013). *Leading for Success facilitator's guide.* Baltimore: Author.

Vaughn, S., Bos, C. S., & Schumm, J. S. (2007). *Teaching students who are exceptional, diverse, and at risk in the general education classroom* (4th ed.). Boston: Allyn & Bacon.

Waxman, H. C., Padrón, Y. N., & Arnold, K. M. (2001). Effective instructional practices for students placed at risk of academic failure. In G. Borman, S. Stringfield, and R. Slavin (Eds.), *Title I: Compensatory education at the crossroads.* Mahwah, NJ: Erlbaum.

8

MEASURING IMPLEMENTATION FIDELITY IN SUCCESS FOR ALL

Rekha Balu and Janet Quint

Success for All (SFA) is one of the most thoroughly evaluated school reforms in the nation.[1] Indeed, the solid body of evidence documenting the program's effectiveness was a major reason for the U.S. Department of Education's selection of the Success for All Foundation (SFAF), the nonprofit organization that provides materials, training, and support to schools implementing the intervention, to receive a scale-up grant in the first round of the Investing in Innovation (i3) competition.

While the Department required new evaluations of the implementation and impacts of all i3 scale-up programs, there is good reason to look again at Success for All. First, the program has changed, with greater integration of technology into classroom instruction. Second, early reading instruction has itself changed, as more schools have adopted the phonics-infused approach called for by the National Reading Panel's influential (2000) report.[2] So, whether students in Success for All schools will continue to register higher reading levels than their counterparts in schools serving similar populations is very much an open question.

SFAF contracted with MDRC to conduct the evaluation of the i3 expansion. The main research question guiding MDRC's study is: *What is the impact of SFA on elementary school students' reading achievement, compared with students in non-SFA schools?* The answer to this question will determine our assessment of whether SFA is successful in improving reading performance in schools serving low-income students. To address this issue, MDRC put in place a cluster random assignment research design. Thirty-seven Title I elementary schools serving grades K–5 or K–6 and located in five school districts heard presentations about SFA and voted to adopt the program if selected. Nineteen of these schools were randomly assigned to the program condition; they received program materials and both initial and ongoing training from SFAF coaches, who made regular visits to the program schools in the study.[3] The remaining 18 schools continued with their "business-as-usual" approach to reading instruction.[4]

Along with the main question, the evaluation will address an array of additional topics in order to deepen understanding of the overall average impact of SFA: How do the impacts of SFA differ for different subgroups of students, defined by such characteristics as ethnicity, gender, and level of baseline reading readiness? What are the program's impacts on such non-cognitive outcomes as attendance and retention in grade? Does SFA produce larger impacts on students with greater exposure to the program? And are impacts on reading achievement higher in districts with stronger implementation of the SFA treatment? These last questions bring us to the subject of this chapter: measuring the extent of implementation and implementation fidelity in SFA schools.

As Slavin and Madden noted in the previous chapter, throughout the program's long history, its developers have been concerned with assessing strength of implementation in order to guide improvement at schools implementing the intervention. Toward this end, the program developers designed the School Achievement Snapshot (the "Snapshot"), an instrument that records students' growth in reading and includes 99 items that describe the extent to which critical program structures, activities, and instructional practices are in place. When they visit the schools, SFAF coaches meet with school personnel, visit classrooms, and examine program documents. Together with the SFA facilitators (school-level personnel who oversee program implementation), coaches complete the Snapshot form, once per quarter if possible but at least at the end of each school year.[5] Coaches then review the forms with school leaders to identify achievements to date and areas for improvement. A number of items on the forms are completed separately for different levels of instruction—KinderCorner (the SFA version of kindergarten), Reading Roots (for beginning readers), and Reading Wings (for more advanced readers)—to further pinpoint improvement needs. The portion of the Snapshot instrument containing the items used in this evaluation appears in the Appendix at the end of this chapter.[6]

Early on, in designing the evaluation of the i3 scale-up, MDRC decided to make the coaches' Snapshot ratings the basis for judging the fidelity of program implementation. There were good reasons to do this. Coaches knew the SFA program far better than researchers did and had a much better sense of what kinds of teacher and student behaviors to look for in classes. Furthermore, they visited the program schools much more often than the evaluation budget would have permitted researchers to be in the field. And the Snapshot itself provides a multidimensional and comprehensive picture of implementation.

On the whole, we still believe that the decision to use an instrument created and used by the developer was the right one, but it is not without its problems and compromises. This is a chapter about tradeoffs. We discuss the advantages and challenges associated with use of the Snapshot. While we want to describe our own experiences, we also suspect that these are typical of the issues that can arise with the use of developer-created instruments.

One other fact is important to note at the outset: Our analysis essentially treats implementation *fidelity* as synonymous with implementation *adequacy*. Schools considered to have implemented SFA "with fidelity" are not necessarily star performers—although some are. But all have done a "good enough" job with implementation: SFA is recognizably shaping school structure, instruction, and other processes in these schools.

The Logic Model

In refining their i3 evaluation designs, all evaluators were instructed to present logic models of the programs under study. This proved to be more challenging than was anticipated. SFA is grounded in a theory of how change occurs, but at the inception of the i3 initiative it was articulated in discursive textual descriptions. It was left to the evaluators and SFAF, working together, to develop a logic model that would specify inputs, outcomes, and the pathways connecting them.

The logic model that now guides the evaluation is shown in Figure 8.1. While the logic model has always included at least three elements—inputs, pathways, and outcomes—the way in which inputs have been specified has been revised over the course of the study. At the outset, there was much back and forth between SFAF and MDRC over a period of several months about which program elements qualified as inputs. Despite a positive and mutually respectful relationship between program developer and evaluator, coming to agreement on a logic model that adequately and accurately described the program's central features was difficult.

The intention of the National Evaluation Team was to ensure that measures of implementation fidelity center on constructs identified in the logic model. But in the case of SFA, the process was reversed: We designed a model to fit the instrument and the constructs it encompassed. We already knew that we wanted to use the Snapshot to measure implementation and schools' fidelity. It seemed sensible, therefore, to construct a logic model whose inputs replicate the categories of the Snapshot.

There are three such categories of inputs. The Schoolwide Structures category represents a varied set of personnel, structures, and processes that apply to the school as a whole: individuals and teams charged with carrying out certain functions, the collection and regular use of data to inform decision-making, periodic regrouping of students on the basis of these data (among other factors), tutoring for students who are not succeeding in the regular classroom, implementation of a schoolwide behavior component, and so on. Items that fall under the Instructional Processes and Student Engagement categories, in contrast, represent classroom behaviors of teachers and students, including use of cooperative learning strategies and questioning techniques.

In describing program inputs, the National Evaluation of i3 called on evaluators of individual programs to differentiate between actions undertaken by program

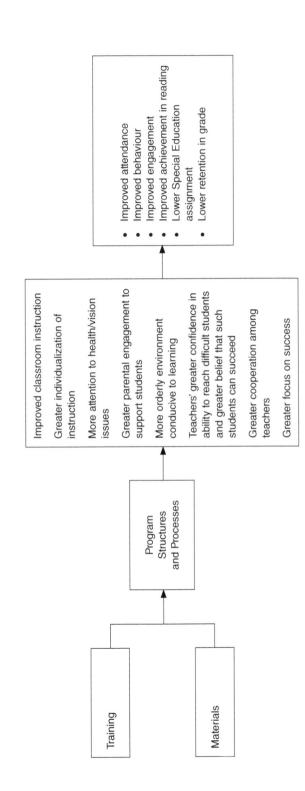

FIGURE 8.1 Success for All Student Impact Logic Model

Training

Materials

Program
Structures
and Processes

Improved classroom instruction

Greater individualization of instruction

More attention to health/vision issues

Greater parental engagement to support students

More orderly environment conducive to learning

Teachers' greater confidence in ability to reach difficult students and greater belief that such students can succeed

Greater cooperation among teachers

Greater focus on success

- Improved attendance
- Improved behaviour
- Improved engagement
- Improved achievement in reading
- Lower Special Education assignment
- Lower retention in grade

developers and those carried out by program sites. As Figure 8.1 shows, the model continues to describe two kinds of inputs (which together constitute the program's "Key Components"): Developer Inputs and School-Level Enactments. For reasons discussed below, the Schoolwide Structures, Instructional Processes, and Student Engagement categories have all been subsumed under the rubric "Program Structures and Processes," a term that is, for all intents and purposes, synonymous with School-Level Enactments.

Measuring Program Fidelity

Prior to the i3 evaluation and for ongoing program operations purposes, SFAF had determined which aspects of the program were critical to measure and created the Snapshot instrument accordingly. But it did so with program improvement, not research needs, in mind. To use the Snapshot to gauge implementation fidelity, MDRC did not modify the items or constructs on the Snapshot. Instead, we worked closely with SFAF to use the existing items in a quantitative analysis. Specifically, we (1) converted largely qualitative ratings of Snapshot items into numerical scores; (2) created additive scales, whereby the numerical scores for individual Snapshot items are summed to yield an overall score for each school, as well as for the separate program elements—Developer Inputs, Schoolwide Structures, Instructional Processes, and Student Engagement—at the school; and (3) developed criteria for determining what constitutes "adequate" implementation at the school and program (i.e., across-school) levels.

SFAF's expectation is that the program will unfold over time and that not all program elements will be in place at the end of the first year. Consequently, coaches rated only two-thirds of the 99 items on the Snapshot in the first year. The measures of fidelity presented in this chapter are based on coaches' ratings at the end of the second year of implementation, when SFAF looks for all program elements to be in place; we will also measure fidelity at the end of year 3.

Converting the Snapshot Into a Scale

The Snapshot includes 43 Schoolwide Structures items (of which two measure Developer Inputs and 41 measure School-Level Enactments), 30 Instructional Processes items, and 26 Student Engagement items. The scale that MDRC developed is grounded in the way that SFAF coaches rate these 99 Snapshot items.

Two items are considered Developer Inputs; they measure whether essential training was provided and whether the necessary materials were in place. These two items, along with the School-Level Enactment items that fall under the Schoolwide Structures section of the Snapshot, are given binary ratings; they are either "in place" or "not in place." On the scale, items "in place" generally get a point value of 1 and items "not in place" get a point value of 0.

Ratings for the items that fall under the Instructional Processes and Student Engagement categories are more refined. Such items are given one of four alphabetical ratings, depending on the percentage of teachers exhibiting the practice. A rating of P (Power schoolwide) indicates that the objective has been verified for 95–100 percent of teachers; M (Mastery) denotes that the objective has been verified for at least 80 percent of teachers; S (Significant use) means that the objective has been verified for at least 40 percent of teachers; and L (Learning) means that staff members are working toward verification of the objective, and that only a minority have attained it. To reflect the proportions of teachers for whom the ratings were verified, the researchers, with the concurrence of the developer, transformed a rating of P into a score of 1, a rating of M into a score of 0.8, a rating of S into a score of 0.4, and a rating of L into a score of 0.

Beyond this, SFA deems some items to be especially important; these items receive a double weight (i.e., the score is multiplied by 2). Items pertaining to Reading Wings also get a double weight, since a school generally has many more Reading Wings than Reading Roots classrooms. And especially important items rated for Reading Wings get a quadruple weight (i.e., the score is multiplied by 4). Thus, the point value of a particular item, depending on its nature, its importance, the level for which it is measured, and its degree of implementation, can range between 0 and 4.

A concrete example illustrating the conversion of the coaches' ratings into weighted scores may be instructive. Cooperative learning is a central element of SFA. Because of its importance, one Instructional Processes item related to cooperative learning—"Teachers provide time for partner and team talk to allow mastery of learning objectives by all students"—receives a double weight. Furthermore, the item is rated separately for KinderCorner, Reading Roots, and Reading Wings teachers. If the coach gave the item a rating of M for Reading Roots—meaning that the item was verified for 80 percent of Reading Roots teachers—it would receive a score of 1.6 (twice the 0.8 score that the item would receive if it were not unusually important). If the coach gave the item a rating of M for Reading Wings, the double weight would become a quadruple weight, reflecting both the item's importance and the large number of Reading Wings teachers; the score for the item would therefore be 3.2.

A school's score on the Snapshot is the sum of its ratings on all items. The maximum possible score on the scale is 144. Of these, 2 points reflect Developer Inputs and the remaining 142 points School-Level Enactments.

Assessing the Validity of Scale Scores and Their Relationship to Fidelity

Coaches conducted Snapshot assessments for the 19 SFA program schools in the study up to four times during each school year and were required to do so for the last quarter.[7] SFA forwarded the Snapshot assessments for the last quarter of each school year to MDRC, which calculated total scores and scores for the program components—Developer Inputs, Schoolwide Structures, Instructional Processes, and Student Engagement—for each school. Total scores ranged between 58.2 and 117.8. On the basis of these scores, the researchers identified four clusters of schools.

In parallel and without knowing schools' total scores, SFAF's president asked coaches to consider a variety of factors, some of which went beyond specific Snapshot items, and to place the schools with which they worked in one of four performance categories: very strong, strong, moderate, or weak. The first three categories include schools considered to be "adequate" implementers, while the fourth category includes schools that were not meeting implementation standards. When MDRC compared the ratings derived from the Snapshot with the SFAF coaches' assessments, the findings were mixed.

Overall, there was only limited consistency between the coaches' categorization of schools and the Snapshot-based clusters.[8] A number of factors probably account for this fact. First, the criteria that coaches were asked to consider in assigning their ratings aligned in part but not in full with Snapshot items. For example, coaches were instructed to rate schools as "very strong" when "classrooms implement cooperative learning consistently and with energy, teachers collect data on classroom performance using paper or online tools and *use the data to guide their instruction*, school-wide systems support attendance, parent involvement, and intervention, and the leadership monitors progress quarterly, *celebrates growth*, sets targets for improvements, and *holds staff accountable for meeting targets*." (Italicized criteria do not have analogues in the Snapshot.) Second, although coaches receive training in conducting the Snapshot assessments, they may have varied among themselves in the weight they attached to some of the non-Snapshot constructs. Finally, the way that Schoolwide Structures items on the Snapshot are rated—either as "in place" or "not in place"—is probably not refined enough to capture variations in strength or quality that coaches may perceive.

On the other hand, the three schools that coaches rated as "weak" also had the lowest Snapshot scores, with a substantial gap between these schools and the school with the next-lowest score. Thus, if the ultimate goal in analyzing fidelity of implementation is to distinguish schools that are implementing the program adequately, if imperfectly, from those that are not, the Snapshot gets the job done.[9]

Our analysis also pointed to another finding, this one with implications for the logic model: Schools could reach a given total score on the Snapshot in different ways and by exhibiting strengths in different areas. For example, the top-scoring school scored higher on Instructional Processes and Student Engagement, but lower on Schoolwide Structures, than the next-highest school. Even among the three low performers, one school had higher subscores on the Schoolwide Structures and Instructional Processes dimensions, but a considerably lower subscore on Student Engagement, than the other two schools. Analyses indicate that Instructional Processes and Student Engagement scores were much more highly correlated with each other (r = 0.83) than either one was correlated with School-wide Structures (r = 0.57 and 0.45, respectively). These results led MDRC and SFAF to conclude that in judging implementation fidelity, total score is much more relevant than are the subscores for Schoolwide Structures, Instructional Processes, and Student Engagement. Thus, in the logic model (shown in Figure 8.1), School-Level Enactment is represented as encompassing Program Structures and Processes. The analysis approach measures Enactment using a single variable that is the sum of the three subscores.

Developing Fidelity Standards

All evaluations of i3 grantees were asked to assess fidelity of implementation at two levels: the level of the organization implementing the intervention ("school-level fidelity") and across all such organizations ("program-level fidelity"). We therefore needed to establish two standards: one to judge whether each of the 19 program schools implemented SFA with fidelity, and a second to determine whether enough schools implemented the model with fidelity to conclude that program-level fidelity exists as well. (Thus, school-level measures contribute to the program-level fidelity measure.) Moreover, we needed to establish standards for measuring school-level and program-level fidelity for both the Developer Inputs and the Program Structures and Processes variables. All standards were developed in conjunction with SFAF.

School-Level Standards: Developer Inputs

While the responsibility for providing training and materials essentially resides with the developer, Developer Inputs are measured separately for each school. Assessing fidelity of the two Developer Inputs variables—Essential Training and Provision of Materials—is straightforward. A school is judged to have implemented each of the Developer Inputs with fidelity if it receives a score of 1 –"in place"—on the Snapshot item that measures the variable.

School-Level Standards: Program Structures and Processes

At the outset of the evaluation, MDRC did not specify a threshold Snapshot score for determining fidelity for two reasons. First, the evaluation standards for a threshold or cutoff score for each school came only in the second year of the evaluation. Second, because the Snapshot had not previously been used to measure fidelity in a research evaluation, any pre-specified criterion would have been rather arbitrary. Instead, we let the distribution of scores be our guide.

The three schools that ranked at the bottom in terms of both total Snapshot scores and coaches' ratings had total Snapshot scores that were less than 50 percent of the maximum possible score. This fact provided us with a ready way to identify a standard for what constitutes adequate implementation fidelity: A school is judged to have achieved adequate fidelity if its score on the measure is 50 percent or more of the maximum possible score.

Program-Level Standards: Developer Inputs

As previously noted, program-level standards involve aggregating across school-level results. SFAF has set a high standard for itself in defining what constitutes program-level fidelity: It must have provided 95 percent of program schools with the essential training and materials (that is, 95 percent of schools must have a rating of 1 on each of the measures) in order for these inputs to be considered to have been implemented with fidelity at the program level.[10]

Program-Level Standards: Program Structures and Processes

SFAF has also set a high standard for this domain: The program is considered to have been implemented with fidelity across the study if 80 percent of the schools have met the school-level implementation threshold.

Results

At the end of the 2012–2013 school year, the two Developer Inputs were judged to be in place at all 19 program schools. With regard to Program Structures and Processes, 16 of the 19 program schools—84.2 percent—had total Snapshot scores that were 50 percent or more of the maximum possible score. These schools were judged to be implementing the program with adequate fidelity. Because 84.2 percent exceeds the 80 percent threshold, we can conclude that at the program level (across schools), Success for All was implemented with fidelity in the schools participating in the i3 scale-up evaluation.

Challenges of Measuring Implementation with a Developer Instrument

The evaluation encountered two types of challenges involving the use of SFAF's Snapshot instrument: those in the data provided by SFAF and those relating to analysis.

Data

The first issue concerns data comparability, both across schools within a given program year and across program years. In the first year of the study, SFAF altered the Snapshot forms between the first quarter of the school year and the last quarter of the school year by reorganizing the form and adding new items. In addition, coaches working with some schools used a different form than coaches working with other schools. To correct for this, our analysis for the first year made use only of the data elements that were common across all forms, which included items essential to launching the program in a school. For the second and third year of the evaluation, coaches completed all items for all schools on the same form.

The evaluation also faced limits on the data that could be compared across years. In the final form of the Snapshot, some items were eligible to be rated beginning only in year 2 of the evaluation, partly reflecting SFAF's belief that it was unreasonable to see these practices in place in the first year of program operations. For example, the socio-emotional components of Getting Along Together or having students identify the intensity of their feelings, are expected to be in place only after schools have instituted other school and instructional structures. The fact that fewer items were rated in year 1 than in year 2 of the evaluation pointed the evaluation team toward comparing results for year 2 versus year 3, in which coaches rate a larger set of items that is consistent across the two years. As a result, we cannot compare the extent of implementation of all items in year 1 to year 3, which would likely show greater differences.

A second issue is that there are often multiple constructs in a given Snapshot item. For example, one Student Engagement item reads: "Students value team scores and work daily to ensure that team members are prepared to successfully report for the team during Random Reporter and to succeed on tests." From an evaluation perspective, it is difficult to know whether this item—with constructs relating to student perceptions, daily effort, cooperative learning, instructional method (reporting out), and test preparation—should be counted as one item (i.e., one practice) or as multiple items. Dividing multiple-construct items into separate constructs, each with its own rating, would have made calculating scores difficult, and would have required validation. Especially because we knew that SFAF's training is intended to create consistency of measures, MDRC chose to follow the developer's convention and treat each item as one distinct practice.

Analysis

Every program has its own language, which may include terms that are well-understood by insiders but mysterious to outsiders. The particular terminology of the Snapshot created a degree of confusion for the evaluators about how some items should be treated in the analysis. For example, as noted in the preceding chapter, SFAF labels each of the 99 items on its form as having one of three implementation "priorities"—"mechanical," "routine," or "refined" implementation—which correspond very roughly with when the items should be implemented. (Items classified as "mechanical" are expected to be implemented during the first year and "routine" and "refined" items are expected to be implemented later.) This fact raised questions about weighting: Should schools receive "extra credit" if they made early efforts to implement items that are generally put in place later? Weights would have made calculation of scores and interpretation of component scores more difficult, and MDRC decided not to apply any weights to these classifications. Rather, the concept of priorities is used for descriptive purposes only.

The evaluators also confronted fundamental questions about which aspects of implementation the Snapshot captures. First, of course, it is intended to record *inputs* (and for this reason can be used to measure *fidelity* of implementation— whether the program is implemented as planned). In some i3 program evaluations, fidelity measures focus on developer inputs. But the Snapshot items, as we have seen, go far beyond the developer inputs specified (i.e., materials and training) to include items relating to processes and outcomes. As the Slavin and Madden chapter notes, the instructional processes and student engagement items reflect measures of *quality* as well.

But are student engagement and behavior really inputs? Our analysis for the first and second years of the study treated items measuring these constructs, along with all the other Snapshot items, as inputs and included them in the implementation score. For comparability across years, the main implementation analysis will continue with this approach. However, we have come to believe that these items might be better assessed as *outputs*, and they will be treated as such in a supplementary analysis for the final report. In this supplementary analysis, we will examine the relationship between intensity of implementation and these behavioral and engagement outputs; we will also consider these outputs as potential mediators of ultimate student achievement outcomes. While these kinds of analysis would obviously be nonexperimental, they would enrich our understanding of how SFA achieves its goal of improving student reading achievement.

Study Constraints

To be sure, the summary of challenges in this chapter is not intended to suggest that use of a researcher-developed instrument would not have encountered its own problems. Instead, it is meant to describe some considerations for researchers when using a developer's instrument to assess fidelity.

First, the evaluator may need to accept the validity of the instrument as is, without an independent opportunity to validate the instrument or individual items. Consider that program staff that rate schools may have already been trained in the instrument, so there may be limited opportunities for 'piloting' or amending the instrument for more consistency or specificity. To this end, it is important for evaluators to collect data from surveys and other efforts to obtain a fuller picture of program implementation in a school.

Second, when employees of the developer organization complete the assessment instrument, the instrument's reliability may be both strengthened and limited. Program staff benefit from prior training and exposure and may bring a high level of understanding of how to rate items. This program knowledge may ensure that each coach provides a consistent rating over time (e.g., does not use different standards when observing different sessions), but cannot substitute for inter-rater reliability (i.e., whether multiple raters would provide the same rating for a given observation session). However, obtaining multiple raters' measures of a school's implementation—which is necessary to demonstrate the reliability of the developer instrument—requires that other SFAF staff members or researchers be involved in the assessment process at a given school. This condition is often infeasible from an economic perspective. Sampling a set of classrooms or schools for multiple raters to visit may be one solution to this challenge.

Third, consider what research questions the developer instrument can and cannot answer. For SFAF, the purpose was feedback on how to implement SFAF's model. It was not to document adaptations to the model or to rate non-SFA schools on the extent to which SFA-type practices are in place. The Snapshot items describe specific ways of operationalizing a set of goals and concepts, by implementing particular structures or procedures; it is these very specific structures and procedures, far more than the underlying goals and concepts, which likely differentiate SFA from control schools. But the language the instrument uses is also specialized, so much so that the relevance of many of its items to non-SFA schools is limited. Even if MDRC researchers or SFA coaches had tried to administer the Snapshot in control schools, the instrument's very specific language would have made it difficult to describe SFA-like practices adequately.

Different research purposes required different instruments. The developer instrument proved the best tool to assess fidelity to a prescribed model. Meanwhile, MDRC employed surveys and instructional logs to describe service contrast and interviews and observations to describe facilitators of, barriers to, and adaptations in implementation. The survey items and interview questions used to ascertain differences between treatment and control schools can capture some broad distinctions but not more detailed, fine-grained ones. For example, during the first year of implementation, high proportions of principals in both SFA and control schools (89 and 77 percent, respectively) reported on a principal survey that an individual or group of people in their school is responsible for "fostering closer relationships between the school and students' families"; this difference was not statistically significant. The Snapshot, however, makes it clear that the parent involvement component of SFA contains a number of essential elements. For example, staff members at SFA schools who belong to the Parent and Family Involvement Team are expected to set targets and chart their progress toward meeting these targets. Further collaboration with SFAF might have allowed us to develop more nuanced survey items to detect potentially larger differences between SFA and control schools' implementation of a more exacting standard.

Conclusion

Readers of this chapter may have been surprised that evaluators working with a long-established, research-based program encountered issues and challenges in measuring implementation. One such challenge was the absence of a straightforward logic model. We would suggest that it is precisely the program's long history that explains this fact. First, the potential value of logic models and theories of change has come to be recognized relatively recently, whereas SFA's developers, including Robert Slavin and Nancy Madden, have been refining SFA for a much longer time.[11] While a detailed narrative description of Success for All was central to the program's implementation and replication over time, a logic model was not. Second, over its history, the program has been modified and improved, as new needs and responses have been identified and addressed. And changes in the way the program is described also reflect new foci of attention in the policy environment (e.g., the crisp delineation of primary prevention versus intervention elements in the preceding chapter).

Second, readers may also remark on the fact that we were limited in our ability to validate or assess the coaches' ratings and the instrument's reliability. This limitation was largely budgetary; the evaluation supported annual site visits to program and control schools, but not the amount of time needed to assess for ourselves the extent of program implementation, especially for those program aspects that require extensive time visiting classrooms. Faced with the tradeoff between independent assessment at considerable cost of staff and travel time (and entailing a steep learning curve) and the developer assessment at lower staff cost and time, we chose the developer assessment.

Finally, readers may wonder whether thresholds for establishing implementation fidelity should have been established a priori rather than empirically, especially in a program with such a long track record. Here, we would again note that the Snapshot was not created for the purpose of quantitative scoring of schools and thus did not have existing numerical thresholds. Comparing the Snapshot scores of schools that coaches judged to be performing well below par with the scores of other, better-performing schools helped us arrive at a cutoff point that distinguished weak performers from the rest. Grounded in reality as it is, we think that our standard for judging school-level fidelity enables us to identify "good-enough" schools, and we think this is the appropriate standard for the i3 evaluation.

In summary, our experience suggests that evaluations benefit from more collaboration with developers and with funders. Advance planning with the funder to understand the requirements for establishing standards to judge implementation fidelity (and early articulation by the funder of those standards), is essential. In addition, advance planning with the developer to design a logic model, to understand the purpose and uses of its implementation assessment tools, and to validate the assessment tools, can improve research evaluations of multi-dimensional programs.

Notes

1. The findings of the most rigorous pre-i3 evaluation of Success for All's impacts are reported in Borman et al. (2007).
2. National Institute of Child Health and Human Development (NICHD) (2000).

3. We subsequently refer to these as program schools, although we note that only a small share of schools that adopted the SFA program under i3 are part of the evaluation.
4. Reading programs in the control schools are broadly similar to SFA. Like SFA, they cover the five reading components (phonics, phonemic awareness, vocabulary, fluency, and reading comprehension) identified by the National Reading Panel report as essential to reading instruction. Like SFA, too, the programs used by the control group schools strike a balance between decoding and comprehension skills. These similarities suggest that it is not the curriculum per se but the specific ways that it is enacted—in particular, the use of cross-grade grouping and the emphasis on cooperative learning—that differentiate SFA schools from control group schools.
5. Ratings are the product of interactions between the coach and school personnel; thus, the ratings are not completely "independent." Ultimately, however, completing the Snapshot is the responsibility of the coach, who must also be able to justify a rating with supporting evidence.
6. In addition to these items, the Snapshot is designed to record statistics on reading achievement, attendance, tardiness, and other variables over time.
7. Ratings are provided by just one coach per school, so that inter-rater reliability cannot be assessed.
8. For example, one school that coaches rated as "very strong" also emerged as a top scorer on the Snapshot. But another school that had an even higher total score on the Snapshot was given only a "moderate" rating by its coach. Of five schools that coaches rated as "strong," one was in our top group based on the Snapshot rating, two were toward the bottom, and the remaining two were in-between.
9. It is important to note that even the weak implementers are making progress toward more complete implementation. All, for example, showed growth between years on at least one program component.
10. While the standards are high, it is notable that in the second year, all schools were considered to have met both standards.
11. For an early treatment of the value of a theory of change in examining program impacts and implementation, see Connell et al. (1995).

References

Borman, G. D., Slavin, R. E., Cheung, A. Chamberlain, A., Madden, N. A., & Chambers, B. (2007). Final reading outcomes of the national randomized field trial of Success for All. *American Educational Research Journal, 44*(3), 701–731.

Connell, J. P., et al. (1995). *New approaches to evaluating community initiatives: Concepts, methods, and context.* Queenstown, MD: Aspen Institute for Human Studies.

National Institute of Child Health and Human Development (NICHD). (2000). Report of the National Reading Panel. *Teaching children to read: An evidence-based assessment of the scientific research literature on reading and its implications for reading Instruction.* NIH Publication No. 00-4769. Washington, DC: U.S. Government Printing Office.

APPENDIX

SUCCESS FOR ALL SNAPSHOT

Schoolwide Structures

B 1 2 3 4   IP = In place; N = Not in place

B	1	2	3	4	Fundamentals
▦	▦	▦	▦	▦	❶ All leaders and staff have received essential training. (1)
▦	▦	▦	▦	▦	❶ Materials necessary for program implementation are complete. (2)
▦	▦	▦	▦	▦	❶ Schoolwide Solutions coordinator has been identified and given time to fulfill Solutions responsibilities. (3)
▦	▦	▦	▦	▦	❶ Facilitator is a full-time position. (4)
▦	▦	▦	▦	▦	❷ Classes in Reading Roots do not exceed twenty students. (5)
▦	▦	▦	▦	▦	❶ A ninety-minute (elementary) or sixty-minute (secondary) uninterrupted reading block exists. (6)
▦	▦	▦	▦	▦	❶ The principal is fully involved with SFA implementation. (7)
▦	▦	▦	▦	▦	❶ Instructional component teams meet regularly to address professional-development needs and connect teachers to online and print resources for program support. (8)
▦	▦	▦	▦	▦	❶ All Schoolwide Solutions teams have been identified and meet regularly as specified. (9)
▦	▦	▦	▦	▦	❶ Getting Along Together structures are in place in every classroom (Class Council meetings, Peace Paths, Think It Through sheets). (10)
▦	▦	▦	▦	▦	❷ Getting Along Together structures are in place schoolwide (Peace Paths; Think It Through sheets; using conflict stoppers in cafeteria, on playground, in hallways, etc.). (11)

▦	▦	▦	▦	▦	❶ Attendance plans are complete and effectively implemented. At least 95% of children are in school on time every day. (12)
▦	▦	▦	▦	▦	❶ The Intervention team meets weekly and uses the Solutions Sheet process to create individualized achievement plans. (13)
▦	▦	▦	▦	▦	❷ Read and Respond forms are collected each week, and return is celebrated. Return rate is 80% or better. (14)
▦	▦	▦	▦	▦	❷ Parent involvement essentials are in place. (15)
▦	▦	▦	▦	▦	❷ Volunteer listeners are in place. (16)
					❸ A positive schoolwide behavior plan (e.g., PBIS, Checkpoints for Success, CMCD) is in place and used consistently. Emergency schoolwide disciplinary procedures are clear and functional. School climate is positive, calm, and orderly. (17)
					❸ A community-supported vision program is in place. (18)

Assessment

▦	▦	▦	▦	▦	❶ An accurate Grade Summary Form is maintained for every grading period. (19)
▦	▦	▦	▦	▦	❶ Formal reading-level assessments with consistent measures are conducted at the beginning of the year and at the end of each grading period. (20)
▦	▦	▦	▦	▦	❶ Teacher cycle record forms or weekly record forms are used by all teachers to record classroom data throughout the grading period. (21)
▦	▦	▦	▦	▦	❷ A Classroom Assessment Summary is submitted quarterly by each teacher. (22)
▦	▦	▦	▦	▦	❸ Member Center (or equivalent) data-collection and reporting tools are used consistently. (23)

B	1	2	3	4	IP = In place; N = Not in place
					Aggressive Placement
▦	▦	▦	▦	▦	❶ Cross-grade regrouping is used each grading period in all grades except pre-K and kindergarten. (24)
▦	▦	▦	▦	▦	❶ Multiple measures are used to determine placement. (25)
▦	▦	▦	▦	▦	❷ Placement is aggressive; students are placed at the highest level at which they can be successful. (26)
					Tutoring
▦	▦	▦	▦	▦	❶ Capacity exists to tutor 30% of first-grade students, 20% of second-grade students, and 10% of third-grade students. (27)

(Continued)

▨	▨	▨	▨	▨	❶ A certified teacher-tutor coaches other tutors. (28)
▨	▨	▨	▨	▨	❶ Tutoring is provided daily for each tutored student. (29)
▨	▨	▨	▨	▨	❷ Team Alphie or Alphie's Alley is used for tutoring. (30)

Leading for Success

					❸ The Leadership team meets monthly to review schoolwide data, monitor Leading for Success teams, and prepare for the quarterly Success Network meetings. (31)
▨	▨	▨	▨	▨	❸ Members of the school Leadership team know the number and percentage of students achieving at grade level and meeting quarterly proficiency goals. (32)
					❷ Leading for Success quarterly meetings are held at the start of school and quarterly to review schoolwide progress toward achievement goals and Leading for Success team reports. (33)

▨	▨	▨	▨	▨	CC/KC	❷ Instructional component teams set SMARTS targets based on program data, chart progress, and work collaboratively to meet their targets. (34)
▨	▨	▨	▨	▨	RR	
▨	▨	▨	▨	▨	RW	
▨	▨	▨	▨	▨	REMS	
▨	▨	▨	▨	▨	REHS	

▨	▨	▨	▨	▨	❸ The facilitator uses the GREATER coaching process to support continuous improvement of student achievement through high-quality implementation. (35)

▨	▨	▨	▨	▨	Attendance	❷ Schoolwide Solutions teams set SMARTS targets based on program data, chart progress, and work collaboratively to meet their targets. (36)
▨	▨	▨	▨	▨	Intervention	
▨	▨	▨	▨	▨	Cooperative Culture	
▨	▨	▨	▨	▨	Community Connections	
▨	▨	▨	▨	▨	Parent and Family Involvement	

▨	▨	▨	▨	▨	❸ The Schoolwide Solutions coordinator supports Schoolwide Solutions teams to identify student-achievement targets that guide the teams' efforts. (37)
					❸ All Leading for Success teams set targets that are aligned with schoolwide quarterly goals. (38)

Please Note: *The shaded areas indicate objectives that may not be rated at your school until the 2013–2014 school year.*

Priorities for implementation: ❶ *mechanical* ❷ *routine* ❸ *refined*.

Instructional Processes*

√	B	1	2	3	4		
						CC/KC	❶ Teachers use the basic lesson structure and objectives. Teachers use available media regularly and effectively. (1)
						RR	
						RW	
						REMS	
						REHS	
						PTM	
						WW	
						CC/KC	❸ Active instruction is appropriately paced and includes modeling and guided practice that is responsive to students' understanding of the objective. (2)
						RR	
						RW	
						REMS	
						REHS	
						PTM	
						WW	
						CC/KC	❷ Teachers use Think-Pair-Share, whole-group response, Random Reporter (or similar tools that require every student to prepare to respond) frequently and effectively during teacher presentation. (3)
						RR	
						RW	
						REMS	
						REHS	
						PTM	
						WW	
						CC/KC	❸ Teachers restate and elaborate student responses to promote vocabulary mastery at a high standard of oral expression. (4)
						RR	
						RW	
						REMS	
						REHS	
						PTM	
						WW	
						CC/KC	❷ Teachers provide time for partner and team talk (and lab activities in kindergarten) to allow mastery of learning objectives by all students. (5)
						RR	
						RW	

(Continued)

√	B	1	2	3	4		
						REMS	
						REHS	
						PTM	
						WW	
						CC/KC	❸ Teachers facilitate partner and team discussion (and student interaction in labs) by circulating, questioning, redirecting, and challenging students to increase the depth of discussion and ensure individual progress. (6)
						RR	
						RW	
						REMS	
						REHS	
						PTM	
						WW	

√	B	1	2	3	4		
						RW	❷ Following Team Talk or other team study discussion, teachers conduct a class discussion in which students are randomly selected to report for their teams; rubrics are used to evaluate responses, and team points are awarded. (7)
						REMS	
						REHS	
						PTM	
						WW	
						RW	❸ During class discussion, teachers effectively summarize, address misconceptions or inaccuracies, and extend thinking through thoughtful questioning. (8)
						REMS	
						REHS	
						PTM	
						WW	
						RW	❸ During class discussion, teachers ask students to share both successful and unsuccessful use of strategies, such as clarifying, questioning, predicting, summarizing, and graphic organizers. (9)
						REMS	
						REHS	
						PTM	
						WW	
						RR	❷ Teachers calculate team scores that include academic achievement points in every instructional cycle and celebrate team success in every cycle. (10)
						RW	
						REMS	

☐	☐	☐	☐	☐	☐	REHS	
☐	☐	☐	☐	☐	☐	PTM	
☐	☐	☐	☐	☐	☐	WW	
☐	☐	☐	☐	☐	☐	RR	❸ Teachers use team scores to help students set goals for improvement, and students receive points for meeting goals. (11)
☐	☐	☐	☐	☐	☐	RW	
☐	☐	☐	☐	☐	☐	REMS	
☐	☐	☐	☐	☐	☐	REHS	
☐	☐	☐	☐	☐	☐	PTM	
☐	☐	☐	☐	☐	☐	WW	
☐	☐	☐	☐	☐	☐	KC	❷ Read and Respond forms are collected each week, and return is celebrated. Return rate is 80% or better. (12)
☐	☐	☐	☐	☐	☐	RR	
☐	☐	☐	☐	☐	☐	RW	
☐	☐	☐	☐	☐	☐	REMS	
☐	☐	☐	☐	☐	☐	REHS	
☐	☐	☐	☐	☐	☐	GAT	❸ Teachers conduct Class Council meetings weekly. The atmosphere is open, and relevant class issues are addressed effectively. (13)
						GAT all day	❸ Teachers facilitate the use of emotion-control and conflict-resolution strategies throughout the day (including use of the Stop and Stay Cool steps, Think It Through sheets, the Feelings Thermometer, and the Peace Path). (14)

Student Engagement*

√	B	1	2	3	4		
☐	☐	☐	☐	☐	☐	CC/KC	❶ Students are familiar with routines. (1)
☐	☐	☐	☐	☐	☐	RR	
☐	☐	☐	☐	☐	☐	RW	
☐	☐	☐	☐	☐	☐	REMS	
☐	☐	☐	☐	☐	☐	REHS	
☐	☐	☐	☐	☐	☐	PTM	
☐	☐	☐	☐	☐	☐	WW	

(Continued)

						Code	Description
☐	☐	☐	☐	☐	☐	CC/KC	❸ Students speak in full, elaborate sentences when responding to teacher questions. (2)
☐	☐	☐	☐	☐	☐	RR	
☐	☐	☐	☐	☐	☐	RW	
☐	☐	☐	☐	☐	☐	REMS	
☐	☐	☐	☐	☐	☐	REHS	
☐	☐	☐	☐	☐	☐	PTM	
☐	☐	☐	☐	☐	☐	WW	
☐	☐	☐	☐	☐	☐	CC/KC	❷ Student talk equals or exceeds teacher talk. (Each student should be engaged in partner/team discussion as a speaker or active listener during half of class time.) (3)
☐	☐	☐	☐	☐	☐	RR	
☐	☐	☐	☐	☐	☐	RW	
☐	☐	☐	☐	☐	☐	REMS	
☐	☐	☐	☐	☐	☐	REHS	
☐	☐	☐	☐	☐	☐	PTM	
☐	☐	☐	☐	☐	☐	WW	
☐	☐	☐	☐	☐	☐	CC/KC	❷ Students are engaged during team/partner practice and labs. If needed, strategies such as talking chips or role cards are in use. (4)
☐	☐	☐	☐	☐	☐	RR	
☐	☐	☐	☐	☐	☐	RW	
☐	☐	☐	☐	☐	☐	REMS	
☐	☐	☐	☐	☐	☐	REHS	
☐	☐	☐	☐	☐	☐	PTM	
☐	☐	☐	☐	☐	☐	WW	
☐	☐	☐	☐	☐	☐	CC/KC	❸ Partners assist each other effectively with difficult words and use retell every day during partner reading. (5)
☐	☐	☐	☐	☐	☐	RR	
☐	☐	☐	☐	☐	☐	RW	
☐	☐	☐	☐	☐	☐	REMS	
☐	☐	☐	☐	☐	☐	REHS	
☐	☐	☐	☐	☐	☐	CC/KC	❸ Students use rubrics to meet expectations (e.g., fluency, writing, vocabulary, strategy use, comprehension). (6)
☐	☐	☐	☐	☐	☐	RR	
☐	☐	☐	☐	☐	☐	RW	
☐	☐	☐	☐	☐	☐	REMS	
☐	☐	☐	☐	☐	☐	REHS	
☐	☐	☐	☐	☐	☐	PTM	
☐	☐	☐	☐	☐	☐	WW	

√	B	1	2	3	4		
▦	▦	▦	▦	▦	▦	RW	❸ Teams are engaged in highly challenging discussions, in which students explain and offer evidence from the text to support their answers, or, for writing, students offer thoughtful responses during the revision process. (7)
▦	▦	▦	▦	▦	▦	REMS	
▦	▦	▦	▦	▦	▦	REHS	
▦	▦	▦	▦	▦	▦	PTM	
▦	▦	▦	▦	▦	▦	WW	
▦	▦	▦	▦	▦	▦	RR	❷ Students value team scores and work daily to ensure that team members are prepared to successfully report for the team during Random Reporter and to succeed on tests. (8)
▦	▦	▦	▦	▦	▦	RW	
▦	▦	▦	▦	▦	▦	REMS	
▦	▦	▦	▦	▦	▦	REHS	
▦	▦	▦	▦	▦	▦	PTM	
▦	▦	▦	▦	▦	▦	RW	❸ Students use strategy cards to assist one another during reading and discussion, or students use revision guides to offer helpful feedback during the writing process. (9)
▦	▦	▦	▦	▦	▦	REMS	
▦	▦	▦	▦	▦	▦	WW	
▦	▦	▦	▦	▦	▦	RR	❸ Students know their reading levels and can articulate what they need to do to increase their reading achievement, or, for writing, students know their writing strengths and what they need to do to improve their writing. (10)
▦	▦	▦	▦	▦	▦	RW	
▦	▦	▦	▦	▦	▦	REMS	
▦	▦	▦	▦	▦	▦	REHS	
▦	▦	▦	▦	▦	▦	WW	
▦	▦	▦	▦	▦	▦	GAT all day	❸ Students use win-win decision-making skills to solve problems that arise through the use of the Peace Path, conflict stoppers, and Think It Through sheets. (11)
▦	▦	▦	▦	▦	▦	GAT all day	❸ Students can identify the intensity of their feelings and use self-control strategies (Stop and Stay Cool) when needed. (12)

√ = Area of focus

P = Power schoolwide—Objective is verified for 95% of teachers.

M = Mastery—Objective is verified for 80% of teachers.

S = Significant use—Objective is verified for 40% of teachers.

L = Learning—Staff members are working toward verification of this objective.

∗Verified by observation or artifacts such as team score sheets, facilitator observation records, videos, audio records, transcripts of instruction, or teacher records of student responses. Leave blank if documentation is not yet available.

© 2012 Success for All Foundation.

9

MEASURING FIDELITY

The Present and Future

Barbara Goodson, Cristofer Price, and Catherine Darrow

The question of program effectiveness and related concerns of program implementation have come to the forefront of educational research. In recent years,
funding agencies like the United States Department of Education (ED) have
required grant recipients to measure the fidelity of implementation of interventions as part of rigorous impact studies. Measuring fidelity requires clear
specification of the program model being tested, including identifying critical
components of the model, their relationship to each other, and their relationship to intermediate and long-term outcomes (Bond, Evans, Salyers, Williams,
& Kim, 2000; Century, Rudnick, & Freeman, 2010; Hall and Hord, 1987;
Mowbray, Holter, Teague, & Bybee, 2003).

Discussion within the field has directly referenced Dane and Schneider's
seminal review (1998) of the ways in which evaluation research reveals varying
levels of implementation, which has given rise to a number of approaches to
measuring implementation. It can be argued that consensus has been reached
over the need for program developers, researchers, and evaluators to clearly define
the program model (Century et al., 2010; Nelson, Cordray, Hulleman, Darrow, &
Sommer, 2012), to indicate the critical elements that are theoretically tied to
impacts of interest (Mowbray et al., 2003; O'Donnell, 2008), to develop original
or use pre-existing measures to assess levels of fidelity (Century, Cassata, Rudnick,
& Freeman, 2012; Hume et al., 2011), and to use fidelity data to interpret program impacts (Durlak & Dupre, 2008; Hulleman & Cordray, 2009).

Ongoing developments in implementation science are impressive, particularly
in the ways education researchers have devoted attention to measuring fidelity to
specific interventions. A wealth of approaches has emerged, including methods in
measuring fidelity to targeted interventions (see Hume et al., 2011, and Pence,
Justice, & Wiggins, 2008, for examples). With an influx of examples on fidelity

measurement comes a pool of approaches that are tied to specific interventions that assess the degree to which unique elements of an intervention are implemented. Diverse approaches to defining and measuring fidelity abound (O'Donnell, 2008). Each system of measurement is seemingly developed and presented in isolation with few connections across educational interventions. Yet, a universal approach in collecting and pooling implementation data—often a large amount from a variety of sources—into quantifiable, analyzable values is underdeveloped. No systematic method of measurement, analysis, or reporting exists that enables fidelity results to be compared across different interventions and across evaluations. This paper adds to the field by offering insight into a process of systematically combining fidelity data to represent the implementation of any complex intervention.

Because researchers find themselves in need of measuring fidelity more deliberately, it has become evident that there are a variety of methods one can use to measure fidelity. The measurement of fidelity, however, has become convoluted as researchers individually establish methods to confirm a successful delivery of an intervention. Each method results in particular findings and serves different purposes in an evaluation. Some evaluations focus on documenting the frequency of developer-controlled supports like professional development or leadership training. In their discussion of key constructs in implementation science, Owens et al. (2013) call a support like professional development "the primary vehicle through which implementers learn the rationale for an intervention, its core components, the mechanisms through which components impact [student] outcomes, and the skills necessary to implement the components with high integrity" (p. 3). Other evaluations focus on assessing the degree to which trained professionals carried out the nuances of the intervention. For example, Pence and colleagues (2008) used a complex, observational checklist to calculate how often teachers use intervention-specific instructional strategies with struggling readers. Owens et al. (2013) and Pence and colleagues (2008) apply different approaches to measuring fidelity: both utilize different methods, consult various sources of data, and focus on answering different research questions about fidelity. These authors represent only a few examples of the different approaches that exist in the field of education research. Yet, rarely if ever is the distinction made between these approaches and their conclusions.

The introductory chapter of this book described the current state of assessment of fidelity of implementation as characterized by (a) general agreement about the importance of studying implementation fidelity as a means to confirm program delivery and interpret program effects and (b) differences in how program developers and evaluators conceptualize and measure fidelity. The chapter also identified ways in which these different approaches to fidelity have limited our ability to compare and interpret findings across studies or to pool implementation data in a meaningful way. The chapter went on to propose a multi-step methodology for systematically collecting and reporting implementation data, which has been implemented by evaluators as part of the i3 program. The first steps include the articulation of the change and logic models, and the identification of critical components. The identification of critical components requires a decision regarding which components of fidelity will be measured—fidelity of implementation (i.e., the extent to which key components of the intervention are delivered as intended), fidelity of intervention (i.e., the extent to which intermediate or proximal outcomes are delivered as intended), or both. In the case of i3, the expectations about fidelity measures focus on fidelity of implementation.[1] Therefore in the context of i3, identification of critical components requires the identification of the elements in the logic model that represent the key structural aspects or inputs in the logic model that define fidelity of implementation to the model. Subsequent steps include the identification of data sources, indices and thresholds, reviewing results, and potentially repeating the steps to produce revised measures.

Chapters 3 through 8 present case studies of three educational interventions in which evaluators have used similar methodologies to create measures of fidelity of implementation. The discussion of the fidelity measurement systems for the three interventions places fidelity squarely in the context of stage of implementation. The first of three interventions represent one program model that is still in the process final development and undergoing its first rigorous evaluation (STEM21 Digital Academy) in a small set of schools. The second model represents an intervention that is no longer "in development," and that has been rigorously evaluated on a small scale, and is in the process of being implemented and rigorously evaluated on a larger scale (the eMints Program). And the third model (Success for All) represents an intervention that is fully developed (it was first implemented in one school in 1987), has been rigorously evaluated on a large scale, and is in the process of scaling up to a national level. For each of these three interventions, the challenges encountered in developing measures of fidelity of implementation and the uses of fidelity data were different and were related to the stage of development of the program model.

Below we talk about what these programs tell us about measurement of fidelity at each of the steps laid out in Chapter 2. All three case studies demonstrated that the development of fidelity measures iterated through all of the major steps of development, through revisions, and back through the major steps.

Articulating the Logic Model and Identifying Key Components

The clear articulation of logic and change models is the critical first stage of the process, regardless of the approach to measuring fidelity. Most importantly for the measurement of fidelity, the logic model identifies essential program components—the resources and activities—necessary to operationalize the change model components for the model. As described in Chapter 2, the critical components define the framework for the assessment of fidelity—whether all key components were present in the implementation and the extent to which they were present. In particular, the three fidelity systems described in these chapters focused on measuring "fidelity of implementation." Also as noted in Chapter 2, the model developer plays an important role in the initial process of specifying key components.

Development Grant: STEM21 Digital Academy

The STEM21 Digital Academy represented the culmination of more than 10 years of funding of school leadership models received by the Education Connection's Center for 21st Century Skills. The STEM21 model that was funded under the i3 program was an expansion of previous activities into a 4-year school career-themed Academy of Digital Arts and Sciences. As stated by the Center directors, at the time that the STEM21 Academy was funded, "From a programmatic standpoint, the Center was aware of the various activities included in the program but could not articulate these aspects or provide a conceptual definition that be used to conduct research on the program" (LaBanca, Worwood, Schauss, LaSala, & Donn, 2013). In this case, the external funding provided much of the impetus for the developer to formally specify the theory of change and the logic model for the intervention. This more detailed conceptualization was necessary not only to communicate with stakeholders (i.e., funders, educators, policy makers, and parents) but also to sustain the growth of the STEM21 program into additional schools and districts interested in replicating the model.

During the early years of program development, prior to this systematic work on the change and logic models for the STEM21 Academy, implementation was studied annually. The questions about implementation that were being asked and the methodologies for addressing them are typical of programs during the early stages of development: Qualitative interviews and focus groups of teachers and students, document reviews and satisfaction surveys were used to answer questions about how well the program met the needs of participants, what implementation challenges were experienced, and suggestions for program improvement. The information on implementation produced by this approach was useful for supporting program improvement and refinement but did not provide systematic data for communicating to outside stakeholders on fidelity of implementation of the model. As described by the internal evaluator, the fact that the intervention model was still in its early stage of development meant that the program also was in the beginning stages of learning about and revising its program model. The program staff and internal evaluators understood that measuring fidelity would involve a change from a culture in which implementation evaluation was seen as an "occasional, additional and unwanted chore" to a view in which the documentation of implementation was considered to be an integral component of the ongoing work on the intervention.

The evaluator describes the process of specifying the change and logic models for STEM21 as involving multiple, iterative discussions among Center staff, including the internal evaluator and the program director, to answer the question, "What are the technology-enhanced and student-centered practices mandated by the instructional model?" As noted by the evaluator, there was a feedback loop inherent in the development process whereby the drive to develop the logic model began the process of systematizing the program definition, which changed the program definition, which in turn changed the logic model. This loop was repeated multiple times during the development of the logic model.

One of the important lessons from the Education Center and the STEM21 Academy is that at the initial stages of development of a comprehensive and accurate logic model for a program model, a strong partnership between the program staff and evaluators is critical. These two groups bring their own unique and critical understanding and perspective on the program, as well as limitations related to their role. In this case, the partners were able to collaborate successfully to develop a shared understanding of the program.

Validation Grant: eMINTS Comprehensive Professional Development Program

The eMINTS Professional Development Program represents an intervention that is at a more mature stage of development. As described by the developer, in its early phases, the program was small, services were newly developed and delivered as needed ("just-in-time") and did not have a well-defined professional development intervention. As was true for STEM21, the early implementation studies of eMINTS were conducted by internal evaluators and were based on more qualitative teacher surveys, informal feedback from teachers and observation. Also similarly to STEM21, as the model was implemented in more sites, this expansion stimulated the developers to undertake a more systematic approach to implementation. That is, across both these interventions, program expansion brought with it both the need to systematize the program model itself and to create frameworks (change and logic models) to support the quality and consistent implementation of the model.

The process, as described by the external evaluator, centered on collaboration between an evaluation team and the eMINTS staff to develop a fully articulated program description that identified and defined the core components of the model. The program description was used to develop a logic model outlining the resources, processes, teacher outputs, and expected student outcomes to be realized as a result of implementing eMINTS. An associated change model was also developed that described constructs, or core underlying changes in teacher and student behaviors, expected to change as a result of implementing the eMINTS program. External evaluators co-developed both of these models with eMINTS staff and used them to inform the evaluation design included in the winning eMINTS i3 validation grant proposal. The fact that eMINTS had included the logic and change models in the i3 validation proposal indicated their readiness to support expansion of the model.

Through the logic model process, five components were identified as core elements for the eMINTS model (technology equipment, technology infrastructure, teacher professional development, administrative support, and ongoing technology support). These components were presented to participating schools and staff to clearly explain the expectations of the program regarding fidelity of implementation. Each school had to indicate its understanding and acceptance of these five components and the expectations for full implementation of each.

Scale-Up Grant: Success for All

At this point in the lifespan of Success for All, after more than 15 years since its initial implementation in a single school, the model's key elements could be expected to be fully articulated and consistently defined. However, the external evaluator describes the challenge presented by this very lengthy history of implementation. The evaluator suggests that the importance of logic models has emerged only relatively recently, after the developers of the Success for All model had been building and refining the model for many years. Although there have been detailed narrative descriptions of the process of school adoption of the model (teacher professional development and support, classroom curriculum content, pedagogical approaches, and formative assessments), the program has been modified and refined without a modified logic model to represent those changes. As a result, despite the maturity of the Success for All program, under i3, the evaluator undertook the challenge of developing a logic model to frame the ongoing work on measuring fidelity of implementation. Creating a logic model that adequately and accurately captured the program's key features, as defined by the developers, required extensive and iterative communication between the program developers and the evaluator.

Under the i3 funding, Success for All received a scale-up grant to support large-scale expansion of the model at a national level. The scale-up grants were targeted to a small number of educational interventions that had well-defined and replicable model specifications as well as strong evidence of effectiveness. A detailed description of the critical elements of the program model is a crucial ingredient if broad replication of an intervention model can be assumed to produce similar impacts to those that have been demonstrated in earlier studies of the model. Large-scale expansion only makes sense if across many implementations of the model, the key elements of the model will be able to be maintained. The contribution of i3 was the impetus it provided for the developers to establish a comprehensive logic model to supporting long-term goals of model expansion and sustainability.

Moving from Model to Measure: Identifying Data Sources and Indices

As described in Chapter 2, and illustrated by the work of the developers and evaluators of the three program models, while defining logic and change models is the necessary foundational work for developing measures of fidelity, it is not sufficient for the purpose of measuring fidelity. Key components in the models must be operationalized in terms of measureable indicators and fidelity scores. An additional part of the process was determining what sources of information were available on each of the indicators of implementation.

This stage of development a fidelity measure was substantially different across the three grants. The fact that the models are at different stages of "institutionalization" directly affects the challenge of determining how to assess the level of implementation of key elements. At this stage in the process of developing the fidelity measure, the realities of the cost and complexity of each potential data source had to be assessed, particularly for programs that were being implemented on a relatively broad scale, such as eMINTS and Success for All.

Development Grant: STEM21 Academy

For STEM21, the fidelity work undertaken under the i3 grant program represented the first effort at systematically measuring and quantifying fidelity. As described in Chapter 4, the "quantitative evaluation of implementation fidelity was a relatively new concept for the internal and external Academy evaluators and the program director." The team, including evaluators and program staff, had to develop a "shared understanding of quality evaluation of implementation fidelity, appropriate levels of implementation fidelity expectations for the Academy; and the importance and value of the collection of implementation fidelity data." Being part of the i3 grant program conferred substantial advantages to the intervention developer and program staff in terms of visibility, but the grant requirements also meant that this work associated with measuring fidelity had to be done.

The initial fidelity system for the STEM21 Academy had some major limitations, particularly from the perspective of the developer. This is because the scoring system for the components of fidelity of implementation was relatively rudimentary and did not reflect either more nuanced differences in the *quality* of implementation nor did it apply any weighting to the indicators within each component. As suggested in Chapter 3, the team of program staff and evaluators were clear that their fidelity measurements would need to evolve over time to provide more information about what is happening during implementation.

Identifying data sources for the implementation fidelity measure also presented some new challenges for the evaluators. While some indicators could be measured relatively easily without requiring additional work on the part of the teachers, such as teacher attendance at professional development workshops.

Others, such as student completion of classroom activities and teacher completion of curriculum content, involved establishing new tracking and reporting systems to ensure that data on implementation could be obtained accurately and consistently. Since this was the first time that the program sought to collect systematic quantitative data on implementation, the data collection tools and strategies changed over time as program and evaluation staff learned what did and did not work. Although the first instruments and methods instituted by the evaluator were ultimately successful at obtaining the desired data on implementation, the implementation team (site coordinators and teachers) found the tools to be sometimes confusing and overly time-consuming, which the evaluators recognized as a potential threat to the positive relationships among the staff members of the program, implementation and evaluation. Subsequently, the evaluator developed more concise and efficient data collection systems for teachers to use to report on classroom activities. The revised instruments were much more successful both from the perspective of the quality of the data and the perception of burden to the teachers. In addition, an unexpected additional benefit was that the data collection system allowed the evaluator to provide useful results back to teachers about the implementation of the program in their classrooms.[2] Finally, the evaluator replaced paper forms with an online portal where teachers could access the forms they needed to complete.

One of the important lessons that evaluators learned concerned the need to provide a rationale to staff in the implementing schools for collecting the data on implementation. The evaluators reported that a clear description of the purpose and use of the implementation data was key to enlisting teacher cooperation and support for accurate data reporting.

Validation Grant: eMINTS Comprehensive Professional Development Program

Prior to receiving an i3 grant, the eMINTS program had contracted for an independent evaluation of the fidelity of intervention focusing on two key components of the program—professional development and in-class coaching of teachers—and the relation of fidelity of implementation and teacher scores on their lesson plans. This previous thinking about fidelity provided a foundation for the development of a systematic measure of fidelity of implementation in the i3 supported implementation of eMINTS. This measure captured key inputs of the model, specifically, the extent to which all of the eMINTS staff and the teachers, school leaders and technology coordinators who participated in eMINTS implemented the core components of the program as planned. The eMINTS program staff and evaluators also felt sufficiently informed about the model to be able to place differential weights on the various components of fidelity to reflect their understanding of the relative importance of each. For eMINTS, as was true for STEM21, the process of developing a final version of a measure of fidelity of implementation involved iterative consultation between the program team/ developers and the evaluators throughout the process.

For the eMINTS team, identifying sources of data on the indicators of fidelity started with reviewing the relevant data that were already being collected in the schools as part of the implementation process itself. Because the program model had been in place for a number of years, for the i3 fidelity measure, eMINTS could take advantage of data systems that had been established. For example, because the program provided stipends to teachers who attended training, and because many of the training sessions occurred outside of the typical school day, a system had been established to document attendance at professional development sessions by teachers and administrators in eMINTS sites. Some of the indicators identified for the fidelity measure required eMINTS to institute new data collection systems involving surveys of students, teachers and technology coordinators in the schools.

Scale-Up Grant: Success for All

Prior to Success for All receiving its i3 scale-up grant, the program had long been concerned with assessment strength of implementation as the basis for guiding program improvement at schools that were using the Success for All model. The program developers had designed a School Achievement Snapshot that records 99 items about the implementation of critical program structures, activities and instructional practices. The Snapshot is completed by the Success for All coaches at least once a year and, ideally, quarterly, after meeting with school personnel, visiting classrooms, and examining program documents. The assessment by the coaches is then reviewed with school leaders to identify areas where there is a need for program improvement. The evaluator and the developer jointly determined that the Success for All Snapshot would be used as the basis for measuring fidelity of implementation for the i3 program. This decision presented some challenges in aligning the existing measure with the guidelines for the i3 measurement. As described in Chapter 8, to use the Snapshot to gauge implementation fidelity, the evaluator, in collaboration with the program developers, had to convert the Snapshot ratings into a numerical scale, develop criteria for adequate implementation fidelity in an individual school, and determine which aspects of the Snapshot would be expected to be fully in place over the multi-year implementation process.

Identifying Thresholds, Reviewing Results, Revising the Measures

The final steps in developing measures of fidelity of implementation involved establishing thresholds for fidelity for each key component, reviewing results, and revising the measures. For all three programs, the identification of thresholds was a new process and, as each of the program-developer teams noted, was made difficult by the absence of evidence on which to establish these thresholds. Although clarity emerged about what full implementation of a component encompassed, it was much more challenging to set thresholds that were less than full implementation but represented what the program staff considered to be an adequate level of implementation. The level of certainly about these thresholds was related to the maturity of the program model, with Success for All having the most data on variation in implementation from many schools over the previous years on which to base thresholds. STEM21 Academy, which was in its early years of implementation as a full model, had only the opinions of the program developer on which to base thresholds. Under i3, reporting on fidelity of implementation was framed around the thresholds for each component; for example, the proportion of units (schools, teachers) who implemented the component at what was established as an adequate level of fidelity. However, since all three of the programs described in this book received funding under i3 for 5 years of implementation, they had the opportunity to adjust and revise their fidelity measures over time as they began to develop empirical evidence on implementation.

Development Grant: STEM21 Academy

In the STEM21 program, program and evaluation staff described the benefits of engaging in the process of refining their logic model, creating definitions and measures of the implementation of key elements, and reporting clear, quantitative results back to schools. This is not to underestimate the challenges faced in changing the culture and context around measurement at all levels of the initiative, but future implementations of the model will clearly be improved by the systems developed and the data collected as part of i3. As reported by the internal evaluator, measuring fidelity of implementation has helped the program examine and improve its own practices.

At the same time, the results on fidelity of implementation had an effect on the conceptualization of the program model itself as well as on the participating teachers. In terms of the program model, the initial results on implementation fidelity, in concert with feedback from participating teachers, led to changes in the program model. The proposed changes to key components were deemed to be substantial enough to require revisions of the logic model and of the fidelity measure. Another change motivated by review of the first data on fidelity of implementation and dissatisfaction among the STEM21 team with the information the measure produced on the professional development component was the introduction of indicators of quality into the measurement of the implementation of professional development.

For the teachers, the program undertook extensive efforts to ensure that teachers were "on board" at all levels with the objectives and methods of the data collection process. As a result, this topic was added to the summer professional development session. The results themselves could be used to help teachers understand the aspects of the program that they were doing well and the parts that they were struggling with. In turn, this has allowed the program to identify schools, teachers, or classes that need additional program support or require changes in the implementation process. As the evaluator states, "This ability [to identify implementation challenges at the individual and program levels] has greatly enhanced program success at ensuring that activities are implemented throughout participating schools, as intended."

Validation Grant: eMINTS Comprehensive Professional Development Program

The results from the first year's assessment of fidelity of implementation indicated that four of the five key program components were being implemented at a level of fidelity. For the program component that was not being implemented at this level, the program developer considered the possibility of redesigning the delivery of the specific professional development, since teachers' ability to enact that aspect of the model was assumed to be adversely affected by the lack of attendance at the training.

The eMINTS evaluators also proposed introducing additional sources of information on implementation for the parts of the measure that depended on a limited set of information and especially where the measurement depended heavily on teacher reports. To address concerns about the reliability of the data on implementation fidelity, going forward, the evaluators are collecting observation data on some aspects of classroom practice. The observation data will be incorporated into the metric for certain of the program components to obtain more reliable estimates.

eMINTS evaluators also reported that some of the measures of fidelity showed no differentiation in the performance of the eMINTS schools. The evaluators want to explore whether the lack of variation is a true indicator of successful implementation or a problem with an overly broad measure.

Scale-Up Grant: Success for All

Success for All had two different methodologies for measuring fidelity of implementation: their School Achievement Snapshot and the adaptation of the Snapshot to align with the expectations of i3. As described by the evaluator, the Snapshot goes far beyond the measurement of inputs that is the focus under i3 to include items related to mediators of student performance such as teacher instructional practice and student engagement and behavior. For Success for All, full implementation includes the presence of these mediating changes as well as the delivery of resources and other inputs. Since the logic model for Success for All was articulated for the first time under i3, it is not unexpected that the first set of results on fidelity of implementation led to changes in the model.

To validate the adapted version of the Snapshot, the program developer obtained ratings of strength of implementation from the Success for All coaches of the schools in which they worked. Although the evaluator reports in Chapter 8 that there was only limited consistency between the quantitative measure of fidelity of implementation and the coaches' global ratings, the two measures were similar in their broad designations of which schools were implementing adequately and which were not.

Lessons from the Field on Measuring Fidelity of Implementation

The experiences of the three programs illustrate the potential benefits of measuring fidelity of implementation, some of the limitations of the measure, and the challenges in the process of moving from logic model to measurement to results. As would be expected, the process appeared to present the largest challenges and to promise the most potential benefits for STEM21. Since the program model is still considered to be in the process of growing and improving, having both a clearly articulated model and an aligned measure of fidelity, particularly if the program shows signs of promise at improving student achievement, could help attract interest from other sites in replicating the model. Throughout its history the eMINTS program and its predecessors have become successively more comprehensive and systematic regarding their measurement of fidelity of implementation. Earlier implementation studies have laid the foundation for program revisions and improvement while their current i3 study is expected to provide a basis for future replication of essential program components while adapting the program where necessary to accommodate new contexts. For Success for All, the measure of fidelity may be able to add information to the previously developed implementation measure, but probably the most important contribution of the process was the articulation of a logic model for the intervention that can serve to help communicate the key elements of the model and the pathways to student achievement.

The descriptions from the program developers and evaluators of these three models clearly demonstrate that developing systematic, quantitative measures of fidelity of implementation requires time and commitment from program staff and evaluators. The process is iterative, collaborative, and challenges all members to think deeply about the theoretical underpinnings of the program model, the ultimate objectives for schools, teachers, parents and/or students, the set of key activities or resources that represent the necessary, but not sufficient, investment, and the desired changes that are the critical changes that mediate the intervention objectives. The goal of i3 is to identify promising intervention models for future replication. This work on logic models and fidelity measures, albeit intensive, will serve the field well in our search for effective models.

The i3 Experience

Chapter 2 introduced the contrast between "fidelity of implementation" and "fidelity of intervention." This distinction is key in the fidelity measurement work among i3-funded interventions, as exemplified by the experiences of the three interventions highlighted in the previous chapters. Figure 9.1 shows the relationship between these two components of fidelity. First, fidelity typically refers to the implementation of a specific intervention as opposed to the implementation as it relates to a comparison or counterfactual condition. Therefore, in Figure 9.1, the boxes labeled Fidelity of Implementation and Fidelity of Intervention are linked to the Program Model. The exhibit indicates that the Program Model has a logic model that specifies the *planned* inputs/activities (resources/activities/structural changes hypothesized as necessary for motivating intended changes), mediators (processes through which inputs/activities as implemented are expected to lead to intended outcomes, sometimes called "short-term outcomes"), and longer-term outcomes. Fidelity of implementation aligns to the inputs/activities, while fidelity of intervention aligns with the mediators.

Measurement of program delivery confirms that the critical components of an intervention, originally designed by the developer and financially supported by a funding agency, are in fact being delivered as planned to the intended target population, which could be important information for the intervention developer who designed the intervention, the funding agency supporting the intervention implementation, and implementers themselves, such as school districts, nonprofit organizations, or the like. Analyses of data about fidelity of implementation can serve an important role in program quality improvement for future implementations as well as in assessing success of a current implementation (Bond, Drake, Rapp, McHugo, & Xie, 2009).

There are advantages and disadvantages to measuring fidelity at this level. By measuring fidelity of implementation, evaluators are able to monitor the delivery of inputs and confirm an intervention's strong foundation. Often funders of grants desire such confirmation and require this approach to fidelity in order to hold grantees accountable for doing what they have received money to do. In addition, the process of collecting and analyzing this type of implementation data is less expensive than other methods, as instruments used in the process are fairly simplistic and reliable (e.g., documentation of attendance, teacher and coach logs). On the other hand, fidelity of implementation focuses on the structural and procedural inputs often with little to no emphasis on quality of delivery. It does not delve into the heart of the intervention like the dose and quality of student-received reading instruction, and therefore has a weak and indirect relationship with distal outcomes (LaBanca et al., 2013).

The guidance for interventions receiving i3 funding is that while, ideally, interventions should develop methods for assessing both types of fidelity, the expectation of the funding agency is that interventions have in place a measure

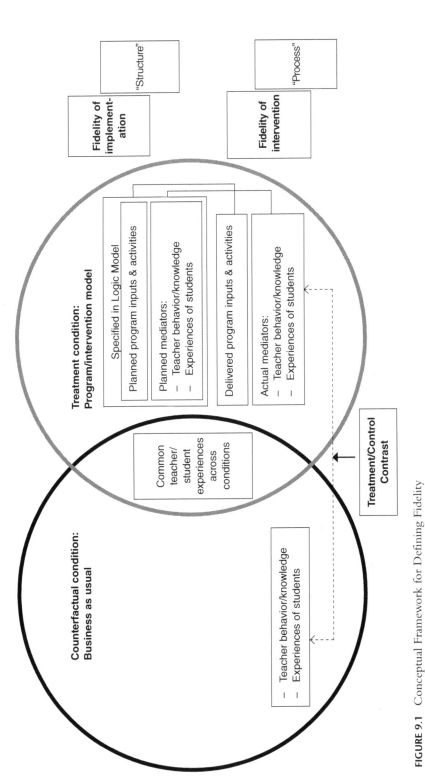

FIGURE 9.1 Conceptual Framework for Defining Fidelity

of fidelity of implementation. This guidance is explicitly not intended to suggest that it is best practice to limit the assessment of fidelity to the fidelity of implementation. Two major considerations led to the approach to fidelity adopted by i3. First, the funding agency acknowledged that expecting grantees to measure fidelity of intervention would be likely to involve measure development (e.g., observation systems to directly assess teacher practice, surveys of administrators, teachers, or parents) and costly and/or burdensome data collection. Expecting grantees to undertake this effort would have to be clearly indicated in the application process itself and likely would require dedicating a greater proportion of the grant funding to evaluation activities. Second, there is a national evaluation of the i3 program that is charged with reporting on the impacts of the full set of i3-supported interventions. As part of this program-wide reporting, there is an interest in also reporting on implementation findings across the interventions. The interest in cross-intervention reporting on implementation is a key motivation for encouraging all i3 grantees to develop a measure of fidelity of implementation, apply it, and calculate a fidelity score, using a common approach.

The i3 approach to fidelity allows the national evaluation to report fidelity findings using a common reporting framework across all grants. Figure 9.2 presents the type of reporting format that will be possible for the i3 national evaluation. The table specifies (1) the key components of the intervention for which fidelity of implementation is being measured, in this example, there are six key components; (2) the threshold for "implementation with fidelity" at the program level that the grantee/evaluator have agreed on, in the example, the percentage of schools that meet the criterion for adequate implementation; (3) the actual percentage of schools meeting the standard for adequate implementation in a particular time period; and (4) the final rating (Yes/No) of whether or not the key component can be said to have been implemented with fidelity, which is defined by whether the actual percentage of schools is equal to or greater than the threshold. All grantees that follow the same process that is described in the prior chapters will be able to complete this same table at the end of their grant period. Not only will this common reporting format help readers look across interventions at the challenges to fidelity implementation, the fidelity measurement system also provides an opportunity for the national evaluation to do some innovative analyses about the content ("key components") of this large program of innovative educational interventions.

The method described and applied above systematizes implementation fidelity data measurement, analysis, and reporting across potentially divergent interventions and provides needed guidance to evaluators on what to measure, why, and how to use implementation data in a meaningful way. There are existing guides available on what to measure (see Century et al., 2010), but the system presented here not only provides funders and evaluators results on implementation of particular interventions, but also offers direction on how to synthesize and report implementation data in a manner that provides large-scale evaluations across

Key Components on Logic Model	Definitions		Findings			
			Year 1		Year 2	
	Measurement of implementation with fidelity	Definition of "implementation with fidelity" at program level	% of schools with adequate implementation of component (based on data collection during year 1)	"Implementation with fidelity" (based on threshold in definition)	% of schools with adequate implementation of component (based on data collection during year 2)	"Implementation with fidelity" (based on threshold in definition)
Technology Infrastructure	Calculation based on 6 indicators	80% of schools implemented with fidelity	89%	Yes	92%	Yes
Technology Use/ Equipment	Calculation based on 3 indicators	90% of schools implemented with or moderate fidelity	86%	No	90%	Yes
Teacher Professional Development	Calculation based on attendance records	75% of schools implemented with fidelity	81%	Yes	80%	Yes
Administrative Support	Calculation based on 2 indicators	80% of schools implemented with fidelity	78%	No	76%	No
Ongoing Technology Support	Calculation based on 3 indicators	70% of schools implemented with fidelity	64%	No	65%	No

FIGURE 9.2 Example of NEi3 Reporting for Program-Level Fidelity of Implementation

multiple studies and a valuable means to report implementation findings systematically and consistently. This system holds promise for complicated initiatives like i3, where no two i3 interventions are the same; this system provides a common metric with which to measure and report intervention delivery across the collection of i3-funded studies.

Notes

1. As is made clear in the i3 guidance materials, focusing on fidelity of implementation is a pragmatic decision, not one based on the belief that this component of fidelity by itself is the standard for quality measurement of fidelity. That is, the i3 grant program does not include the requirement that grantees include measurement of the short-term outcomes of the intervention inputs, that is, changes in mediators such as teacher behavior, student behavior, school structures, etc., which represent the pathways by which the inputs lead to longer-term improvements for student performance and achievement. Measurement of mediators requires measurement in both treatment and comparison units and often entails more expensive data collection (observations, individual surveys, etc.), which the grant program did not feel could be required.
2. In the i3 context, the grant notices articulated an expectation that the evaluations would provide ongoing feedback on implementation to program implementers. It is important to note that in other evaluation contexts the opposite expectation is sometimes applied. In these contexts the expectation is that the evaluation captures a real-life implementation where an external evaluator would not be present to support implementation. In these scenarios, the expectation is that the evaluator does not provide implementation feedback to the evaluator during the evaluation.

References

Bond, G. R., Drake, R. E., Rapp, C. A., McHugo, G. J., & Xie, H. (2009). Individualization and quality improvement: Two new scales to complement measurement of program fidelity. *Administration and Policy in Mental Health and Mental Health Services Research, 36*(5), 349–357.

Bond, G. R., Evans, L., Salyers, M. P., Williams, J., & Kim, H. W. (2000). Measurement of fidelity in psychiatric rehabilitation. *Mental Health Services Research, 2*(2), 75–87.

Century, J., Cassata, A., Rudnick, M., & Freeman, C. (2012). Measuring enactment of innovations and the factors that affect implementation and sustainability: Moving toward common language and shared conceptual understanding. *The Journal of Behavioral Health Services & Research, 39*(4), 343–61.

Century, J., Rudnick, M., & Freeman, C. (2010). A framework for measuring fidelity of implementation: A foundation for shared language and accumulation of knowledge. *American Journal of Evaluation, 31*(2), 199–218.

Dane, A. V., & Schneider, B. H. (1998). Program integrity in primary and early secondary prevention: Are implementation effects out of control? *Clinical Psychology Review, 18*(1), 23–45.

Durlak, J. A., & Dupre, E. P. (2008). Implementation matters: A review of research on the influence of implementation on program outcomes and the factors affecting implementation. *American Journal of Community Psychology, 41*, 327–350.

Hall, G. E., & Hord, S. M. (1987). Change in schools: Facilitating the process. Albany, NY: State University of New York Press.

Hulleman, C. S., & Cordray, D. S. (2009). Moving from the lab to the field: The role of fidelity and achieved relative intervention strength. *Journal of Research on Educational Effectiveness, 2*, 88–110.

Hume, K., Boyd, B., McBee, M., Coman, D., Gutierrez, A., Shaw, E., et al. (2011). Assessing implementation of comprehensive treatment models for young children with ASD: Reliability and validity of two measures. *Research in Autism Spectrum Disorders, 5*(4), 1430–1440.

LaBanca, F., Worwood, M., Schauss, S., LaSala, J., & Donn, J. (2013). *Blended instruction: Exploring student-centered pedagogical strategies to promote a technology-enhanced learning environment*. Litchfield, CT: EDUCATION CONNECTION.

Mowbray, C.T., Holter, M. C., Teague, G. B., & Bybee, D. (2003). Fidelity criteria: Development, measurement, and validation. *American Journal of Evaluation, 24*(3), 315–340.

Nelson, M. C., Cordray, D. S., Hulleman, C. S., Darrow, C. L., & Sommer, E. C. (2012). A procedure for assessing intervention fidelity in experiments testing educational and behavioral interventions. *The Journal of Behavioral Health Services & Research, 39*(4), 374–396.

O'Donnell, C. L. (2008). Defining, conceptualizing, and measuring fidelity of implementation and its relationship to outcomes in K-12 curriculum intervention research. *Review of Educational Research, 78*(1), 33–84.

Owens, J. S., Lyon, A. R., Brandt, N. E., Masia Warner, C., Nadeem, E., Spiel, C., & Wagner, M. (2013). Implementation science in school mental health: Key constructs in a developing research agenda. *School Mental Health*. doi:10.1007/s12310-013-9115-3

Pence, K. L., Justice, L. M., & Wiggins, A. K. (2008). Preschool teachers' fidelity in implementing a comprehensive language-rich curriculum. *Language, Speech, and Hearing Services in Schools, 39*, 329–341.

CONTRIBUTORS

Rekha Balu, Ph.D., focuses on experimental and quasi-experimental impact evaluation techniques, implementation and cost analysis, and managing large-scale projects with complex data sets. Currently, she serves as Deputy Project Director for the evaluation of Response to Intervention under a federal contract with the Institute for Education Sciences to examine impacts on early reading outcomes. She is leading the scale-up and cost study components of the i3 evaluation of Success for All, a whole-school reform model focused on early reading.

Monica M. Beglau, Ed.D., served as the Executive Director of the eMINTS National Center at the University of Missouri in Columbia, Missouri, from 2002 until her retirement in 2013. During her tenure, the program was awarded a highly competitive Investing in Innovation (i3) grant. Dr. Beglau also oversaw the e-Learning for Educators online professional development program. Her experience in education includes positions as Executive Director of the Partnerships for Educational Renewal at the University of Missouri and at the University of Wyoming, and as an elementary principal and special education teacher in Cheyenne, Wyoming. She was recognized by the International Society for Technology in Education (ISTE) as the 2011 Outstanding Leader.

W. Christopher Brandt, Ph.D., is Principal Researcher in the Education Program at AIR. Dr. Brandt leads and supports federally sponsored education research, evaluation, and technical assistance projects. He is Deputy Director of the Regional Educational Laboratory Midwest, a $45 million research center funded by the Institute of Education Sciences, overseeing multiple project teams in applied education research and evaluation. Brandt is the Principal Investigator of a $2 million randomized control trial that evaluates the effectiveness of a technology integration program through the U.S. Department of Education "i3" grant program. He is the author of several technical reports and published articles in the areas of teacher professional development, educator evaluation, and formative assessment. Before Joining the American Institutes for Research, Dr. Brandt taught as an elementary school teacher in Naperville, Illinois, and later earned a doctoral degree in educational psychology from the University of Georgia.

Catherine Darrow, Ph.D., is an Associate at Abt Associates, Inc. in Cambridge, MA. She works as the lead on analysis of implementation findings for the i3 National Technical Assistance Contract, funded by the Institute of Education Sciences (IES). She also provides support and assistance on issues of implementation fidelity across projects and divisions within Abt. In addition, she has consulted on issues around measurement and analysis of implementation fidelity for a number of external clients such as the U.S. Department of Labor (DOL), U.S. Department of Education (DOE), as well as a number of not-for-profit educational organizations. Dr. Darrow came to Abt from the Frank Porter Graham (FPG) Child Development Institute at the University of North Carolina-Chapel Hill. At FPG, she completed an IES postdoctoral fellowship and directed an IES-funded, randomized control trial (RCT) examining the efficacy of a K-1 reading intervention. As a result, she has developed expertise in experimental research design, issues of implementation and intervention fidelity measurement, as well as statistical analysis (e.g., multi-level linear regression, meta-analysis) appropriate for classroom- and school-based evaluations.

Sonica Dhillon is a Research Associate for the Education group at the American Institutes for Research. She has 6 years of experience in cognitive psychology with a specific interest in learning mechanisms and their applications. As Research Associate at AIR, her responsibilities include data management and analysis, technical report writing, survey development, event planning, and outreach. Prior to her work with the American Institute for Research, she managed the Northwestern University site location of the Spatial Intelligence and Learning Center (SILC), one of six National Science Foundation's Science of Learning Centers. Ms. Dhillon acquired her Master's degree in Social Science from the University of Chicago in 2006. In 2005, she graduated with a degree in Applied Psychology Cum Laude with Distinction from the University of Illinois at Chicago.

Barbara Goodson, Ph.D., is a nationally recognized expert in the field of educational research and policy, with more than 35 years of experience designing and implementing intervention impact and implementation studies. She currently has her own consulting firm. Previously, she was a Principal Scientist at Abt Associates for 30 years, where she was the senior early childhood researcher in the company, functioning as a company-wide resource on early childhood research as well as on design and measurement more broadly. Dr. Goodson is an expert in the field of measurement of implementation fidelity. Dr. Goodson currently is the PI on the IES contract to provide Evaluation Technical Assistance to the Investment and Innovation grant program in the Department of Education. Dr. Goodson is the lead of the technical assistance on implementation studies, including working with more than 120 evaluations of educational interventions on developing high-quality logic models and systematic measures of fidelity of implementation. Dr. Goodson has presented her approach to assessing fidelity of implementation at national conferences and is an author on an in-process special journal issue on measuring implementation. Dr. Goodson also is the director of the evaluation on the National Cross-Site Evaluation of Project LAUNCH, a federal grant program funded by the federal Substance Abuse and Mental Health Services Administration. Dr. Goodson developed an electronic data collection system for implementation data on the more than 100 child and family service programs funded by the 35 LAUNCH grantees.

Lorie F. Kaplan, Ph.D., is a professional in the field of educational technology and received her doctorate degree in Educational Leadership and Policy Analysis from the University of Missouri-Columbia. She has worked with the University of Missouri for the past 18 years, most recently as the Executive Director of the enhancing Missouri's Instructional Networked Teaching Strategies (eMINTS) National Center and as an Assistant Clinical Professor in the College of Education's School of Information and Learning Technologies. Dr. Kaplan also serves as Project Director for the Investing in Innovation (i3) eMINTS Validation Grant awarded to the program in 2010. She started her work with eMINTS as an Instructional Specialist, providing professional development and in-classroom coaching to teachers learning how to integrate technology with inquiry-based instruction. Previously, she spent time in Japan teaching English to junior and senior high school students. She also received her Master's in Educational Technology in 1996 and her Bachelor's in English in 1993, both from the University of Missouri-Columbia.

Frank LaBanca, Ed.D., is a teacher, educational researcher, and change agent. As the Director of the Center for 21st Century Skills at EDUCATION CONNECTION, he directed and managed the implementation of innovative Science, Technology, Engineering, and Math programs in high schools across Connecticut. During his classroom career, Dr. LaBanca taught Biology and Applied Science Research at Stamford, Newtown, and Oxford High Schools. He has been recognized as a National Education Association Innovation Teacher; a GTE GIFT (Growth Initiatives For Teachers) Fellow; a RadioShack National Teacher for Excellence in Science, Math, and Technology; and the Teachers' Insurance Plan Teacher of the Year. Dr. LaBanca is currently the Principal of Danbury Public School's Westside Middle School Academy magnet and supervises dissertation research in Western Connecticut State University's Instructional Leadership program. He holds a BS in Biology, an MS in Science Education, and an EdD in Instructional Leadership.

Mhora Lorentson, Ph.D., is the Director of the Center for Collaborative Evaluation and Strategic Change at EDUCATION CONNECTION. Dr. Lorentson earned a doctorate in Education and a certificate in Organizational Change Management from Cornell University, an MS in Hydrology from the University of Minnesota, and has a strong background in STEM education. She has 15 years of high-level experience as a researcher and evaluator on state and national projects, including National Science Foundation-funded projects involving competency-based STEM education in K-12 and higher education (Noyce, Innovative Technology Experiences for Students and Teachers, and Advanced Technology Education Program areas), has successfully served as the internal evaluator for a Nellie Mae Education Foundation Research & Evaluation Project, and was recently selected as the external evaluator for a Carnegie Grant implementation project in Washington, DC. Dr. Lorentson is currently the Internal Evaluator for EDUCATION CONNECTION's Investing in Innovation Program (i3) and is responsible for assessment of the fidelity of implementation of all program activities. Her work has won national recognition as a best practice as part of the William T. Grant Foundation and Spencer Foundations' i3 learning community. Dr. Lorentson has published multiple peer-reviewed articles and is primary author of a book chapter on evaluation of fidelity of implementation accepted for publication by Routledge.

Nancy A. Madden, Ph.D., is a professor at the Center for Research and Reform in Education at the School of Education at Johns Hopkins University and part-time Professor at the University of York Institute for Effective Education. Dr. Madden is the President and co-founder of the Success for All Foundation which develops, researches, and disseminates educational programs to increase achievement, particularly for disadvantaged students. Dr. Madden graduated from Reed College in 1973, and received her Ph.D. in Clinical Psychology from American University in 1980. From 1980 to 1998, she was a research scientist at the Center for Research on the Education of Students Placed at Risk at Johns Hopkins University, where she directed the development of the reading, writing, language arts, and mathematics elements of Success for All, a comprehensive school reform program. An expert in literacy and instruction, Dr. Madden is the author or co-author of many articles and books on cooperative learning, mainstreaming, and education of disadvantaged students, including *Effective Programs for Students at Risk* (Allyn & Bacon, 1989) and *Two Million Children: Success for All* (Corwin, 2009). Current research interests include practices to increase social-emotional learning and use of interactive whiteboard technology and electronic response devices to increase student success.

Coby V. Meyers, Ph.D., is a senior researcher at American Institutes for Research. Dr. Meyers is Project Director of AIR's work in the Regional Educational Laboratory (REL) Northeast and Islands. He also leads the REL Midwest Beating the Odds Alliance, working to identify schools achieving at levels higher than expected and analyzing organizational factors that might be related to those achievement levels.

Dr. Meyers also plays integral roles in various school turnaround initiatives, an area in which he has presented and published, including coauthoring the book *Turning Around Failing Schools: Lessons from the Organizational Sciences* and multiple journal articles. He was recognized in 2012 with the Emerging Scholar Award by the American Educational Research Association special-interest group School Turnaround and Restructuring. He is also co-PI of the $2.5 million randomized controlled trial evaluation of the i3 eMINTS Validation Study. In addition, he has expertise in aspects of urban education, including the achievement gap and school reform, as well as teacher incentive pay. In 2010, he received training from top research methodologists at the Institute of Education Sciences–sponsored Randomized Controlled Trials Summer Institute, an experience that remains key in his work on multiple randomized controlled trial evaluations. He became a What Works Clearinghouse reviewer in the summer of 2012. Through his projects, publications, and presentations, he has demonstrated quantitative, qualitative, survey, and synthetic research skills. He also has had practical in-class experience as a middle school and high school English and literature teacher. He received a Master's degree in secondary education at the University of Kentucky and earned his doctoral degree in education leadership, policy, and organizations at Vanderbilt University.

Ayrin Molefe, Ph.D., is a senior statistician and methodologist at AIR with more than 15 years of experience in statistical analysis, consulting, and teaching. She has expertise in formulating scientifically based research designs and in analyzing complex educational data sets. She is the lead statistician for two i3 (Investing in Innovation Fund) grants: an evaluation of TNTP's (The New Teacher Project) Teacher Effectiveness and Certification (TEACh) Initiative, and an evaluation of the enhancing Missouri's Instructional Networked Teaching Strategies (eMINTS) program. She was the lead statistician in a recently completed two-year Institute of Education Sciences–funded randomized control trial evaluating the Measures of Academic Progress (MAP) program. Dr. Molefe collaborates with various teams as a methodologist and consultant. She develops or provides advice on study design and statistical methodology, leads or conducts statistical analysis, writes and reviews research proposals and evaluation reports, and resolves statistical issues and questions. She has expertise in hierarchical linear modeling (HLM), multiple imputation, propensity score analysis, Rasch analysis, and many other methodologies. She has a passion for learning and has undergone extensive training with leading experts in experimental and quasi-experimental designs, causal inference, HLM, missing data methods, structural equation modeling, and complex sampling designs. Dr. Molefe has more than 20 years of solid SAS programming experience and is well versed in R, Stata, and HLM software. Prior to joining AIR, she was a statistics professor at the University of Central Arkansas.

Youn Joo Oh, Ed.D., is a Project Director II at EDC who conducts research and evaluation activities in STEM impact and fidelity of implementation studies in K-12 education. Dr. Oh is currently a Co-PI and primary Research Scientist and

Evaluator on the Nellie Mae Educational Foundation's Research & Evaluation Program, ED-i3, and NSF-ITEST grants. She has extensive research and program evaluation experiences leading national-level STEM research studies. Her work has won national recognition, including inclusion in the William T. Grant Foundation and Spencer Foundations' i3 learning community. She also develops measurement tools in motivation, statistics and probability, the 21st Century Learning and Inquiry Skills and the 21st Century Skills Teaching Scale. She has disseminated her work through peer reviewed journals, a practitioner book, book chapters, and research and evaluation conferences. She holds an EdD in Educational Psychology and Technology and Postdoctoral Research Fellowship in Outcome Research and Evaluation and Statistics & Measurement from University of Southern California.

Cristofer Price is a Principal Scientist who has extensive experience with conducting, leading, and providing high quality guidance for rigorous impact evaluations. Mr. Price has over two decades of experience in behavioral and educational research. He is an expert in study design and the formulation of statistical models of longitudinal and clustered data for continuous and discrete outcomes, including the analysis of complex survey sample data. Mr. Price is the senior technical lead on a wide variety of projects representing a multitude of different types of sampling designs, data elements, units of analysis, and analytical methods. Recently, he has been the Director of Analysis on five separate studies that used individual-level or cluster-randomized evaluation designs. He has been a technical assistance lead on three contracts that have provided technical assistance to researchers conducting 134 different evaluations to help them design and implement their impact and implementation studies.

Janet Quint, Ph.D., has led or participated in a number of mixed-methods studies of education reform initiatives in community colleges and K-12 schools, as well as evaluations of programs for young mothers and welfare recipients. She is currently Project Director for MDRC's evaluation of Success for All, a reading-focused whole-school reform effort that is one of four initiatives initially selected for scale-up under the federal Investing in Innovation (i3) competition; the study involves the random assignment of 37 schools in five school districts to treatment and control conditions. She also directed the Developmental Education Initiative Evaluation, in which she headed a team that examined the implementation of developmental education reforms in 15 community colleges, with a view toward identifying the factors that facilitate or constrain scale-up. Before joining the K-12 policy area, she played major roles in the organization's evaluations of two programs aimed at improving the educational attainment, employment prospects, and parenting skills of teenage mothers receiving welfare, as well as helping the young women defer further childbearing until they were better prepared economically to care for their children. A graduate of Harvard University, Quint received a Master of Arts in Teaching degree from the University of Chicago and a Ph.D. in sociology from the City University of New York.

Robert E. Slavin, Ph.D., is currently Director of the Center for Research and Reform in Education at Johns Hopkins University, part-time Professor at the Institute for Effective Education at the University of York (England), and Chairman of the Success for All Foundation. He received his BA in Psychology from Reed College in 1972, and his Ph.D. in Social Relations in 1975 from Johns Hopkins University. Dr. Slavin has authored or co-authored more than 300 articles and book chapters on such topics as cooperative learning, comprehensive school reform, ability grouping, school and classroom organization, desegregation, mainstreaming, research review, and evidence-based reform. Dr. Slavin is the author or co-author of 24 books, including *Educational Psychology: Theory into Practice* (Allyn & Bacon, 1986, 1988, 1991, 1994, 1997, 2000, 2003, 2006, 2009), *Cooperative Learning: Theory, Research, and Practice* (Allyn & Bacon, 1990, 1995), *Show Me the Evidence: Proven and Promising Programs for America's Schools* (Corwin, 1998), *Effective Programs for Latino Students* (Erlbaum, 2000), *Educational Research in the Age of Accountability* (Allyn & Bacon, 2007), and *Two Million Children: Success for All* (Corwin, 2009). He received the American Educational Research Association's Raymond B. Cattell Early Career Award for Programmatic Research in 1986, the Palmer O. Johnson award for the best article in an AERA journal in 1988, the Charles A. Dana award in 1994, the James Bryant Conant Award from the Education Commission of the States in 1998, the Outstanding Leadership in Education Award from the Horace Mann League in 1999, the Distinguished Services Award from the Council of Chief State School Officers in 2000, the AERA Review of Research Award in 2009, the Palmer O. Johnson Award for the best article in an AERA journal in 2008, and was appointed as a Member of the National Academy of Education in 2009 and an AERA Fellow in 2010.

Christine E. Terry is the Associate Director of the eMINTS National Center. Over the past 12 years with eMINTS, she has helped educators improve student outcomes through professional development focused on technology and instruction. She directs the e-Learning for Educators online professional development program and assists in coordinating the development of new programs and partnerships for the eMINTS National Center. She began her career teaching math and science in rural Mississippi with one computer for 30 students. She has also taught third grade self-contained and was the lead teacher for a small progressive community school with multi-age classrooms and a focus on student inquiry.

INDEX

Printed by PGSTL